THE REFORM OF
PARLIAMENT

GOVt
242

Born in London, Dr. Bernard Crick received his B.S. in economics at University College, London, and his Ph.D. at the London School of Economics, where, until recently, he was Lecturer in Government. Dr. Crick spent five years studying and teaching in the United States and Canada. From 1952 to 1954 he was a Teaching Fellow at Harvard Graduate School; in 1954–55 he was assistant professor at McGill University, Montreal; and for two years he was a Visiting Fellow, first at the University of California at Berkeley (1955–56), and then at Harvard (1960–61). He is presently a member of the Politics Department at the University of Sheffield.

Dr. Crick's publications include *In Defence of Politics; The American Science of Politics: Its Origins and Conditions;* and a Fabian pamphlet, *Reform of the Commons.* He has also written a number of articles for such magazines as the *Reporter, Review of Politics, Commentary, Encounter,* and *New Statesman.*

THE REFORM OF PARLIAMENT

Bernard Crick

ANCHOR BOOKS

DOUBLEDAY & COMPANY, INC.

GARDEN CITY, NEW YORK

The Reform of Parliament was originally published in hard covers by Weidenfeld and Nicolson in 1964. The Anchor edition is published by arrangement with Weidenfeld and Nicolson.

Anchor edition: 1965

CONTENTS

It is both necessary and desirable that the government of a democratic people should be active and powerful; and our object should not be to render it weak or indolent, but solely to prevent it from abusing its aptitude and strength.

TOCQUEVILLE

PREFACE TO THE AMERICAN EDITION

This book may have mercifully little to offer the college student of 'Comparative Government', if by that is meant, as it is now fashionable to mean, the search for 'cross-cultural' generalisations. It may have a little more to offer those to whom Comparative Government still means the 'brick by brick' method, or one good thing at a time. It will mainly be of interest to any American who just happens to be interested in how Britain is governed, just as there are Britishers who are interested in how the United States is governed. Of course, what cannot be compared can always be contrasted: but an imaginary foreign country, like Ruritania or China, would be just as useful a point of perspective (if that is what we are looking for) as a real one, and perhaps both would be less rewarding than some model of what the country in question could be.

There may perhaps be a general problem of the decline of British-style Parliamentary institutions, but with this I am not concerned here. But even if I were, the 'general problem' is sometimes misconceived. Parliamentary institutions, we are told, have failed to work throughout former British Africa—but failed to do what? To provide a two-party system? But why should they? Such an assumption may reverse cause and effect badly. For they have not failed to provide a framework in which organised government is possible. This is surely some achievement and it is not by any means to be taken for granted. There were those who thought that some African cultures were not ready for self-government at all, in the sense that self-government would in fact mean no government, the breakdown of ordinary law and order, anarchy—as in the Congo, or at the best a relapse into local and provincial rule. Certainly it is right to be disappointed that political liberties for each individual are about as precarious in contemporary Ghana as in contemporary Mississippi, yet one can argue that preparation for self-government has, at least, maintained government at all, even if autocratic. Freedom and order do not always go hand in hand. The British Parliamentary form is, indeed, extremely flexible. It is compatible with deliberate one-party autocracy just as much as with political systems which actually flourish on public conflict about the means and ends of governments. All depends on context.

Another general problem, thus one which would have to be treated comparatively, is often seen as a general tendency for the legislature to lose powers to the executive. This, in some broad historical sense, is often so. Bertrand de Jouvenel has pointed out, in a brilliant essay 'On the Evolution of Forms of Government' in his *Futuribles* (Geneva, 1963), that we dwell in a time of great economic optimism and great political pessimism. But we must be very sure, in each actual case of legislative decline, what the historical starting point of such an analysis is. When, for instance, did Parliament ever dominate the Crown in British history on any stable and regular basis? Answer, never: Ministers of the Crown came to dominate Parliament by themselves exercising the powers of the Crown. The *influence* of Parliament over the executive has certainly diminished, but power was never there. But even if we work more subtly with 'authority' and 'influence' than crudely with 'power' and 'command', we still have to be careful not to pick factors of stability and decline simply to fit our optimism or our pessimism. As in the State and Federal government controversy in the United States, the broadest truth may be that both have gained greatly in power in recent years, and not always even in different spheres. The matter is strictly relative.

Equally, I am sorry to have some scepticism that lessons can be drawn for Congress from this book, or lessons for Parliament from Congress. Congress is Congress and Parliament is Parliament. A congress could not govern Great Britain and a parliament could not govern the United States. Both are embedded in different social systems and arose in response to different problems. Congress may work well or badly, but it works in American terms. It arose to achieve minimum agreement among thirteen existing governments and continued as an engine of sectional conciliation. Parliament arose to strengthen the tax-gathering capacity of an already centralised and unified Crown and continued as a device for selecting Ministers strong and popular enough to take over the full power of the Crown. If there was to be 'a more responsible two-party system' in the United States, there would have to be a different national history; *no* amount of contemporary social engineering by democratic means could make it work. A single-party system might work if it forced the facts to fit the theory, by a fantastic degree of coercion (involving, among other things, either the rewriting of history or the destruction of memory). But a competitive party system would immediately take on the characteristics of the people for whose support the parties were competing. Americans act more pluralistically; the British public sweeps away independents and has only the most limited tolerance of regional variations in politics; the average American, both history and surveys tell us, is indeed mobile and aspirant; and the average Englishman, settled and deferential.

The time is long past—and almost incredible to remember—when a kind of institutional Anglophilia dominated the American political science profession. Professor William Yandell Elliott's *The Need for Constitutional Reform* (New York, 1935) was a fair and powerful example of a tune first called in Woodrow Wilson's *Congressional Government*. Broadly speaking, the idea was to turn Capitol Hill into the Palace of Westminster, just as, equally incredibly (as we in Britain enter into a period of refreshing self-doubt), the Canadian publicist Professor Robert McKenzie wishes to turn the British Labour Party into the American Democratic Party, and many others think that the French machinery of *planification* and of technical higher education can cross the channel whole and intact, or at least on the half-shell, much as Venus was borne from Cyprus to Attica. And if Professor Samuel Beer, more subtly and delicately than McKenzie, asks whether the Labour Party may not be growing more like the Democratic Party, rather than the old obverse speculation, this is only fair play in return for the many English writers who have professed surprise at not finding the Junior Lords of the Treasury on Capitol Hill, and who start talking about the late Senator McCarthy whenever it is suggested that the Estimates Committee might well have seven subcommittees rather than five to aid its work of sporadic investigation.

To say that one cannot transfer bits and pieces of one political system to another (for the very reason that it is right to use the word 'system') is *not*, however, to deny that political systems can change, can be changed, and often should be changed. Nor need we say that the language of practice used by politicians to describe what they think they are doing is *always* superior to the more technical language of some

scholar's theory when he tries to describe what in fact they
are doing. Here is no case for conservatism disguised as
methodology. If *direct* lessons cannot be drawn for the practice of one country by the study of another, comparisons
even between chalk and cheese can often be of indirect value
in suggesting possibilities and limitations. And broadly similar social processes do occur in similar conditions in what
we accept as broadly similar societies. Taken together the
American and British systems may seem like chalk and
cheese, but, compared to Indonesia or Mexico, they are birds
of a feather. It simply depends on what kind of question one
is asking: there is no 'subject' that speaks for itself. So I am
not arguing against the generous hope of finding something
small but acceptable abroad, but only for a greater realism
than has sometimes been the case. The persistent reformer
and the lasting scholar both need a fairly odd mixture of
cynicism and passion: they must avoid the feckless optimism
of those who only launch paper darts.

I could not put this point of realism better for Parliament
than Professor Ralph K. Huitt put it for Congress in a paper
delivered to the American Political Science Association last
year on 'Congressional Reorganisation: The Next Chapter'
and published in part in the November issue of *Nation's Business*:

> It is important in the beginning of any analysis of the
> prospects for institutional change to say clearly and repeat-
> edly: Institutions *can* change. Institutions *do* change. They
> *must* change; it is a law of collective life. Criticism and
> proposals for change *are* legitimate and necessary to the
> good health of institutions. These statements should be
> made, written on the blackboard (marked 'Do Not Erase'),
> and perhaps worn around the neck like a sandwich ad-
> vertisement—because even with these precautions, the pro-
> cess analyst who suggests that more than good will is in-
> volved in institutional change still will face the charge: You
> are a defender of the status quo. You are saying 'What-
> ever is, is right.'
>
> There is nothing about the procedures or structure of
> Congress that should be defended for its own sake. Con-
> gress, like other institutions, goes about its business in cer-
> tain ways because at some time or other in its history these

ways have proved to be convenient to most, or enough, of
the members. . . . When they become inconvenient to
enough members, or they obstruct the will of an effective
majority, they are changed. . . .

What must be said, of course, is that such changes do
not come easily. For one thing, there is great toughness
in an established way of doing something. An institution is,
after all, a pattern of anticipated behaviours; it is made
strong because its procedures are formal, stable and
predictable. . . .

Furthermore, no institution stands alone. Congress is a
part of the American political system, a complicated network of relationships which have been fashioned by our
national history and pre-history. No really fundamental
aspect of Congress can be altered without affecting changes
in other agencies with which it is bound up, and in many
cases the other changes must come first.

American readers should have this in mind when they come
to wonder why on earth such ideas as found in my book have
stirred up such controversy in Britain—since they leave un-
criticised such 'flagrant contradictions of democratic principle'
(as even an English student put it to me) as the extent of
party discipline among MPs, the complete control of the Government over legislation, the lack of Parliamentary control
over finance, the injustice of the electoral system to the Liberal Party, and the oligarchic methods of choosing candidates.
But these together constitute the system. I seek to show that
the system is not working well by its own terms, and to convince fellow countrymen of how much worth-while change
is possible within even such—apparently—harsh limits.

One thing strikes me vividly about these harsh limits as
I reread and prepare my book for publication in America.
There is astonishingly little in it explicitly about *the* essential
peculiarity of the British political system—party and party
discipline. But almost every line assumes the fact and the
effect of such intense party discipline. The things we take for
granted and treat explicitly are commonly of the greatest
importance: basic factors are often suppressed—as I have often
jibbed at others (see the appendix 'A Footnote to Rally the
Academic Teachers of Politics' to the Pelican edition of my
In Defence of Politics). Now is the biter bit indeed. It is
parties that vote in divisions. It is a party which exclusively

composes a Government; and it is parties for which the electorate vote. There are no MPs at the moment who are not members of one of the three parties. It is a national event when an MP votes against his party; if he persists, almost certainly he will have fatal constituency trouble. The ablest or the most appealing candidate (or the most well organised local campaign) does not seem able to gain votes more than 2 per cent against the national trend for his party (though the last election did show unusual signs that particularly unpopular Ministers could lose up to 8 per cent against the trend). Some modern Disraeli might well say that 'All is Party'. In Britain, Government is Party and Party almost exclusively aims at being Government. For a full and explicit description of this system and an explanation of the discipline in party in terms of *deference,* the American student could not possibly do better than to turn to Professor Leon Epstein's case study *British Politics in the Suez Crisis* (Urbana, 1964) and to Professor Harry Eckstein's contribution on Britain to Samuel H. Beer *et al., Patterns of Government* (New York, 1958), an unusually brilliant textbook; or for a complementary, more than rival, explanation in terms of the historical power and unity of *the Crown,* to the late L. S. Amery's 'The Nature of British Parliamentary Government' in Lord Campion *et al., Parliament: A Survey* (London, 1952), an essay whose insidious Tory influence on my own thinking I should recognise, at last, and cheerfully acknowledge. All this is *very* —and, you may think, happily—un-American.

So my book is interesting if one is interested in British government. For this reason I have presumed some familiarity with the ordinary accounts of British government and have not 'adapted' or further explained my original text in any way, only made a few corrections. But I have added a Postscript to bring the matter up to date to after the election of 1964, and to show how the political and legal strength of a British government and the need for reform are little, if at all, affected by even—as I write—the knife-edge majority of three votes.

London
February, 1965

PREFACE TO THE FIRST EDITION

Parliamentary Reform is one of those things, as Mark Twain remarked about the weather, which everybody talks about, but nobody does anything about. Seldom has there been so much public agreement that something should be done, but seldom so much private agreement that nothing is likely to be done. The Frontbenches of both parties view it as a threat—forgetting that power always rests on authority which is, in turn, a product of public confidence. Backbenchers think of it, if at all, merely as ways of getting more time for each of them to speak on the floor of the House—forgetting that repetition may weary everyone before ever it wears down or diverts the Ministers in question. And some liberal publicists and journalists have sounded very radical by advocating an anachronistic 'restoration of the rights of private members'—forgetting that good colourful copy does not always mean effective control of the executive. Perhaps it takes the peculiar perspective of a student of politics, half engaged and half dispassionate, to suggest that there is an urgent need for Parliamentary reform in Britain *for the sake of the effectiveness of government itself*.

As a student of a subject called 'Government' or 'Political Science', which ranges all the way from what Plato meant to what the Council on Tribunals intends, I do not believe that I or any of my colleagues have any special competence to tell governments how to govern or people in parliaments how to go about their business. But I do think that our peculiar intellectual and professional preoccupations should have, and unavoidably do have, some relevance to politics. We at least have the time and leisure, and are quite well placed, to bridge the gap between understanding how a system works from day to day (which is seldom appreciated by an outsider), and what is likely to happen to it in the future (which is seldom appreciated except by outsiders). We recognize that the wood is composed of trees, but we tend to start with the wood.

This book is both an interpretation of what our system of government does and an advocacy that it should be reformed in certain directions—reformed *both* in order to continue to do what its practitioners have always claimed to do so well, and in order to deal with new problems in new circumstances. So I will not be unhappy if it is not clear whether this book is itself an act of politics, a work of institutional description or an essay in political theory. For it is intended to be all three. I think that we only draw such distinctions for the purposes of study, or for purposes of keeping scholars in their place, and that they should be put together again, as one field and flow of experience, for the sake of practice. For we find ourselves at one of those times of crisis in the life of a nation when theory and practice must commune together as a matter of some urgency. For, quite irrespective of debates about policy, great and sudden doubts have arisen about whether our whole machinery of government, which includes the way we think about it, is adequate to deal with modern problems.

The primary task of political theory is not to state principles or to set out new details or possibilities, but to describe and explain the general relationships which characterize any particular system of government. There is really no ultimate distinction between 'ideas' and 'institutions': ideas are meaningless, or simply not political at all, if they do not seek some institutional or procedural form; and institutions and procedures are regressive if they do not embody living purposes.

No theories, however, are more powerful than those held by men who think themselves to be 'purely practical' with, indeed, 'a proper contempt for mere theory'. For, after all, it was a blind and passionate allegiance by practical politicians to a highly abstract concept of 'Parliamentary Sovereignty' which once made compromise with the American colonies impossible (and in 1962 threw the suburbs into a kind of metaphysical panic about 'what would happen to the *Crown*' if we went into Europe). Today, the most intellectual Ministers adhere to a concept of 'Ministerial *Responsibility*' which firstly means that no one else can control the actions of their civil servants, and secondly means that they are not to be blamed if they can't themselves.

But even if we can uncover the theories involved, there is still always need for choice. But the one choice which would at this time prove completely self-defeating is, I will seek to show, to accept that the relationship of Government to Parliament can continue much as at present. There are times when, in Burke's great phrase, one must 'reform in order to preserve'; and also times when, as Hazlitt argued in a celebrated essay on Burke, one has to ask, 'preserve what?'

I believe that it is possible and desirable to write about complicated matters of government in such a way as can appeal to the judgement of both specialist and layman, particularly as they both form part of an electorate or, more specifically, if they look at such books as this at all, part of an active opinion-making group. Mutual comprehension is, after all, a fairly obvious and elementary, but not always attained, criterion for a just and effective relationship between governments and governed. Even the most complicated systems of electoral representation are not so much devices arising from ideas of 'right', as responses to the need of governments to know accurately what people want or what they will stand for. One of the weaknesses of British government today is that Ministers are too apt to hide themselves from both information and criticism by invoking concepts of 'official secrets', Crown privilege, or 'please just trust us' discretion. There is a virtual revival of *'raison d'État'* (that the *real* reasons for actions cannot ever be publicly stated, that the 'mystery' or craft of government is inexplicable). Ministers have grown foolishly hostile to devices which cast light on such majestic mysteries, such as investigations by Parliamentary Select Committees, or the presumption of the press in trying to report accurately the debates of Party committees (who shelter, in turn, behind antique notions of 'Parliamentary Privilege').

So most of what I have to say will not be new to 'specialists', whether those who practice politics, those who study it, or the many 'agents' or 'servants' of Government and Parliament. But the occupational vice of the specialist is narrowness of vision. He rarely has occasion to consider all the relevant factors set out at once—neither the conservative who fears that if one thing is changed, everything will change, nor the reformer who does not care to consider the 'side-effects' so long as his one Wonder Drug of the moment works its immediate cure. The vice of the layman is either impatience or indifference: he may not be aware of the technical and practical difficulties involved in some reforms he might regard as 'self-evident', although quite as often he is misled into passivity by the expert who tells him that things are impossible which are merely difficult or which are merely a threat to the particular expert's habitual routines. But the general reader is not much impressed by the mere reiteration of 'general principles' if the grounds and evidence in favour of the brief are not set out fairly fully. So I try to do so, even though I am not a specialist in Parliamentary procedure myself. But I do believe that there are no techniques or arts of government so complicated but that their general nature cannot be taken in by the ordinary man of affairs. Those who claim the contrary usually have something to hide or some particular interest to maintain (and this is as true for the 'Law and Custom of Parliament' as it is for the 'Defence of the Realm').

Here, indeed, is a point of theory as well as of practice. For there are many who do believe, as Walter Bagehot did in his *English Constitution,* that it is necessary to deceive in order to govern a free and democratic country. This very view is, I will try to show, part of the present trouble. But I write in the sober belief that free governments are governments that can state publicly the true reasons on which they act. Truth may not always be the victor in a conflict with falsehood, but at least it can never do good governments any harm. Of all the governments in the free world the British administration is certainly the most restrictive in giving access to information about its operations to either scholars or journalists: this I take to be not just the old arrogance of an administrative and political élite which is used to minding its own business, but a new uncertainty about the efficacy of the system.

So I have drawn heavily on the labours of others. Acknowl-

edgement is paid where the principal debts occur, but I have
not provided a bibliography, since excellent ones exist already
in Hansard Society's survey of previous writings, *Parliamentary Reform, 1933–1960* (1961) and in their *Government and
Parliament in Britain: A bibliography* (1964) by John Palmer.
Some Appendices on more specialized or purely factual matters creep after so as to keep the text as plain and clear as
possible. Good government and plain language do, I am sure,
somehow go together—whether by way of describing something or criticizing it. The student of politics is under a particular duty to politicians in this at least.

My own political prejudices and beliefs should become
clear. This book had its germ in my Fabian Tract of 1959,
Reform of the Commons. I am grateful to the Fabian Society
for generous permission to reprint and revise parts of that
pamphlet, as also from my own work in Lord Chorley,
Bernard Crick and Donald Chapman, MP, *Reform of the
Lords* (Fabian Research Series, 1954). But they are in no
way responsible for or to be connected with the opinions expressed here. And I would venture the opinion that I am
writing on something which is likely, now as then, to command support in all Parties (or to split them about equally).
I will here salute as fellow labourers the Conservative authors
of *Change or Decay?* (Conservative Political Centre, 1963),
though also take the chance to execrate those of the Bow
Group who in a special number of their journal *Crossbow*
on Parliamentary reform (New Year, 1960) were so embar-
rassed by their degree of agreement with my Fabian tract
that they were reduced either to plagiary or hairsplitting.
Parts of the sections on the House of Lords draw on articles
which appeared originally in *Parliamentary Affairs, Political
Quarterly* and the *Observer;* and my remarks on the good
old 'pendulum theory' of British elections appeared in *Public
Law.* I thank these journals for permission to reprint with the
usual mutual disassociations. I am especially grateful to the
Observer and to Mr Rudolf Klein for permission to reprint
as an Appendix his most valuable survey, 'What MPs Think
of Their Jobs'. And a former student of mine, Mr Allan Segal,

who has worked in television, contributes an Appendix on 'The Case for Not Televising Parliament'.

I would have liked to have thanked heartily and by name several officers and members of both Houses for help they have given me, but I think that in view of the somewhat polemic nature of this book, the best public thanks is, for once, a politic and evasive generality. I should put on record that I have been stimulated and much helped by the various writings on Parliament and Parliamentary reform of Professors Victor Wiseman and Harry Hanson; and also by Professor John Griffith's contribution to *Law Reform Now!* (Gollancz, 1963) and his informal and friendly advice, for the use or misuse of which I take full responsibility. And, above all, I am eager to thank most warmly Mr William Hampton, of the Extra-Mural Department, Sheffield University, for the very great and intelligent help he gave me, while my temporary research assistant at LSE; he has contributed the Appendix on 'The Facilities of the Library of Congress'.

Two writers who have put their mark upon the present debate about the changing character of British government, have both criticized my Fabian pamphlet for seeking to exaggerate the possible powers of Parliament: Professor Brian Chapman in his *British Government Observed* (Allen and Unwin, 1963), and Mr J. B. Mackintosh in his *The British Cabinet* (Stevens, 1962). I own that I might have been open to that charge. But here will be no possible misunderstanding. This is not another sad and nostalgic appeal for the clock to be put back; the thesis is not that 'the rights' of Parliament are being ignored, but that the effectiveness and efficiency of British government itself is suffering from the lack of informed criticism from those still best fitted to give it and those still directly responsible to the electorate—still MPs themselves, not NEDCs, NICs or even the Fourth Estate itself. Once policy is decided by the Cabinet and the Ministries, and the Acts or Statutory Instruments are pushed through the legislature by party whip and drum, then Ministers and MPs should be dialectic partners, not complete rivals in the scrutiny and control of the administration and in the consideration of future needs and resources.

I should add that in writing before the election of 1964 I have a high degree of confidence, alas, that this book will be unhappily relevant whatever happens.

December, 1963   B. R. C.
London School of Economics and Political Science

CHAPTER I

PARLIAMENT AND
THE CRISIS OF GOVERNMENT

The Decline of Parliament

The first business of a government is to govern. As much as
we want protecting from the State, this is, historically and
politically, a sophisticated afterthought compared to the
primal need for the powers-that-be to do things actively for
the preservation of the community and the common welfare.
To say that all government rests upon consent is true enough.
But it is true for all governments. The concept is mere rhetoric
if we use it to put the cart before the horse: first there is always the fact of being governed, only then do we begin to
question the manner in which we are governed. We do not
consent to be governed. We grow up into a world in which
we are governed. On this the Conservative and the Socialist
at least agree, in contrast to the old-fashioned Liberal. Indeed, much of the growth of 'democracy' in Britain, which
still means little more than the extension of the franchise, is
plainly to be seen not as a response of governments to the
power of abstract ideas of right, but rather the realization
that for government to be carried on at all in an industrial
society, the basis of support has to be widened. The strongest
governments are those who can mobilize consent on the
widest scale; modern governments can attempt tasks impossible before the democratic era. But this is true both for
governments of free and of un-free societies alike. All modern governments rest upon the need for mass consent, whether
it is given voluntarily or manufactured in controlled conditions.

The need for strong government can be taken for granted.
But strong government needs strong opposition both if it is

to be free government and if it is, in the long run, to be efficient and effective. There is much historical evidence to suggest that in a complex, modern industrial society decisions
which cannot be questioned publicly are likely, in the long
run, either to prove obviously inept or to need a degree of
violent enforcement that civilized societies should not stom-
ach. There is much contemporary evidence to suggest that
Britain so lacks effective scrutiny of the workings of the Executive that a situation is created in which popular esteem
for Parliament and Government declines and its own effectiveness crumbles.

There is something out of the ordinary about the degree of
worry in Britain today both about policies for the future and
about control of the executive. Part of the trouble is that we
too often think of these things separately. What is at issue is
really the whole machinery of government of which Parliament is part, only part, but still an essential part.[1] The worries are many and topical: lack of proper and responsible
machinery for long-term planning; the character of recruitment for public service and for political life; the control of
the administration; the apparent confusion, perhaps even
breakdown, in the accepted notions of Ministerial responsibility; seemingly unnecessary secrecy about the ordinary operations of government; the lack of effective control of Defence
expenditures; the apparent divorce between scientists and administrators; lack of knowledge of the ways and means of
pressure groups in Whitehall and Westminster; continued
uncertainties about Parliamentary powers in relation to the
Nationalized Industries; the control of the powers and
methods of the police; confusion and collision in the twilight
zone between political and judicial functions; the discretion-

---

[1] This has been said recently, though in somewhat different
terms, by Brian Chapman in his *British Government Observed*
(London, 1963) and by Joseph Grimond, MP, in his *The Liberal
Challenge* (Hollis and Carter, 1963). I am in complete agreement
with Part One of the latter, apart from a persistent pun on 'liberal'
and 'Liberal'. See also R. H. S. Crossman, MP, in his introduction
to the Fontana Library's Walter Bagehot, *The English Constitution* (Collins, 1963).

ary powers of the Home Secretary and the police in relation to public meetings and demonstrations; the adequacy of the machinery of justice itself; the complexities of electoral law; the status and control of immigrants and other aliens; the rights and duties of the press, radio and television; the scope of Parliamentary privilege—particularly touching the press, radio and television; the existing machinery for the redress of grievances and administrative faults, and the arbitrariness of whether tribunals or other forms of public inquiry exist at all in different spheres of the administration—this is a long sentence and it could be longer, and recent cases will be cited in all these spheres. These worries go far beyond the competence or incompetence of a particular Government. They have in common a feeling that Parliament and the Executive are both not doing things which should be done and also not finding out, through some failure in their relationship, whether things that are done are in fact done well. If political leaders do not see this connection in all these things, they are then themselves demonstrating the degree to which an alienation between the government and the governors has already progressed.

There is no incompatibility between strong government and strong opposition. Changing circumstances demand both. It is neither relevant nor helpful to recall or invent some golden age when Parliament 'really did' govern the country, or when independent and encyclopaedic Backbenchers 'really did' make Ministers tremble.[2] Even if the facts were ever so, it is not a sensible intellectual method to compare everything in terms of a falling off from some ideal image of the past. For the question then arises, what next? Parliament has always been in the process of change. We will see that many of the 'ancient traditions' are in fact very modern. The relative stability of Parliamentary procedure in the last fifty years is the exception rather than the rule. (And it has been far more

[2] See, for instance, Michael Foot, MP, *Parliament in Danger* (Pall Mall Pamphlets, 1959); Christopher Hollis, *Has Parliament a Future?* (Liberal Publications Department, 1960), and John Grigg (formerly Lord Altrincham), 'The Commons in Eclipse', *Observer,* 10 March, 1963.

stable, or rigid, than the organization and methods of the Executive.) The modern executive must dominate the House to get its legislation through. But this has been true since the time of Parnell. The whole process is older than most people think. The dominance of the House by the Executive is not a product of the 'rise of the Welfare State', but a product of habits born in the Parnellite struggles, when the majority had to ride rough-shod over attempts to obstruct, not particular measures, but the whole system; and these habits were rendered compulsive by the two World Wars. The wars have had more to do than the Welfare State in creating the fundamental problem of the decline of Parliamentary control.

For this fundamental problem is *not* lack of Parliamentary time, as is usually said. It is rather an attitude of mind about the nature of British government and politics which has grown up, fortified by wartime experience, in the Ministries and on both Frontbenches. More Parliamentary time could be found if anyone wanted it strongly enough. This will be shown. But governments have grown to feel that they are neither representative, nor in any real sense themselves Members of Parliament, but simply remote and all-powerful trustees for the electorate, only answerable to anyone at General Elections. The prejudice grows that proceedings in Parliament are a waste of Ministerial time. It is this prejudice which has to be met. Party leaders talk of Parliamentary reform only when they face the facts of life as an Opposition. The Ministerial mind is not much moved by demonstrations that there is public disquiet with Parliament. For the Ministry shares this view, indeed is part responsible for it. To them Parliament is a pretty futile place. There has actually been an increasing tendency of recent years for senior Ministers to be put in the House of Lords *in order* to shield them from 'the time-wasting turmoil' of the Commons. And if this lofty attitude might appear to threaten popular confidence in the whole system, then this only shows, it is held, that most people are an ignorant lot in not distinguishing between the real government and the shadow proceedings of Parliament; in not realizing that Parliament does not legislate, but only criticizes. And, after all, it is shrewdly said, the whole legislative process is really like a great iceberg: only a tenth of it may appear above the surface, the most important part is that which goes before legislation ever appears on the floor of Parliament. But this is to beg the whole question. It will be seen that Parliament does, indeed, spend far too much time on criticizing the inevitable and far too little in examining the submerged processes of administration and influence from which the pinnacles of legislation emerge—let alone what happens to them afterwards. But at the moment as usual we do not build enough roads; we simply put up more warning signs.

No Magic Stabilizers

Right at the beginning it is as well to meet three common objections to the assertion that there is a problem at all. First, there is the super-realist who asks why the gradual demise of Parliament cannot be taken for granted and accepted, so long as there are general elections and so long as the press and the Courts, in all their forms, remain free and active—as they will while the British people remain what they are, etc. What is important is simply that opposition should exist at all, in its broadest sense, not any particular recipe of procedures for opposition and criticism, etc. The answer is not one of principle, but of practice. The Courts can only examine matters that fall within Statute or Common Law; and one of the things at issue is the extent of Ministerial and administrative discretion. The press can offer criticism only on the basis of information coming from somewhere; and one of the things at issue is the *growing* secrecy attached to the operations of government. Parliament is still the most effective device we have for scrutinizing the work of government and for focusing news, opinion and criticism relevantly. The Courts cannot question its proceedings. Parliament could do more itself and could do more to help the Courts and the press, but it is hard to see that any other body, or process, could even do as much.

Second, there is the procedural or antiquarian-romantic who says that adjustments have in fact taken place—though too subtle for outsiders to see; who maintains that although Parliament apparently allows governments to get away with too much too easily, in fact informal checks and balances will have arisen elsewhere—for instance, in the private meetings of the parties themselves. We were beginning to hear it said that the real opposition is always within the Government Party. All this is at best a dangerous half-truth. More often it is a piece of plain man's metaphysics, a subtle version of the old mechanistic theories of heaven-sent 'checks and balances' and 'divisions of power': now of the fatuous belief that we are dealing with an organism which always somehow and wonderfully brings Executive and Government into equilibrium or—to be fully modern—ecological balance. Cut off a toe and another one grows, or anyway the good old Constitution silently adapts. It may adapt, however, by sitting down and never moving again or by falling over every time it needs to run. There is some evidence for the latter view.

The third objection is more comprehensive: that nothing matters as much as that the electoral system creates a regular alternation between the two parties. This view goes very deep. It is worth examining. But it is almost entirely false. Whatever the result of the General Election of 1964, the evidence of 1959 will remain and is quite enough.

Never before had a British political party succeeded in gaining a working majority in three successive elections—let alone adding to both its seats and votes each time. This feat alone should destroy the myth that in a two-party system there is some inevitability about alternation. Our two-party system is clearly an historical product of the type of social division which has dominated English politics since at least the industrial revolution, and of the religious divisions between 'Church established' and non-conformity which went before. The modern Cabinet system, together with all those tendencies of electoral law and practice which make it difficult for third parties to keep or gain an effective number of Parliamentary seats, clearly solidified, but did not create, the two-party system. It is endlessly disputable what is the right strength to be attached to each link in the chains of historical cause and condition which have come to bind the system together; but it is not seriously disputable that all these causes and conditions normally add up to two and to two only. And the idea of necessary alternation, while it cuts deep into our political preconceptions, yet bleeds more than binds our body politic. There should be no doubt that the idea, however empirically implausible, does cut deep. Free government, liberty itself, we are often told (or overhear ourselves lecturing), ultimately depends on a government's supposed knowledge that it is likely to be followed, indeed pursued, shortly afterwards by another. Don't cheat or you will be found out—and electoral consequences will follow; don't kick, or you will be kicked in turn; and keep time for five years, but you'll still get knocked down by the pendulum.

Now the idea of 'alternation' is, in a strict sense, 'liberal'. It is part of an era that has vanished but of liberal assumptions that have not. An examination of the work of James Bryce, both as Liberal statesman and liberal 'political scientist', would illustrate this point. He really did believe, as his American friend President Lowell of Harvard tried to demonstrate statistically, that the political universe oscillated in a dignified and definite rhythm. His *American Commonwealth* and his *Modern Democracies* sum up a whole climate of opinion and are the kind of books which influence subsequent thought almost to the degree that they become known only at second hand. Bryce transmuted into politics the assumptions of Manchester political economy. Given perfect competition and perfect knowledge of the market, that is, a free electoral system based on manhood franchise (with bits of proper property bias) and a free press, then the demand of the rationally self-interested electorate for a particular party would automatically decline in favour of the other party as the price of the first (in terms of mismanagement) rose. If Disraeli mismanaged Ottoman affairs, the Grand Old Man would come in; and if the GOM could not govern his own friends, let alone Ireland, back would come the Tories. An enlightened public, glued to the *Morning Post's* exhaustive parliamentary reports, weighed and reweighed the issues. They might occasionally flinch from this formidable task out of sheer laziness; but it was the statesman's duty to exhort them back again into their responsible agony of (liberal) ever-open-mindedness. 'Slackness', in politics as in the rest of life, was the only real natural vice—and one that people could always be 'shamed out of'. And, anyway, sooner or later, if anything went far enough, a 'reaction' (to something) would set in—a concept as current and as fatuous in liberal thought as it is in Marxist. In a sense, this 'rational alternation' view has only to be stated to see how absurd it has become; indeed neither Conservative nor Socialist would think that alternation was inherently likely or even desirable. Bryce's brand of liberal political mechanics was, at the best, the dominant ideology of a particular period of English politics.

The evidence of contemporary history does not argue even a contingent, let alone a necessary alternation. The electoral history of the Conservative Party in this century, despite the recent astonishingly close division of popular votes, shows that it is still the party overwhelmingly the most likely, unless there are quite exceptional circumstances, to govern. Hence the question before the British electorate nearly always simply appears as: 'shall we trust the Tories again?' rather than the Liberal 'what are both offering and are they sincere?' The identification of the Conservatives with—never mind definitions—the great felt-thing, the Establishment, strengthens this anti-alternating tendency, this bias in the system arising from the snobbery of the mean streets every bit as much as from the conceit of the clubs. (And, indeed, from the famous electoral bias arising from the piling up of Labour votes in safe urban seats.) But the very establishing of Conservative power, the quite 'constitutional' status of the Conservative Party, is itself the factor which enables the natural dissidence of dissent to coalesce into one Opposition. Historically, the Labour Party cannot be sensibly pictured (by friend or foe) as a Socialist movement with a programme driving towards perpetual office; it is rather a gathering-up into coherent opposition of diverse tendencies: nonconformist England united by dislike of, or ostracism by, the Establishment. Thus there is a two-party system, but one in which the chances are unequal.

So far so abstract; but the practical point is obvious. Many of our traditional liberties have been held to depend on the alternation of the parties. To many, 'liberty' could be defined (in minimum if not complete terms) as those rights and conditions necessary to ensure regular and peaceful changes of government. We are now in great danger of taking for granted the beneficent effects of a process that does not take place. It is no accident that a rash of demands has suddenly sprung up for legal safeguards against all sorts of actions hitherto trusted to the discretion of public authorities; phone-tapping, immigration procedures, press access to council meetings, employment policy regarding race, the 'right' of assembly, etc. And, even from those most enamoured of the meaningless dogma of the 'sovereignty of Parliament', murmurs of vexation have arisen at Parliament's wildly elastic and erratic interpretations of 'privilege'. Talk is drawn more and more towards the American concept of 'civil liberties', a concept quite un-English so long as the essential foundation of English political liberties was held to be a natural rhythm of alternation which made formal safeguards unnecessary. What is fundamental to (reasonably) free government is not regular alternation as such, but the constitutionalizing of an already established Opposition. There must be an opposition —it cannot be artificially created when, for instance, a young country is dominated by a nationalistic rage for unity; but an Opposition at all, if it is to be effective, must be given special abilities to criticize, and also special protection from prosecution—such as members of governing groups normally only share among themselves: privilege, immunity, pay, honours, etc. Grave doubts could be raised about the suitability for export to 'underdeveloped' areas of British institutions based on the assumptions of a two-party system. But what is also forgotten is that, even in Britain itself, the effectiveness of Opposition is likely to decline sharply if one party succeeds in staying in power for long consecutive periods of time and if, at the best of times, conscious efforts are not made to strengthen the facilities for opposition when the powers of the Executive increase. And it may be that an Opposition will itself become infected by the 'Executive mind' and act

on the theory that its primary function is to furnish a 'responsible alternative government' rather than, quite simply,
to oppose.

So perhaps it is not always wise to raise the blanket-bogey
of 'not understanding the (hidden) spirit of the British system', etc., whenever any attempt at all is made to consider
whether Parliament is effectively fulfilling its function. How
can it possibly be supposed that at any given time there is
always a 'balance' between the two great functions of Parliament, that of creating a strong government and that of trying
to criticize its hide off within the hearing of the electorate?
But this is commonly assumed—and by people who are not
normally considered either simple or metaphysical. There is
in fact a great deal of cant from MPs in which the word
'organic' mechanically figures, or else the tag from Tenny-
son about precedents broadening down, which argues that
the procedures of Parliament necessarily evolve (Burke-
through-Darwin-out-of-Aristotle) until they are near perfect,
and that there is always a sensible response to any challenge
which threatens the divinely ordained balance between criticism and support of government. Yet if the public is suspi-
cious that the legislative and procedural history of recent
years had always weighted the scales in the same direction,
that of vastly and deliberately strengthening the Ministers
against the House, the public is surely right. There is no
question of a balance: we are approaching the point when
it will only be a question of how much initiative the Frontbenches will be graciously pleased to allow the Backbenches.
We are already at the point where demands from Parliament
and public for an inquiry into certain acts or omissions of
government cannot ensure that the form of such an inquiry
is in any way likely to meet their demands. If the Prime Minister says 'One Judge', acting in heaven knows what capacity,
then it will be one Judge, and not a committee of either or
both Houses, or any other form of responsible public inquiry.

Public Interest and Reform

No one in their senses nowadays questions the broad basis on
which Parliament goes about its business. Root and branch

schemes for reform, such as were canvassed in the 1930s, are no longer the fashion and, indeed, no longer relevant. Few intelligent men in the 1930s could have imagined, amid the economic events of the time and the seeming incapacity of Parliament to deal with them, that the coming to power of the Labour Party in 1945 with a large majority would not lead to the most radical changes in the purposes—and therefore the procedures—of the highly decrepit old Mother of Parliaments.

The procedures of the House did not allow an easy delivery for such a uniquely large and contentious programme as Mr Attlee's between 1945 and 1950. But the fact that it could get through at all—with the need for only relatively minor procedural alterations—showed that Parliament still possessed a quite unexpected flexibility, if pushed hard enough. In other words, it is a long path from the innovating zeal of even such a respected and judicious writer on the Constitution as Sir Ivor Jennings in his *Parliamentary Reform* of 1934, to the apostrophe to institutional tradition of Mr Herbert Morrison's *Government and Parliament,* written exactly twenty years later.

But, as usual, the truth lies between extremes: the danger of ceasing to think big is ceasing to think at all. The welcome decision that, after all, there is no place like home can become all too often sheer parochialism. The reputation of the House of Commons in the outside world is now far in excess of its merits. By comparison with the popular assembly of almost any other free country, Parliament has fallen hideously behind the times both in its procedures and in the facilities that it extends to its Members, and there is good ground for thinking that it would benefit from some fairly drastic internal alterations and repairs which would go far beyond mere patching. Despite the general complacency of MPs themselves, there has been evidence lately of public concern: flare-ups of indignation and mockery in the popular press, worried soul-searchings and reassurances in the heavier papers. Parliamentary reform has actually become a newsworthy topic. Some MPs are aware of a growing scepticism, even hostility, certainly bewilderment, among the public; but the House as a whole seems to react only by an increasing touchiness about 'privilege'—such as telling journalists not to be rude to them and not to tell the public what goes on in the 'private' party meetings.

True, the House itself has appointed several Select Committees of recent years to inquire into its domestic affairs and procedures, but these bodies have, we will see, come up with almost nothing of real importance; they have limited themselves to almost ritual acts of reassurance about the 'complex and subtle' nature of our Parliamentary institutions. Meanwhile, the public has little help in trying to form a sensible image of what Parliament is doing and, in particular, what it is doing for them.

The declining effectiveness of the House has been paralleled, as we will see, by a rising efficiency of the Executive. But there is no necessary contradiction between wanting a strong Executive and wanting a more effective and efficient House of Commons. The more power we entrust to a Government to do things for us, the greater the need for it to operate amid a blaze of publicity and criticism. But there is such a contradiction at the moment because Parliament has not improved her own instruments of control, scrutiny, criticism and suggestion to keep pace with the great improvements of efficiency and the increase of size in the departments of executive government. Small wonder that public comprehension of Parliament is so low and that confidence is declining. Unless Parliament does something to repair its hide-bound ways, this confidence may degenerate from the typical affectionate scepticism (at times so good for the pride of Ministers) into an indignant cynicism (hitherto, of course, a purely foreign phenomenon).

While the public is interested in the content and substance of what Parliament discusses and the legislation it approves, concern is more rare with the methods by which Parliament fulfils its function. Partly this is because the Mother of Parliaments is not shy of hinting that the way she conducts her business is the wonder of the wise; partly because the study of Parliamentary procedure seems to many just so dry and dull; and partly because there is widespread confusion about what the functions of Parliament should be. Yet the purpose of any institution, or the operative ideals of any group of men, are only realizable through procedures and so existing procedures must constantly be examined in light of the great radical question: 'Do they serve the public interest?' The procedures and principles of Parliamentary government are inextricably intertwined and the one cannot be understood without the other.

There is perhaps a primary level of confusion in the public mind about the function of Parliament which can be put out of the way: the belief that Parliament should deliberate and legislate as a body of some 630 independent minds, irrespective of party, passion or pedigree, dies hard and is the source of much confusion. Any student of politics worth his salt will, on the utterance of this fallacy by even friend or family, settle himself easily into a familiar and forceful rebuttal: that party organization is necessary both in Parliament and the constituencies, if you want to be able at elections to hold any group of politicians clearly responsible for anything; and that strong and enforcible party discipline is necessary if there is to be a coherent development of policy. It is recognized that an MP has something very technical called a 'conscience' which he may exercise by not voting at all on matters concerning capital punishment, divorce, gambling, conscription, sex, religion and—at various times—Egyptian and then European affairs; but it is also recognized—whatever Edmund Burke said at Bristol—that, to adapt a once famous phrase of Ernest Bevin at Brighton, an MP cannot hawk his conscience around to every issue that turns up.

Much of the undoubted public scepticism about Parliament and the growing antipathy towards the whole profession of politics admittedly stems from this fallacy of self-defeating individualism. It is, in a silly but safe form, the dominating motive of many of the young Liberals of the moment; it gets more sinister with those who speak, sometimes innocently, of 'wanting to get rid of politics'. But the MP or the student of politics, however secure and sound he feels in refuting such muddle, should at least ask himself whether all alienation of the elector and the elected is due to ignorance on the part of the former, and whether, in any case, verbal rebuttals by the latter cut much ice at all.

Certainly there is no self-evident reason for assuming that

Parliament is functioning in the best possible manner. The control of the Executive over the House increases during some great Parliamentary crises, notably the obstructionism of Parnell and the Irish Party in the 1880s, above all in the two World Wars, and by the exceptional pressure on the time-table during Mr Attlee's two Ministries; but when these particular crises are past, the Executive never fully relaxes its new grip. It would be simple if it were merely a question of bad leaders needing strict discipline, but even with the best of generals habits of blind command, as well as of blind obedience, outlive the campaign.

Certainly it is no longer eccentric to suggest that Westminster needs to reform itself to keep pace with the technical efficiency and expansion of Whitehall, indeed in order to allay the public suspicion that Members have become mere Ministerial voting machines that rarely even backfire in protest. Certainly there is a declining sense of assurance in individuals or particular groups involved in some conflict with their local authorities, some planning authority, public board or government department, that their local MP is likely to be of any help to them. The *cliché* of the popular press is, indeed, a broadly correct description: most MPs have become mere 'rubber stamps'—and not, unfortunately, because they are literally forced to become so, but because they themselves seem happy to become so. We will see that this is partly because, with the size of governments, the proportion of jobs to boys is quite high, certainly compared to most professions; and the prospects for promotion are fairly good if one does not blot one's copybook too publicly. But we will also see that there have been occasions in recent years, notably the creation of the Select Committee on Nationalized Industries, when Backbench opinion has proved too strong to resist.

A leading article in *The Times* of 23 December, 1957, complained that the House of Commons had 'far too many little men' who were 'engaged in desperate fighting over things that do not matter'. This is a fairly typical and sweeping indictment. But different things, of course, matter to different people; top people and little men live differently and think differently. The wide scatter of matters raised in Question Time and in debates on the Adjournment is, for example, surely a good thing; something matters to everyone, depressing though at times this truth is, and the range of topics keeps the whole executive at least somewhat awake and aware. What is depressing is not that so many things in themselves do not matter, but that they cannot on occasion be made to matter more. What so often happens is not that MPs are not brilliant enough men to ask the really searching question, but that they lack the office facilities and the authoritative sources of information to follow through such a question against the well-briefed reply which turneth away a river of wrath into a delta of confusion. Rarely is the 'desperate fighting' inherently trivial, but often it lacks depth. British MPs, like British boxers of recent years, still have a classic straight left lead which can pierce most guards, but they rarely develop anything to throw after it. And that they do not is because they are not supposed to; their role is that of perpetual sparring partner who must never injure the champion (which is fair enough), but who must also never be allowed seriously to influence his style (which is unfortunate). If the champion gets the worst of it, he simply gives himself better equipment and removes some from his sparring partner. This has unhappy results on his training, but apparently it matters little in terms of his popularity, for however often our champion is plastered by foreign opponents, he is still our lad; masochism is perhaps the great national vice, in politics as well as sport and other things.

It is just possible that we might do better by other methods. But since in politics we work with the material we have at hand we can only see what methods might fit, if we first examine the present situation.

CHAPTER II

THE STRENGTH OF BRITISH GOVERNMENT

The Concentration of Power

Of all governments of countries with free political institutions, British government exhibits the greatest concentration of power and authority. Nowhere else is a Government normally so free to act decisively, so unfettered by formal restraints of Constitutional Law, by any Federal divisions of power, by any practice of strong and active local government, or by any real likelihood of defeat in the Parliament. The British system of government is in essentials quite simple: a Prime Minister dominates a Cabinet which in turn dominates a Party majority in the House of Commons; this Party, under the same leaders, has to fight periodic General Elections: if the Party wins the elections, then the Prime Minister and his Cabinet control the entire machinery of legislation and administration, if they lose they go into Opposition.

There are no overriding legal restraints whatever upon a British Government's actions. A Minister may break the existing law, but then there is no law to stop the Government passing a new law to give retrospective validity to the previously illegal act. The only restraints are political. Governments are restrained by what they think the country will stand for come the General Election, and they adhere to things like General Elections because they *prefer* (whether out of ethics, habit or prudence, or all three) to settle disputes politically rather than despotically and coercively. If the time ever came when a British Government chose to extend its life indefinitely without facing elections, the only restraint would be the general one of 'opinion' reaching towards its most unpolitical form, rebellion.[1]

This makes British government both superbly strong and somewhat insensitive. It can act, for good and ill, with an unparalleled concentration of power; but it will be restrained only by its own morality and good sense and by the broad, crude, drastic test of a General Election. Abuses which are not likely to affect which way people vote are not likely to worry governments. Parliament itself now functions primarily as the place where weapons are forged, propaganda given and information extracted, that are likely to be useful in the elections. It is no longer itself the decisive battle-ground except in circumstances as extraordinary as those of 1940.[2] The rival accounts of the 'conduct of the late administration' and the announced policies over which elections are fought (though other factors may decide them) present a 'take it or leave it', 'lump it or like it' aspect to the electorate in which even a member of a Party feels helpless to influence any points of relative detail. But he would be even more helpless if Parties were not growing aware that elections may be won and lost not just by who votes, but also by who does not vote. Neither party can count on all of its followers always voting for it whatever it has done or says it will do, even though it can usually count, to an astonishing degree, on their not switching in large numbers to the other party. British government is 'an autocracy', as A. L. Lowell said in his *Government of England* (New York, 1908), but an autocracy which operates in the open light of public opinion, and with the need to carry that opinion with it.

In time of war even the statutory requirement for periodic

[1] Both the Parliament Acts of 1911 and of 1949, however, left the House of Lords with the power to reject absolutely any Bill to extend the life of a Parliament. But all this means is that a Government would first have to introduce a Bill abolishing the House of Lords, which could only be delayed by their Lordships under the terms of the 1911 and 1949 Acts.

[2] Some kind of Birthday Honour may well be given to the first author who plainly states that it would be *unconstitutional* for MPs to frustrate the wishes of the electorate by voting so as to defeat their own Party in Parliament.

General Elections is waived with very little public disquiet. Indeed, in the Second World War British government achieved a degree of centralized control and of effective total planning which plainly surpassed that of its totalitarian enemy. This did not mean that the Nazis were not really totalitarian, or that Britain had become so. The aspirations of the Nazi ideology of Leadership, Expansion and Power, and Racial Purity were all too real and were implemented; but their machinery of government was grossly imperfect: the absolute authority of one man alone could not prevent, indeed partly caused, constant rivalry between and among the Party and the bureaucracy. British government in wartime exhibited the classic efficiency claimed by the Romans for their doctrine and institution of 'Constitutional Dictatorship'. For the limited purposes of winning a war, of dealing with an emergency, a Prime Minister was able to initiate and authorize a totally planned allocation of resources, but to share the burdens of initiation, execution and mutual adjustment of policies with an established hierarchy of political leaders used to acting in concert. The machinery of British government is highly flexible between extremes of action and inaction.

There was Churchill's famous utterance: 'All I wanted was compliance with my wishes after reasonable discussion.' The real point of his remark illuminates the whole British system: that decisions made after 'reasonable discussion' are likely to be more effectively carried out than those made purely autocratically. Decisions can usually be more drastic, more authoritative and less tentative, if other leaders agree that the edicts are likely to be followed: and Churchill's 'wishes', while nearly always pills to be swallowed whole by his colleagues, yet frequently emerged after discussion as coated with substances more palatable to the public.

We all comment, in and out of season, on the wisdom and adequacy of particular British Prime Ministers. But the system is always held to be stronger than any particular man. The character of British government will change remarkably between the Premierships of an Asquith and a Lloyd George, or a Baldwin and Churchill, yet the system always pushes forward someone, however inadequate at times, to fill in so big a role.

Even foreign comment is rarely unfriendly, however, about the basic system. Long generations of American students of government, both 'firm government' Republicans and reforming Democrats, have looked with envy at what they rightly regard as the greater political power of the British Prime Minister compared to that of the American President. For the President is less powerful and established as Party leader, he lacks control by direct patronage over Congress, and he is always likely to be faced either by openly hostile majorities in either House, or (as with Roosevelt after his second great victory in 1936), by a nominally friendly majority of Congressmen who are, however, under no electoral compulsion to stick together, still less to view themselves as the President's almost ever faithful liegemen. The basic reason for this is historical: that American Congressmen are elected far more on local issues, whereas the British MP since 1867 is elected almost entirely on national trends or national party issues. (In this sense the British people get the type of government they want.)

This American envy has not always been well placed, in that if the first business of government is to govern, then it is unlikely that an administration as unified and centralized as the British could have ever held together a country so much more politically diverse as *the* United States (indeed until the Civil War settled it by bayonets, 'these United States'). But this envy has recognized British government for what it is: a system whose whole dynamic rests on the carrying on of government, not on the niceties of a truly representative electoral system (which it is not),[3] and whose limits rest on the ultimate check of the General Election, not on the day to day results of votes in Parliament.

So strong is the power of British government that it can be seriously doubted whether there is a British Constitution at all, in any sense of 'constitution' in which it is not simply true by definition that all governments have one (that is we know there would be nothing necessarily Whiggish about a book sim-

[3] See how harshly we all brush aside the case for electoral reform as being irrelevant to the business of Government: we all unite in calling British Government 'Responsible Government', but hardly 'Representative Government'.

ply titled *The Constitution of the USSR*). If a constitution is
'a system of effective restraints upon governmental action',[4]
then certainly *legal* safeguards do not explain the regular restraints upon British government—which, after all, does fly in
the face of one of the longest speculative and practical traditions in European politics: that good government is the 'government of laws and not of men'. Pitt the elder was the last
British Prime Minister to believe that there were some things
which Parliament had done, such as taxing the unrepresented
colonies, or would like to do, which were in fact 'unconstitutional' and illegal.

The remarkable concentration of political authority in Britain, and its equally remarkable flexibility, arises from the almost continuous history of power being exercised in the name
of the Crown. The phrase 'King-in-Parliament' has been a
proper description of political reality in Britain ever since
Plantagenet times. The content of the symbol has changed, but
not the underlying reality of a centralized administration governing in some forum of debate. The forum has moved from
a Great Council, through many forms of Parliament to the
present system of Cabinet facing a mass electorate. But the
predominancy of government has changed less than the character of the forum, or the institutions of opinion, in which it
takes place. 'Parliamentary Government' has, indeed, been the
exception, not the rule. In a strict sense of a government dependent on uncontrolled, critical, hence shifting and uncertain, majorities in Parliament, Britain has only known Parliamentary Government in the period between the Reform Bills
of 1832 and 1867. Before that, even in the late eighteenth
century, the dominating assumption was that the King's Ministers would normally be supported *because* they were the King's
servants and because the King, even after 1688, was held to
be ultimately responsible both for the conduct of administration and for the initiation of important legislation (as indeed
he was so long as he had a real choice of Ministers).

After 1867, the dominating assumption was that a Cabinet
should normally be supported *because* it was composed of the

[4] Carl J. Friedrich, *Constitutionalism and Democracy,* rev. ed.
(New York, 1950), p. 26.

leaders of the majority Party. In this early modern period, first characterized in Walter Bagehot's *The English Constitution*, the system was called either 'Cabinet Government' or 'Party Government' (both being descriptions which were really theories, and correct theories, to explain how Britain was governed). Now the question arises, whether or not some new description is needed to account for the great growth in importance in, as it were, some 'second modern period', of the office of Prime Minister and his role in a continuous strengthening of both Party discipline and ever more uniform and integrated procedures in an ever more expanded Civil Service.[5]

Sovereignty and Convention

At any time after 1688 the system of British government has had some theoretical coherence in the doctrine of 'the Sovereignty of Parliament'. But this may now obscure more than it explains. There is an habitual clinging to this highly abstract theory by many would-be purely practical men which helps to hide even from themselves what is actually happening; and there are even traces of a deliberate obscurantism by which the concept is used to conceal from the public the continuously declining role of Parliament in British government and politics. This concept must be examined because even the most untheoretical call it 'a convenient short hand' to describe and explain the whole British system.

What does the concept of Sovereignty explain? It explains that Parliament, as great Blackstone said in his *Commentaries on the Laws of England*:

. . . hath sovereign and uncontrollable authority in the making, confirming, enlarging, restraining, abrogating, repealing, reviving and expounding of laws, concerning matters of all possible denominations, ecclesiastical or temporal,

[5] See John P. Mackintosh's masterful *The British Cabinet* (Stevens, 1962), and R. H. S. Crossman's forceful, if somewhat derivative, Introduction to the Fontana Library's edition of Bagehot's *The English Constitution* (Collins, 1963).

civic, military, maritime, or criminal: *this being the place where that absolute power, which must in all governments reside somewhere, is entrusted by the constitution of these kingdoms. All* mischiefs and grievances, operations and remedies, that transcend the ordinary course of the laws, are within the reach of this extraordinary tribunal. It can regulate or new-model the succession to the Crown; as was done in the reigns of Henry VIII and William III. It can alter the established religion of the land; as was done, in a variety of instances, in the reigns of Henry VIII and his three children. It can change and create afresh even the constitution of the kingdom and Parliaments themselves; as was done by the Act of Union and the several statutes for triennial and septennial elections. It can, in short, do everything that is not naturally impossible.

This is formidable, whoever in fact controls Parliament: Blackstone was making a deliberate and decisive assault on all those who held Whiggish notions that Parliament was, or should be, restrained by the Higher Laws of some unwritten, or written and reformed fundamental constitution. And the official modern guide to Parliamentary procedure states:

> The constitution has assigned no limits to the authority of Parliament over matters and persons within its jurisdiction. A law may be unjust and contrary to sound principles of government; but Parliament is not controlled in its discretion, and when it errs, its errors can only be corrected by itself. To adopt the words of Sir Edward Coke, the power of Parliament 'is so transcendent and absolute, as it cannot be confined either for causes or persons within any bounds'.[6]

This depends on what is meant by 'Parliament'. But if, in fact, the Prime Minister-in-Cabinet controls the Commons, is this not, then, still true? The theory may still be true in essentials even though some use it to make the unhelpful, even silly, assertion that 'Parliament' (meaning all MPs and Lords) could

[6] Sir Thomas Erskine May's *Treatise on the Law, Privileges, Proceedings and Usages of Parliament*, 16th ed., edited by Sir Edward Fellowes and T. G. B. Cocks (London, 1957), p. 28.

still 'in theory' (that is never in practice) exercise these powers. But it may still seem to describe the original source and
the present extent of the power of the Government. Then the
dilemma seems dark indeed and the stark picture we have
painted of government checked only by General Elections
would seem to need no qualification. But the theory depends
on an assumption which is not just 'one of theory', but of fact
and evidence. The critical italics in the above quotation from
Blackstone are my own.

The assumption he makes, that in every government there
is a clear place of such absolute power, is plainly false. The
example of Federal Constitutions alone refutes it. Thus, of
course, generations of English lawyers, from Blackstone
through Dicey even to the Colonial Office today, have regarded Federal Governments as, at the best, bastard forms of
life—which is plainly absurd or, at best, the confusion of British preferences with foreign realities. It may be true that Federal systems are prone to run into difficulties in times of
emergency when they cannot, or cannot readily, summon and
assert such sovereign power; but it is equally true that the British system does not normally use it. What the concept of the
'Sovereignty of Parliament' does explain is that there are no
possible *legal* limitations on the sovereignty of Parliament.
But this is a very formal and fleshless thought. For what is
interesting is not what could be done, but what is likely to be
done politically. It tells us little to tell us that no Court or other
body can challenge an Act of Parliament or a proceeding in
Parliament. This led A. V. Dicey to distinguish between 'legal
sovereignty', exercised by the Queen-in-Parliament, and 'political sovereignty', exercised by the electorate. The one is what
is possible, the other is what is likely. But this distinction is
not as helpful as it seems. For plainly Parliament as well as the
electorate plays a role in political influence; and everybody
(including Members of Parliament) form part of an electorate, which is itself only to be defined in legal terms. The real
distinction is between what people may do in legal and in political capacities; but this does not correspond to any precise
distinction between, as Dicey suggested, institutions like 'Par-

liament' and 'the electorate'.[7] They are in fact, linked indissolubly by the political processes of party.

The concept of sovereignty is best reserved for the conditional assertion that all governments may face circumstances of emergency in which normal constitutional rules have to be ignored if the State is to survive. Thus we can say that British government has a capacity for *sovereign* action, as shown in the Second World War, but this capacity is not normally to the fore. Sovereignty exists whenever the function of government is held to be reduced to one overwhelming consideration: survival. Thus to speak of the 'Sovereignty of Parliament' is, at best, only to assert that Parliament can act (or allow actions) in this manner. It is highly misleading to use the concept *either* to argue that something fundamental called 'Parliamentary rights' has been infringed of late by the powers of the executive—the Liberal fallacy; or that since the Prime Minister-in-Cabinet is now the Sovereign Parliament in this sense, therefore 'let no dog bark'—the high-Tory fallacy.

It is necessary to put this abstract concept in its place since it does obscure for many, seemingly practical men, the real restraints there are on any British Government. These restraints are, of course, all political. The framework in which these political restraints operate is what Dicey technically called 'the Conventions' of the Constitution. They are, as it were, the habitual extra-legal rules by means of which politicians accept that new legal rules can be made by the Queen-in-Parliament, or powers exercised under old ones. That conventions are often difficult to define precisely and are, in any case, subject to change, does not detract from their power. Their flexibility adds to their importance in helping to give British Governments the ability and scope to govern decisively, which in turn is partly because British Governments are forewarned by procedural devices, resting on conventions, as to which way the cat of public confidence will jump.

Breaches of conventions are not so much likely to lead to

[7] This follows Geoffrey Marshal and Graeme C. Moodie's excellent *Some Problems of the Constitution* (Hutchinson, 1959), pp. 16–18.

breaches of the Law itself, as Dicey argued, but to a deliberate change of the Law.[8] For instance, when the House of Lords threw out a Budget in 1909, it led to the passing of the Parliament Act of 1911; or when Franklin Roosevelt broke the 'third term' convention, it led to the passing of the Twenty-second Amendment to the United States Constitution. They are at least that important politically. But even this is too legal and too little political. Breaches in Conventions may merely lead to the emergence of new Conventions. So why are they obeyed at all if they are not legal rules and if breaking them does not always lead to breaches of the Law or to new Laws? Sir Ivor Jennings writes that 'conventions are obeyed because of the political difficulties which follow if they are not'; and Marshal and Moodie offer the worthwhile amendment: 'conventions describe the way in which certain legal powers must be exercised if the powers are to be tolerated by those affected'.[9] George V, for instance, had the undoubted legal right to break convention and refuse to sign the Irish Home Rule Bill of 1913—as excited Conservative lawyers, including Dicey, were arguing in the correspondence columns of *The Times*. But plainly great 'political difficulties' would have followed for the Crown, and is unlikely that the use of such powers would have been tolerated by the Liberal Government affected.

Very many of the conventions of the Constitution define the relationship between Parliament and the Government, and also the manner in which the Government may exercise the powers of the Crown. The special positions of the Prime Minister and of the Leader of the Opposition are purely conventional; so are such rules as: that a Government defeated in the House of Commons should normally be required to resign; that the Monarch should dissolve Parliament, and can only, when requested by the Prime Minister; that a Government if defeated in the general elections should resign before meeting the new Parliament; that the majority Party in the Commons should have the right to have its leader called as Prime Minister by

[8] See Marshal and Moodie, *Some Problems of the Constitution*, pp. 28–46.
[9] *Ibid.*, p. 40.

the Crown, and even that there ought to be at least one session of Parliament a year.

What has all this to do with our original contention that British government has become more and more a matter of a Prime Minister governing absolutely, only restrained (from doing too little as well as too much) by the knowledge that his Party sometime must face a General Election? A great deal— for by the very token of the importance of elections, governing has now become a prolonged election campaign. (This is meant in no invidious sense; one is all in favour of elections, particularly General Elections.) But this now means that the Conventions of the Constitution should be seen by analogy to the laws and practices which govern the small period of the statutory 'election campaign'. Conventions should now be seen realistically as the agreed devices by which *the continuous election campaign* of the whole life of a Parliament is fought. Britain is not, after all, in any danger of falling into a legally institutionalized 'plebiscitory democracy' in which two Parties simply contend at general elections at fixed periods with no Parliamentary restraints in between. Parliament, on the lowest and most ultra-realistic construction of its present function, is still the agreed arena in which most of the continuous election campaign is fought.

Does this simply reintroduce Whiggish 'Parliamentary Sovereignty' by the back-door after having been thrown out the front? Yes, but not simply: only in a very chastened and spare form. The Conventions which are important are now not those required for some past era in which Parliaments overthrew governments and regularly modified legislation, but for the present-time in which only electorates can do so. Parliament is fundamentally the device by which the Parties obtain something like equal access to the ear of the electorate in the long formative period between the official campaigns. It is not the only device, for the idea of the continuous campaign makes the press, radio and especially television of more importance than of old; but it remains the most important device (certainly these other media of political campaigning give most of their thought and time to other purposes, and in any case focus their political reporting, rightly or wrongly, on Parliament). If this view is accepted, certain profound consequences follow.[10]

Parliament is to be seen as a forum of publicity. This has often been said, but now it must be meant. Its real functions are those of alerting and informing the public on matters relevant to the decision which way (or whether) to vote. This may call for much rethinking. For if this is the criterion then it is patent that Parliament spends relatively far too much time discussing the details of legislation and far too little examining and publicizing the conduct of administration. It would mean that attempts to reduce the Government majority by a few votes in divisions are a great waste of time compared to work spent in committees which may report on things to be done or on things left undone. It would mean that Backbench MPs

[10] The 'continuous election campaign' appears to be more fully accepted, consciously or not, by the last three Conservative administrations, to judge by their expansionist economic policies in the year before each election, than ever by Labour—at least on the limited evidence of Mr Attlee's plain refusal to think in such terms at all: his political instincts and economic optimism were always limited by somewhat *a priori* and old-fashioned ideas of constitutional rectitude. One is tempted to assert the validity of what a former student of mine has called 'the theory of fourth year democracy' (in which the only hope for steady economic growth would then be to revive the old Chartist demand for annual elections). But certain factors limit the applicability of this theory (and make me hope for acceptance of my theory of Parliament as a continuous election campaign). For instance, the Labour Party prided itself on the brilliant election campaign it fought in 1959; but it took some time to realize that even 'images' are not made or remade over night. And whoever loses this coming election, they will realize that they did not begin the campaign early enough. If Governments lose, or even fear defeat, with such advantages as they now have for managing the economy, then they may eventually be driven back, in their reprehensible desire to win elections (especially if the electorate becomes aware of the theory of fourth year democracy), simply to trying to practice responsible government every year. We said that sovereignty exists whenever the function of government is held to be reduced to one overwhelming consideration: national survival. We should add that corruption exists whenever the function of a Government is held to be reduced to one overwhelming consideration: political survival.

should be given far greater facilities for informing themselves and in a way *not* dependent on government sources. It would mean that many traditional devices for controlling the executive in Parliament can be abandoned or diminished, since they are not likely to affect the Government's chances of re-election (and do not affect the immediate content of legislation anyway); but then this frank recognition could lead to developing those practices and contentions which do have more relevance to the actual conduct of British government and the course of British politics. If these things are not done, because governments may simply concentrate on the immediate task of winning elections, then it could lead, through a radical contradiction between theory and practice and between appearance and reality, as well as through an understandable reaction that the economic and political system was being managed corruptly, to a dramatic loss of public confidence in the whole system, not merely in particular governments. Incomprehension by the governed has been not the least cause of the decline and fall of free governments; and inability to regard the ordinary as rational has often made men prone to snatch at violent actions and crazy dogmas.

The constitution is what people with political influence (thus including the organized electorate) accept as a proper way of reaching political decisions. Their views on what is proper will plainly be affected by the theories they hold about the aims of the system of government itself. If the system becomes incomprehensible or seems purposeless, then great evils could follow. But if people see correctly that government has become stronger and stronger, and that its purposes and limitations depend more and more on the dialogue it conducts with the electorate, and less and less with Parliament itself, then it is perfectly proper, not ignorant or unrealistic, of people to demand that Parliament should give the electorate all the help it can. All this is to reverse the classical constitutional theory of responsible government: that the electorate influences a Parliament which has the real power to control the Government. The theory which now best fits the facts is that Parliament in-

fluences the electorate which has the real power to control the
Government. Here is no argument that it *should* be so, but
simply that it *is* so and therefore *should* be recognized and
acted upon to adapt past habits to present conditions. This
flexibility had always been part of the strength of the British
system of government. But it is a *system* and so will be that
much less strong if government changes become stronger
while the Conventions that govern its operation prove less
flexible, hence weaker.

The Continued Strengthening of the Executive

Let us come down to earth, in case this still seems to the practical man to be an attack on a straw-man in a mare's nest, and
show some of the grounds for asserting that the power of the
executive has increased in such a way as to give rise to real
concern. For this has been denied. A recent author of great
ability tells us that while there have been 'changes in the practice' and 'the tone' of British government since the First World
War, that nothing has altered 'in any fundamental way'.[11] But
this remark, as his own evidence shows, is unduly legalistic;
true, none of the forms and relationships has changed sufficiently to warrant new descriptions, but a change in scale has
made the change in 'tone' very significant. The 'tone' is now
far more authoritarian, partly because of the sheer increase
in size and scope of the administration—leading men 'to think
big', but partly because of changing ideas about the proper
exercise of executive authority—which ideas can now be more
swiftly and easily implemented.

The changing ideas of government in relation to changing
scale are most apparent if one simply considers the growth in
size of Ministries.[12]

[11] John B. Mackintosh, *The British Cabinet*, p. 381.
[12] Taken from David Butler and Jennie Freeman, *British Political Facts* (Macmillan, 1963), p. 44. See also F. M. G. Willson,
The Organization of British Central Government (Allen and Unwin, 1957), *passim*.

GROWTH IN SIZE OF GOVERNMENTS

	1900	1910	1917	1920	1930	1940	1950	1960
Cabinet Ministers	19	19	5	19	19	9	18	19
Non-Cabinet Ministers	10	7	33	15	9	25	20	20
Junior Ministers	15	22	33	33	27	32	35	35
Royal Household	16	14	14	13	7	11	8	9
Total	60	62	85	80	62	77	81	83
No. of MPs in the Government	33	43	60	58	50	58	68	65
No. of Peers included in the Government	27	19	25	22	12	19	13	18
Parliamentary Private Secretaries	9	16	12	13	26	25	27	36
Total No. of MPs involved in Government	42	59	72	71	76	83	95	101

This table includes the Whips as Junior Lords of the Treasury among Officers of the Royal Household, but it has not included the unpaid Assistant Whips who vary in number between four and a dozen according to circumstances; these swell the Ministerial numbers still more. Simply observe the growth in absolute numbers and the very high proportion that the Ministry now constitutes of all MPs in the majority party. Something between a third and a quarter of such MPs will be in the Government, in some manner. A Backbencher must be exceptionally clear-headed and candid if, with such short odds, he does not believe that fortune will smile his way one day. Such numbers, then, do not apply their discipline merely upon those directly concerned; great expectations are created in others. A modern Prime Minister has a patronage beyond the wildest dreams of political avarice of a Walpole or a Newcastle.

Now part of this growth is an obvious response to the sheer complexity of modern government and the increased scope of State intervention that the electorate has demanded and obtained from the major Parties. But the remarkable growth in numbers of Parliamentary Private Secretaries seems to arise far more from the *attitude* that modern governments have towards Parliament. Parliament is not seen primarily as a controlling body, but as a recruiting ground for the Ministry. No one doubts that for a Backbench MP to look after the 'private' political business of a Minister, and to have an office in the Ministry which gives him contacts and knowledge, is valuable training for Ministerial responsibility. But one can doubt whether the price is worth paying in terms of the loss of prominent Backbenchers, particularly when much of the most effective Parliamentary control of the Executive takes place in the committees of the Government Party itself, not in the official proceedings of Parliament. PPSs do not have the absolute constraint in speaking their mind in such meetings which their chiefs must accept. But they cannot speak critically of the things they are most interested in, their own department matters, and they will be more than normally prudent and politic in talking about anything else for fear of embarrassing their chief or their own career. There is, in other words, a strong case for senior Ministers, certainly Cabinet Ministers, to have a PPS, but a far weaker one for every Minister to take a man, as it were, half-out of Parliament; some, indeed, to take two.

Notice also how the total number of Ministers has shown its greatest rate of increase in wartime; they went back to pre-war figures in the 1930s, but did not decline after the Second World War, or even after the end of Mr Attlee's two administrations. The total numbers of MPs involved in the Government shows a more steady progression since it includes the

PPSs and others more concerned with normal Parliamentary relations and management; but even this figure clearly shows that the influence of the wars has been at least as great as that of the high periods of legislative activity associated with Asquith's and Attlee's administrations.

So here is both change in scale and in—'tone' is too weak—character. The exigencies of wartime are carried over into peacetime as being too useful to drop, both for Parliamentary management and for the efficiency of the executive.

Consider also the increase in size of the Civil Service. These figures are for the total of non-industrial Civil Servants:[13]

GROWTH OF NON-INDUSTRIAL CIVIL SERVICE

1901	116,413	1939	387,400
1911	172,352	1943	710,600
1914	280,900	1950	684,800
1922	317,721	1962	669,800

Notice that again the greatest rate of expansion seems to be a product of war. The structure of the State-at-War may then be turned to the purposes of the Welfare State, but it is obvious that much of the character of the great periods of growth will carry over: extreme centralization, a great stress on secrecy of operations and a habit of regarding Parliament simply as a place of obstruction and 'mere politics'.[14] Again it seems that a change of scale may well involve something more than a change in 'tone'.

And put this in the context of an ever-increasing degree of Treasury control over the whole Civil Service and the increasing importance of the Treasury with its responsibilities both for budgetary arrangements and economic planning. After all,

[13] See W. J. M. Mackenzie and J. W. Grove, *Central Administration in Britain* (Longmans, 1957), p. 7 and *Annual Abstract of Statistics* (HMSO, 1962).

[14] See C. H. Sisson, *The Spirit of British Administration* (Faber, 1959)—an example of this attitude.

it was as recently as 1920 that formal recognition was given to the Treasury's general responsibility for the organization of the Service; and that more power was given to the Treasury to classify jobs and control administrative methods in all the Departments. Previously there had been considerable differences in the organization and methods of major Departments and very little movement between them. This was undoubtably less efficient than the modern integrated and co-ordinated Service, but it did involve more informal checks and balances than now exist. The strengthening of central control and uniformity of practice within the Service might be thought to have made the task of Parliamentary control more easy. From a narrowly institutional aspect, this could have been so; but it did not happen simply because a large part of the impetus behind this very process of centralization was the same as that behind the steady decline in Parliamentary control: the executive attitude of mind that sees British government as something best kept as far apart from Parliament as possible. This is often called a 'bureaucratic' frame of mind. This is palpably unfair to actual Civil Servants in that the impetus has always come from Party leaders. But, if we look at the time-scale of the maximum rates of growth, it might be more revealing to call this frame of mind 'military'. By 'military' is meant not that it is warlike, but that it is (for politics, at least) excessively hierarchical and believes that it cannot function properly if exposed to public criticism. (One is often tempted to the view that neither armies nor civil services can function properly *unless* exposed to public criticism.) This is no place to discuss the whole issue of 'Treasury control' and whether there might not better be two, even three, Ministries doing the same work. But it is relevant to point to the almost grotesque air of confidentiality hanging over the Plowden Report on the organization of the Treasury—an 'inside job' if ever there was one;[15] and to the role that the Treasury has played in the continued strengthening of the executive. It should be evident that the high level of

[15] See D. N. Chester's clear and caustic remarks, 'The Plowden Report: Nature and Significance', *Public Administration,* Spring, 1963. A 'Treasury view' in that of S. C. Leslie's 'The Treasury's New Look', *The Times,* 1 October, 1962, p. 13.

Defence expenditures exacerbates the situation, though this bureaucratic-military-hierarchical-secretive frame of mind could plainly survive even total disarmament.

To this could be added the familiar story of the increase in Delegated Legislation and the continued decrease in the powers, though not the size, of Local Government. The story is familiar but its significance is often misunderstood. There is nothing inevitable, for instance, about the particular pattern (and chaos) of relationships between Central and Local Government by which the Welfare State is administered; nor is there anything inevitable about the vast delegation of authority which Ministers have obtained from Parliament to make laws and statutory instruments. The particular practices of the moment are not to be explained in terms of size alone, but also in terms of certain attitudes to size, which, it is suggested, are more a produce of war than of the tradition of British politics.[16] Put it at its simplest. Great increases in the scale and the functions of Government can evoke two different kinds of response; that of administrative decentralization (or 'pluralism' on the plane of abstract thought) or of increased centralization (or sovereignty theories on the plane of abstract thought). Broadly speaking, the former was the traditional reflex of English statesmen and administrators, while the latter has become the modern—and more modern in time than we think. And it is interesting that this distinction cuts right across Party lines: there are Conservatives and Socialists who share a common view of 'the State' as the sovereign vehicle of civilization (simply differing on who should use it and, sometimes, for what); but there are also Conservatives and Socialists who attach far more importance to Burke's 'small platoon' or William Morris's 'company of fellows' which is 'itself a small Republic'. A fruitful way of looking at Parliament would be to see it as the body that mediates between these two views of social action, the unitary and the pluralistic. Plainly neither view can stand on its own: the risk is that either could destroy both if followed exclusively.

[16] Though it could be suggested that the Cold War has made even free governments think and act as if in a continuing state of emergency rather than in any return to 'normal politics'.

Prime Minister and Party

Walter Bagehot's *English Constitution* described the 'efficient secret', as distinct from the 'dignified façade', of British Government 'as the close union, the nearly complete fusion, of the executive and legislative powers. . . . The connecting link is *the Cabinet*. By that new word we mean a committee of the legislative body selected to be the executive body'. But as a consequence of the Reform Bill of 1867, which had stimulated Bagehot's new realism in the first place, even his account became quickly dated: by the end of the century the 'efficient secret' of British Government was clearly the connection between Cabinet and Party. The need to forge mass organization in the country created a great strengthening of party discipline in Westminster. And this new discipline had a ready-made pattern to follow in the great tactical successes of Parnell's resolute small band, and became hardened and sharpened in the long and bitter political wars, not on the Social Question, but on the Irish Question.

Cabinet Government became not merely Party Government but, as the century progressed, something completely implausible to view as a *committee* chosen by the legislature and of the legislature. It became a committee of the Party chosen by the Prime Minister from Parliament. The Prime Minister as Party Leader has now a unique position, very different from that of the era in which the main principles of Parliamentary procedure were settled.

This Prime Minister was not merely Party Leader, but secure as never before as Parliamentary Leader by the great patronage he wielded as the size of Ministries grew ever greater. And his control over the Civil Service increased. The creation of a Cabinet secretariat, directly under the Prime Minister, was as recent as the First World War. This put the keeping of minutes and circulating of papers on a regular basis and enabled great use of sub-committees of the Cabinet to be made. Much of this was seen as a wartime exigency when Lloyd George established a small War Cabinet of five members and erected the famous Garden Suburb for his secretariat, official and unofficial, in the garden of No. 10. But, as usual, what was created for pressing need became habitual for normal convenience. This new Cabinet Secretariat enabled Prime Ministers to begin to plan in a way not directly dependent on the advice of individual Ministers. And it went together in time with the growth of Treasury control and the further unification of the Civil Service, so that, having one head and not many, the Civil Service became easier to control; and the many departmental heads declined, like the Cabinet, in importance.

Despite the easy going habits of Baldwin, the First World War saw an end to the Cabinet system as Bagehot had pictured it, and many still do, of between a dozen and score of great men debating with each other around a table. Churchill enjoyed such talk, but there was no doubt where the initiative and the final decisions lay. Attlee did not even enjoy such talk. And even the urbane and clubable post-war Conservatives found that Eden could involve the country in war without the clear consent of his Cabinet; that even he followed in the footsteps of Chamberlain, against which he had once protested, and made the great decisions either alone or after real discussion with two or three more trusted intimates.

It is clear that Lord Morley's famous description of the position of the Prime Minister is now inadequate: *'primus inter pares'*—perhaps best translated as 'top dog among champions'. He is now a creature different in kind, not merely status, from the other party chieftains. For the Prime Minister, as well as being leader of the Government as a collective body, is now undisputed leader of the majority Party. The heart of the matter is that after 1867 the Prime Minister has become more and more the choice of the electorate; no Party can afford to recognize a leader, however able an administrator and a Parliamentarian, who does not appear to be the best man to lead the Party into a General Election. And he is the man who controls the nominations to all other offices and also the honorific patronage: if the Queen is still the Fount of Honour, he is the tap who controls and directs the flow. Patronage becomes seen more and more as the key to his day to day power over his followers, not the famous right to obtain a dissolution when he requires it. For dissolution could never in fact have been a weapon for disciplining his own followers any less clumsy than a boomerang with its risks of striking down the whole Party. Thus Morley's phrase is too weak, and so is his 'the Prime Minister is the keystone of the Cabinet arch'. He is not merely the keystone, but the foundation stone and cement for all the other stones as well. He appoints his colleagues, he holds them together, and his reputation must carry the Cabinet and the Party forward to victory at the next election. And he controls the Party machine as well; even careers in the Party organization depend ultimately on his positive blessing.

For as long as the Prime Minister carries with him the conviction of his Party that he will get them victory again, his power remains almost absolute. He may have difficult colleagues with a following in the country who cannot be excluded from the Ministry, even from the Cabinet; but inclusion can be a device for muzzling a rival far more effective than exclusion. The rival thoroughbred is chained by the doctrine and practice of Collective Responsibility and is likely, if he does resign, to earn some general detestation for 'rocking the boat' or for being a *'Prima Donna'* when there is plainly only room for one. For the Prime Minister alone decides who takes what posts, and some posts are clearly more helpful than others in furthering—or not—a colleague's public reputation. He need not even be faced with continued dissent within the privacy of the Cabinet room. For he controls the agenda. Nothing is raised which is not on the agenda and nothing finds its way on to the agenda which has not been raised with the Prime Minister beforehand and premeditated by him. He may even forbid papers or policy memoranda to be circulated by Cabinet Ministers among each other if they appear to grind some axe contrary or unwelcome to his purposes—as Chamberlain did on several occasions.[17]

The former Foreign Secretary, Lord Home, put the matter fairly clearly:

[17] See Mackintosh, *The British Cabinet,* p. 395.

Every Cabinet Minister is in a sense the Prime Minister's agent—his assistant. There's no question about that. It is the Prime Minister's Cabinet, and he is the one person directly responsible to the Queen for what the Cabinet does.

If the Cabinet discusses anything it is the Prime Minister who decides what the collective view of the Cabinet is. A Minister's job is to save the Prime Minister all the work he can. But no Minister could make a really important move without consulting the Prime Minister, and if the Prime Minister wants to take a certain step the Cabinet Minister concerned would either have to agree, argue it out in Cabinet, or resign.[18]

But 'argue it out' may make even this home truth another understatement. The modern Cabinet does not normally settle down happily to long discussions of alternative policies, let alone of 'first principles'—as is the received picture of Asquith's stimulating, turbulent but collectively ineffective Cabinets. It normally registers decisions already nine-tenths made and co-ordinates their implementation (and resigns itself to the fact that many of the most important decisions of Foreign Policy, Defence, Security and Budgetary matters will have been made in its name by the Prime Minister without the least thought of prior and collective consultation). This change of the Cabinet from a political decision-making body to an instrument of administrative co-ordination has been made possible, and accelerated, by the great and continued development both of Standing Committees of the Cabinet (such as Defence, Home Affairs, Economic Policy, Future Legislation, Foreign Policy and Atomic Energy), and of *ad hoc* committees which are constantly being set up to report on particular problems. Needless to say, the Prime Minister appoints and selects these committees, they consult with him before anything goes up to Cabinet, and he either takes the chair himself at their meetings or sees to it that they are guided by one of his most trusted colleagues: there exists informally, at every stage, an 'inner Cabinet'.

The evidence is great that the Cabinet no longer makes pol-

[18] See the *Observer*, 16 September, 1962, quoted by Crossman, *op. cit.*

icy and that, in any case, little reliance is to be put on the old concept that the Cabinet represented a kind of coalition of the diverse forces in a great Party and was, therefore, in itself an effective check on the powers of the executive. As Mr J. B. Mackintosh puts it:

> . . . a successful, strong and opinionated Prime Minister can put his impress on a whole government. . . . The Cabinet falls into place as a forum for informing his colleagues of decisions that have been taken. In these circumstances it is very hard for a Minister who begins to have doubts to intervene with effect. He has insufficient knowledge, he is always too late, and is contending with the Prime Minister and the men whom the latter has elevated to a position of trust. And when decisions have been taken, there is little that can be done, except protest in the secrecy of the Cabinet, or resign.[19]

Examples of resignations since 1945 do not suggest that the power of a Prime Minister is shaken even when such rare events as the resignation of a Bevan or a Thornycroft take place. Certainly, Cabinet Ministers can take part in the final stages of a revolt to replace a Leader who has already lost the confidence of a clear majority of the Parliamentary Party that he can lead them to victory come the elections. But his authority must already have been diminished by failure before this is likely to take place. There are several examples of the Conservative Party's being able to get rid of a Leader in this century, but in none of them is it likely that the revolt began in the Cabinet.[20] Revolt is possible, as the events of October 1963 showed, but even there the power of the retiring Prime Minister to influence the choice of his successor appears to have been unexpectedly great. For a revolt to be fully successful, there must be already a widely accepted heir-apparent.

Normally the Prime Minister can make and remake his Cabinet almost at will. The Great Purge of July 1962 is an instructive incident. Here was what the *Daily Telegraph* rightly called 'the most sweeping government reconstruction in mod-

[19] *The British Cabinet,* p. 420.
[20] See Dr Robert McKenzie, *British Political Parties,* 2nd ed. (Heinemann, 1963), especially chapters II, III, X and XI.

ern times'. It was aimed at restoring confidence in the government after a vexing period of decline and disaster in by-elections—as *The Times* put in a leading article on 14 July, 1962: 'The requirement was to give a flagging government new ideas and new drive and that means new men.' Seven Ministers left the Cabinet and there were twenty-four governmental changes in all, including nine resignations and the entry of eleven Backbenchers into the Government for the first time; and only ten members of the Cabinet of twenty-one retained their previous posts. It was thorough. It was even unprecedentedly candid—the ever-memorable first sentence of Mr Selwyn Lloyd's letter of resignation read: 'You have told me that you would like me to resign, and this I willingly do.' But it was universally recognized, both in the short and the long run, to have been a failure. At the best, it left the repute of the Government much as before—the by-election reverses continued; and at the worst it brought opposition to the Premier from within his Party out into the half-light of the lobbies—some seventy Backbenchers had a meeting of protest over the treatment of Mr Lloyd and his policies.[21] But if the failure of this reshuffle led to the revolt of October 1963, yet Mr Macmillan was able to carry on for a whole year and it can never be clear whether he would have gone, even after Mr Profumo's adventures, had there not been the accident of temporary, physical incapacity.

His action in the Great Purge has been freely described as 'ruthless' and it was unprecedented in scale, but there were many who reminded us that Prime Ministers had ever been so and of necessity. A correspondent to *The Times* could even quote Gladstone as saying that: 'The first essential for a Prime Minister is to be a good butcher.'[22] One letter, however, so crystallized the whole problem that it deserves to be quoted in full:

Sir,
    What in constitutional *practice* is now meant by collective Cabinet responsibility for policy?
        Your obedient, Conservative, bewildered servant,
                                    Rt Rev Dr John Vance

[21] See reports in *The Times*, 18 July, 1962.
[22] A letter in *The Times*, 24 July, 1962, from Mr Clifford Roberts.

Certainly the traditional and still common interpretations of the constitutional doctrines both of Ministerial Responsibility and of Collective Responsibility are weak straws to lean upon in any search for effective restraints on the Executive in the existing British system.

Not since the 1850s and 1860s has it been possible for the Commons to censure a Minister without overthrowing the Government. Governments grew to treat all such votes as votes of confidence in themselves. The blanket of Collective Responsibility has been thrown over any holes in individual Ministerial Responsibility ever since the tightening of party discipline which followed 1867, and also since the time, roughly coincident, when it was no longer reasonable to assume that a Minister could watch over every detail of work in his Department. Responsibility is now almost entirely political except when an individual Minister personally feels that he is culpable—as with Sir Thomas Dugdale over the Crichel Down affair in 1954 (a popular Minister whom no one held 'really responsible'). This feeling may have nothing to do with legal responsibility at all or with the Parliamentary conventions about who is responsible for answering questions about what—as with the Minister of Health, Aneurin Bevan over German rearmament in 1951. Or it may be that a particular Minister will be sacrificed by his colleagues in the interest of his Party for what was clearly a matter of Collective Responsibility—as with Sir Samuel Hoare and the Hoare–Laval Pact in 1935. Otherwise 'responsibility' is simply 'accepted' collectively and politically: if it will do less political harm for a man to stay, he stays; if it will appear in the public eye to remodel a Ministry, he goes. In 1958 the Devlin Report censured the Colonial Secretary, Mr Lennox-Boyd, in the report on the disturbances in Nyasaland and in the inquiry into the deaths of eleven men in the Hola detention camp: the Cabinet accepted Collective Responsibility and he stayed, just as Mr Selwyn Lloyd proved immovable from the Foreign Office for an astonishingly long time after Suez, when even his transfer might seem to have shown that the new Government did feel culpable either for the adventure or for its failure. So unless someone actually breaks the law, deceives his colleagues or goes by his own light of conscience, he will not go at all if it is to the political disadvantage of the Government which, as ever, has public opinion and the next election in mind.

Collective Responsibility now simply means: (i) that all members of a Government must be unanimous in support of its policies on all public occasions; and (ii) that they are all in the same boat, personally, morally and politically, when it comes to success and failure in the General Elections. The Denning Report held the Prime Minister responsible for not questioning Profumo himself at an early stage of the whisperings and rumours. *The Times* said in an editorial:

> If, on the evidence then before the Ministers, he had tackled Mr Profumo himself, he might not have come to any conclusion other than that arrived at by his colleagues, but that does not excuse him from the omission. A Prime Minister selects his colleagues and he may dispense with their services; responsibility for their fitness for office is his and serious imputations on their character must concern him personally and, one would have thought, necessitate personal confrontation.[23]

But that was only to state the obvious. Did anyone therefore really expect that the Prime Minister would resign—or even should resign?

For the point of this account of the strength of British government is not to say that any of these tendencies should necessarily be reversed, or can be reversed, but simply to show that, amid so much power, the need to revise the procedures by which it is open to criticism is almost self-evident.

The system of Prime Minister leading a Party and administering through a Cabinet (which is not a group of colleagues as much as the focus of the network of committees that he controls) is not necessarily a bad system. It has obvious advantages over many other systems of government in strength, stability and flexibility. It is far from beyond all control even at the moment, even on the bleakest reading of the decline in Parliament's influence. The need for the Prime Minister to carry his Party with him is a very real restraint when all have to work the ship together in foul as well as fair weather. When

[23] *The Times,* 26 September, 1963.

Mr Macmillan was struggling to keep control of his Party, Mr T. E. Utley reminded his fellow Tories that: 'A Conservative MP should at all times have an almost overwhelming pre-disposition in favour of supporting his Parliamentary leader', but that 'this extraordinary measure of trust is rendered tolerable only by the Leader's acceptance of his Parliamentary supporters'; and since 'loyalty' is itself one of those '*convictions*' (not mere *opinions* note), it is 'a thing to be honoured not exploited'.[24]

But these restraints from within the governing Party suffer from at least three obvious and inherent defects as substitutes for Parliamentary control. Firstly, they work in private, amid secrecy and rumour far from the public eye; events may be important, so reports will appear in the press, but rarely can anyone feel confidence in their accuracy and relevance —thus public understanding even of *how* we are governed suffers. Secondly, they are so informal as well as secret that they place an extraordinary need for honesty on politicians, both to deal openly with each other and to report accurately the findings from 'soundings'—the Conservatives' way of finding a new Leader is only the most obvious case.[25] And

[24] See T. E. Utley, 'The Tory Tradition: Leader's Duty Towards his Followers', a long letter in the *Daily Telegraph*, 25 July, 1963.

[25] This process of selection or 'emergence' may be sensible and responsible (it may often be a better way, than the voting habits of the Parliamentary Labour Party, of finding who is most likely to hold the Party together, not merely who has the most popularity and support). But it does not readily appear to be so and it is wide open to abuse. Coming so close after the Profumo affair, the tangled events by which Earl Home came to be Premier will probably mark the end of the Conservative tradition of excessive informality based upon loyalty and friendship. This system has often been ungenerously, sometimes even inaccurately, called 'nepotism'; but this sneer fails to understand the strength of such a system, so long as manners remain what they were. Burke mocked Chatham's 'Mosaic Ministry' because he claimed, with caricature, that Ministers had to be introduced to each other; Burke thought it ridiculous to attempt something so complex as governing a free country except between men who knew each other well. This explains Mr Macmillan's apparent inability to take the constitutional point seriously of his responsibility for Jack Profumo, and the apparent irrelevance

thirdly, they may work against the public interest, even prove corrupt now that the economy can be so easily managed in short periods—for a Party collectively is likely to think what no one member of it would think individually: that nothing is more important than re-election.

From the very virtues of British government we must return to our point that if the basic check on any British Government is the General Election, then that election must be seen as a continuous campaign, beginning on the first day of each new Parliament, in which the factors most relevant to its conduct are the procedures and practices of Parliament—the permanent hustings.

---

of his sincere and heartfelt demand for public sympathy that he had been *lied to* by a political friend.

This footnote is no digression, but points to both a key fact and a symbol of the whole 'so long as it works' and 'trust us informally' attitudes of British government—and what is wrong with them. There must, to turn the American political story, indeed be a Constitution even among friends. And friends are more likely to do such things to friends in the very type of commercial society which Mr Macmillan probably detested, but politically encouraged.

CHAPTER III

WHAT THE COMMONS DO INDIVIDUALLY

The General Functions

To be too commonsense and practical is too often to lose touch with the importance of symbolic actions and constitutional conventions in government, particularly where they touch public confidence and understanding. So it is not just a sore wound of the moment, something quickly forgotten in the day to day movement of fronts in Party warfare, but a highly suitable beginning to a modern account of the role of the Commons to remind Parliament of how it was kept waiting for a fortnight, in October 1963, while the Prime Minister made himself a commoner and an MP.

The Times was not alone in weighing the many practical considerations which must have led the Prime Minister to think that he was obliged to do so, but it concluded:

> . . . this obligation stops well short of actually postponing the assembly of Parliament, for that is both to depress its standing and to elevate the Parliamentary standing of the Prime Minister. It implies either that the normal Parliamentary calendar is adjustable to suit the convenience of the Prime Minister, or that the Government's policies cannot usefully be presented and defended at the beginning of a session without his presence: and that is to forget that the system of government here is not yet fully Presidential, and that responsibility for the Government's actions and policies is the collective responsibility of the Cabinet.[1]

No one doubts that governments must govern and Parliaments follow after. But the manner in which this is done is vital. The incident vividly illustrates how little even the most

[1] The First Leader of 23 October, 1963.

realistic and minimal account of Parliament's function is taken seriously by modern Governments.

Realism about Parliament has been current for a long time, even though the formal theory of *Parliamentary* sovereignty still has a remarkable hold on the public mind, even in elementary books of instruction in schools. Gladstone once said to the House of Commons: 'Your business is not to govern the country, but it is, if you see fit, to call to account those who govern it.' It all depends what one means by 'call to account'. One must now say that the 'call' is more important than the 'account': Parliaments will not bring down Ministries by votes in either House, but will call aloud with grievances and criticisms to the public who become the electorate. Sir Ivor Jennings has put it clearly and baldly: 'the true function of the House of Commons is to question and debate the policy of the Government'.

Here, for once, Bagehot was as realistic as he claimed. Firstly, 'the main function of the House of Commons is one which we know quite well, though our common constitutional speech does not recognize it. The House of Commons is an electoral chamber; it is the assembly which chooses our President'.[2] This may need some qualification, but not much. He need not necessarily come from the Commons, as we have just seen, but this Convention, held to have been created in 1924 when Stanley Baldwin was summoned instead of Lord Curzon, will only need rephrasing: he cannot actually be in the House of Lords while Premier. Other voices may have a say in the selection, Peers, candidates and Party officials, but it will be the collective opinion of the Party in the House of Commons that finally recognizes whether a man is Prime Ministerial timber or not, and it is there that a man must make his reputation even if not his whole career.

'The second function of the House of Commons,' continued Bagehot, 'is what I may call an expressive function. It is its office to express the mind of the English people on all matters

[2] This and the following four quotations from Bagehot are from pp. 150–3 of the Fontana Library's *The English Constitution* (Collins, 1963).

which come before it. Whether it does so well or ill I shall discuss presently.' And so shall I.

'The third function of Parliament is what I may call . . . the teaching function. A great and open council of considerable men cannot be placed in the middle of a society without altering that society. It ought to alter it for the better. It ought to teach the nation what it does not know. How far the House of Commons can so teach, and how far it does so teach, are matters for subsequent discussion.' This is a bit lofty of Bagehot, rather too much in keeping with his whole thesis that England is only saved from the ravages of democracy by devices which maintain the deferential nature of her society. It is only acceptable if we construe true teaching to include constant inquiry on the part of the teacher himself, always discovering how much more he himself needs to know. But then this would merge into Bagehot's fourth category.

'Fourthly, the House of Commons has what may be called an informing function . . . that to some extent it makes us hear what otherwise we should not.' Again this needs amendment away from its rather deferential premise: it should not be assumed that Parliament is always knowledgeable; its informing function may first involve informing itself.[3] And this, as we will see, in modern conditions implies the use of methods of inquiry either novel to it or too little used.

'Lastly,' Bagehot concluded, 'there is the function of legislation, of which of course it would be preposterous to deny the great importance, and which I can only deny to be *as* important as the executive management of the whole State, or the political education given by Parliament to the whole nation.'

Bagehot puts the matter well. He does not claim too much. We may question how well Parliament fulfils these functions, particularly considering the very few new strengths that Parliament has gained since his day, and the very many the Executive; but that it fulfils some of them somewhat is beyond question. The tendency is more and more for Governments to

---

[3] One could placate Bagehot that this amendment is due not to any marked change in English society, but to—as he would think —an unfortunate change in the social composition of Parliament.

deal directly with the electorate, but Parliament is still the essential intermediary with considerable power to determine the issues on which elections will be fought. The whole life of Parliament adds up to this much at least.

In some ways the informing function works better than when Bagehot wrote. Lord Campion, the former Clerk of the House of Commons, has written that Questions 'are the one procedural invention of the democratic era'.[4] Their importance is hard to exaggerate. They are a fairly quick way of publicizing acts and omissions for which any Minister is legally responsible, for extracting information even, and for keeping the whole administrative machine on its toes—for the civil servant has to think not merely of the Questions that are asked, but of all those that might be asked. They are essentially a device of publicity, for it was and is always possible for a Member to extract information by direct correspondence with a Ministry; and Questions put down for a written answer, though usually answered more quickly, are markedly less popular. But their importance *can* be exaggerated.

Despite the great growth of the administration since the 1900s, when the modern Question Time became firmly established, 'the really significant feature . . . is not that there has been an increase [in the number of Questions] but that the increase, however measured, is so small'.[5] This is due to the growth of devices limiting Ministerial responsibility, at least in the sense of 'answerability', in all kinds of individual cases arising out of delegated powers and from the day to day administration of the Nationalized Industries and other Public Corporations; to a great growth of Members' correspondence with Ministers; to restrictions on the number of Questions for oral reply that any MP can ask on any one day; and to the sheer congestion of Question Time.[6] Certainly the picture of Ministers under daily fire, intensified by the post-war develop-

[4] Lord Campion and others, *Parliament: A Survey* (Allen and Unwin, 1952), p. 165, quoted in D. N. Chester and Nona Bowring, *Questions in Parliament* (Oxford, 1962), p. 269.

[5] Chester and Bowring, *Questions in Parliament*, p. 91, and generally Chapter 4 on numbers of Questions.

[6] *Ibid.*, p. 92.

ment of the Supplementary, is a false one. Chester and Bowring have shown in remorseless detail the extreme variations there can be between the time it takes to get an answer to an oral question—anything from three days to eight weeks;[7] and, due also to the rota system of answering questions, the infrequency with which even important Ministries are questioned.[8] 'It will indeed come as a surprise and a shock to many,' they write, 'to learn that the opportunity to question the Foreign Minister in the House occurred on only nineteen occasions during the Session of 1959–60 and that the possibility of questioning most other Ministers was even less.'[9]

The basic restriction is time. Question Hour is not even an hour, but anything between forty-five and fifty minutes. Yet no one has seriously proposed, or seriously expects, that any modern Government would allow the time even to become a modest hour.

> The indifference of Frontbenchers and the unwillingness of Backbenchers to press for more time to be made available . . . may explain but can hardly be said to justify a state of affairs in which the amount of time available for questioning Ministers remains the same as it was half a century ago and is less than it was at the beginning of the century. The House of Commons has conferred vast new powers on Government Departments, yet appears unable or unwilling to provide even an extra half hour on four days a week for questioning Ministers.[10]

Thus even the most famous device of Parliament's informative and critical functions, the one that least threatens the Government's ability to govern, turns out to be something less than is commonly thought. The limiting factor here may be partly sheer lack of time, or possibly less Executive hostility than indifference; and that the institution should exist at all is still a highly important thing. Yet when its two closest students have examined every possible strength, they are forced to conclude:

[7] *Ibid.,* p. 156.
[8] *Ibid.,* pp. 145–66.
[9] *Ibid.,* p. 281.
[10] *Ibid.,* p. 276.

But it could equally well be argued that the House is getting the worst of both worlds, for the present procedure ensures neither that Ministers are frequently and regularly available for questioning, say, once a week, nor that, once available, there is time to cross-examine them thoroughly. It can hardly be denied that once again the procedures of the House have failed to keep pace with the increasing powers of the Executive.[11]

If time is so precious, how does the House spend the time it does give itself? This usually gives some clue to the true character of an institution—or a person.

Recent changes in the time available to Government, Opposition and Private Members have *not* been very dramatic. Consider this table:

DISTRIBUTION OF TIME BETWEEN MEMBERS[12]

(*average time in days*)

	Private Members	Opposition	Government	Indeterminate Remainder	Length of Session
Inter-war years	25	34	69	21	149
Post-war years	29	41	75	13	158

May one be rather simple-minded and make three unusual comments? One is surprised at *how much* time the Opposition has at its disposal.[13] One is surprised at how little the broad

[11] Chester and Bowring, *Questions in Parliament*, p. 285.
[12] From 'Appendices to the Minutes of Evidence Taken Before the Select Committee on Procedure', *Report of the Select Committee on Procedure* (HC 92), 1959, p. 194.
[13] Certainly the time available for the moving of Private Members' Bills has declined since between the Wars, but not their rate

pattern has changed. One is surprised at the shortness of the session. The table shows how seriously the critical and inform-ing function of Parliament is taken. But it suggests that if there is real shortage of time preventing government business going through, or preventing reforms in procedure or the use of more committees of investigation which would otherwise be acceptable, then this shortage of time is not absolute, but is a product of how MPs distribute the time they have. There is in fact plenty of time to play with if MPs could ever look at the problem as a whole.

For instance, obviously the efficiency of the executive would suffer if Parliament sat for even 200 days in a year.[14] But there are obvious public advantages for its Session to cover a longer span of time (the events of this last summer while Par-liament was in recess are not so very unusual, or unlikely to recur). It could spread its sittings more loosely over the year, giving everyone, Government and Opposition, more respite for (perhaps) 'real work'. Or the House could sit the same num-ber of days, but for five weeks longer so as to have a mid-week Wednesday adjournment—a scheme with obvious advantages for Ministers and for chairmen of committees of all kinds.[15] This is not the chapter to argue these details. It is simply clear that time, as such, does not limit any such possible changes.

The use that is made of the time in one typical Session is shown in the next table. Some of this table's implications will be considered later in detail. But again an unusually simple remark: when all authorities seem to agree that Parliament

---

of acceptance, nor the time available to Private Members, and, in any case, there is much to be said for this decline: the Government must be responsible for major legislation and there are better ways of ventilating grievances. Between the wars an average of 67 such Bills were moved each year, an average of 11 becoming Law; from 1950 to 1957 an average of 27 were moved each year, and an aver-age of 10 accepted. See Strathearn Gordon, *Our Parliament,* 5th ed. (Hansard Society, 1958), Appendix 8, pp. 208–9.

[14] About 150 working days is also the time of most University Sessions. I use this analogy since here too it should not be lightly suggested that time not on the site is necessarily time not on the job.

[15] An elaboration of a suggestion by Mr Airey Neave, MP (Con-servative), in the debate on Parliamentary reform of 15 March, 1963, HC *Debates* (673), col. 1735.

DISTRIBUTION OF TIME, SESSION 1957–58[16]

How the days were spent (the House sat on 156 days)	Number of days
Debate on the Address	6
Supply	26
Consolidated Fund Bills	6
Government Motions	11¾
(Gas and Electricity, Privileges, Procedure, Wales, Economic Situation, Civil Aviation, Hydro-Electric Board, Bank Rate, Defence, Malta, Privileges, Coal)	
Special Debates on the Adjournment	3½
(Foreign Affairs, Rhodesia and Nyasaland, Middle East)	
Opposition Motions	1
(Bus dispute)	
Orders and Regulations, etc., for approval	2
Prayers Against Orders	1
Government Legislation	56¾
Budget, Finance Bill and Ways and Means	16½
Opposed Private Business	½
Private Members' Bills	10
Private Members' Motions	10
Adjournment at Recesses	4
Prorogation	1

no longer should even try to legislate, what an extraordinary amount of time it spends on the Floor of the whole House considering Government legislation! The Government is never defeated and the rules of relevance are so strict that the public may be less well informed than by a general debate on the

16 From, *Report of the Select Committee on Procedure, op. cit.,* p. 215.

subject. One thing that Parliament wastes too much time on is going through old forms and rituals, often with a painstaking masochism, which have lost any present power. The Finance Bill is the great case in point—but more of that anon.

There is time for anything if Parliament were to take a long cool look not at details of procedure, but at its whole function. Time is no excuse. And neither, with all respect, is the burden of work. This has increased in recent times, but far less by any test than is usually supposed. Consider this table:

THE AVERAGE NUMBER OF PUBLIC BILLS RECEIVING THE ROYAL ASSENT, THE AVERAGE NUMBER OF DAYS SAT AND THE AVERAGE NUMBER OF HOURS OF SITTING IN DECENNIAL PERIODS FROM 1885–1954[17]

	Average No. of Public Bills	Average No. of Days Sat	Average No. of Hours of Sitting
1885–1894	86	139	1,178
1895–1904	54	127	1,099
1905–1914	56	146	1,177
1915–1924	75	145	1,092
1925–1934	58	148	1,156
1935–1944	61	144	1,050
1945–1954	66	162	1,316

Admittedly Public Acts have increased remarkably in length, though not in number. The total number of pages in Public Acts in 1900 was 198, in 1920 it was 560 and in 1957 it was 1,103. But the burden has not been so great as to lead to anyone's even hinting at a proportionate increase in the time Parliament sits.

[17] *Ibid.*, p. 194.

The burden, of which MPs make so much, must arise from three factors. Firstly, the unequal way the burden is divided, particularly of committee work, between those who are in fact full-time and those who are merely part-time MPs. It is not easy to estimate, but Parliamentary opinion often speaks of 'about 200' as the number of regular, dependable attenders, in addition, of course, to the Ministry. But this is almost certainly an exaggeration and refers to the *average* number who attend Standing Committees on any day when they are all meeting, not to the actual number of Members who attend often enough to have a proper grasp of business.[18] A minority of MPs work extremely hard, often force themselves to work excessively hard; but the majority—it must be roundly said—do not. (And it is quite clear that sympathy for Parliamentary reform is far greater among the dedicated minority than among the more casual majority.) Secondly, there would still be an excessive burden of work, even if more Members shared in it, because the House tries to cram too much into too short a time. And, thirdly, there is the peculiar and badly concentrated incidence of the Budget and the Finance Bill in the Parliamentary time-table. As we will see, there are many reasons for thinking that the time is not sensibly divided and is probably too short anyway; and there are some reasons for thinking that some of the things MPs willingly spend so much time on, such as legislation, have too much attention, and that some of the things they would like *more* time for, such as for Members to speak more often on the floor, serve no public interest whatever. The public interest is not advanced by the numbers of moderately well informed Members who are able to repeat the same point again and again, but by those who are at least better enough informed to make some new point. Time is needed not for speeches on the floor so much as for the procedures that can give those speeches authoritative depth —work in committee.

[18] If the criterion was attendance at Standing Committees at least once a week, then in the Session 1961–62 only about seventy Members would qualify, see p. 86 below.

The Man for the Job and the Tools at Hand

Yet who spends this time however it is spent? The character of the men who work an institution explain much about that institution. Is there any common characteristic of MPs? The most common and important is that they are now *all* elected as Party men. The most generous estimates measure the ability of even the most favoured candidate to shift the vote against the national trend by no more than two or three per cent. This may be crucial in some marginal seats, but it is perfectly clear that men become MPs by their Party regularity. Some Constituency Parties may put up candidates whose support the Party leaders might wish to do without. And the Constituency Parties have a firmer control over their nominations than was once thought;[19] but it is Party none the less. The Labour leadership seems more apt to intervene to prevent certain people being nominated by Constituency Parties than the Conservative, but they have less success in finding seats for their own nominees.

The social, educational and occupational background of MPs has been much studied.[20] The conclusions are fairly familiar. Neither Party is precisely 'representative' of any of these categories when applied to the country as a whole, but the Labour Party is markedly more diverse and representative (in this sense), whereas the Conservative MPs (even compared to unsuccessful Conservative candidates) are still drawn from an astonishingly narrow élite. The facts are undisputable, but the interpretation to be put upon them seems purely subjective: many people appear to prefer to be represented by a much superior person, rather than 'by one of us'.

[19] See Leon D. Epstein's excellent study, 'British MPs and Their Local Parties: the Suez Cases', *American Political Science Review,* June 1960, pp. 374–90; also Laurence W. Martin, 'The Bournemouth Affair: Britain's First Primary Election', *Journal of Politics,* November 1960, pp. 654–81.

[20] See David Butler and Richard Rose, *The British General Election of 1959* (Macmillan, 1960), pp. 124–30; J. Blondel, *Voters, Parties and Leaders* (Penguin, 1963), pp. 131–58; and W. L. Guttsman, *The British Political Elite* (MacGibbon and Kee, 1963), *passim.*

The only viable theory that would describe the actual practice of representation in Britain today is that it is 'Party representation', or what one of the shrewdest and most learned observers of British politics has called 'the collectivist theory': that Members are sent to Parliament by the electorate because they represent parties which, in turn, represent great collective social and economic interests.[21]

Much public disquiet about Parliament is plainly self-contradictory. The public votes against independents, supports Party-wheelhorses and, except in occasional by-elections, punishes third Parties, and yet the pubs, the clubs, the canteens, the restaurants and the trains, in both first and second, are full of grumblings at the 'lack of independence' of MPs and, from rare face to face confrontations, full of stark disappointment at their ordinariness.[22]

The public in its coolness to Parliament is on very weak ground, it is agreed, if it thinks that the House of Commons should consist of the 630 pre-eminently independent and intelligent minds of the nation. Members themselves, particularly of the Conservative persuasion, are surprisingly prone to grumble about a steady decline in the calibre (or class) of their fellows. Even if this decline were true (which is doubtful), the grumble would not be very sensible. What would Parliament do with such a picked six hundred? Would they in

21 See Samuel Beer 'Representation of Interests in British Government', *American Political Science Review,* September 1957. Professor Beer sees four stages in the modern period: the 'Old Whig theory' that interests, ranks, orders and estates were to be represented, even if only 'virtually'; the 'Liberal theory', which had its heyday between the first two Reform Bills, that individuals who were independent of interests were to be represented; the 'Radical theory' that *the People* as a whole were to be represented—democracy against both individualism and the interests; and the 'Collectivist theory' in which democracy has become periodic conflicts between two great Parties.

22 See, for example, the results of a survey carried out in January 1963 by Mass Observation and Public Attitude Surveys as reported in *New Society* (No. 23), 7 March, 1963, p. 26. More than half those interviewed regarded MPs as 'out of touch with their constituents', and just over half either could not name, or named incorrectly, their local Member.

any sense be representative?—and this question is asked not in point of theory, but in point of fact: could the 630 'best men' represent even a rough index of what the general public want and will stand for, as distinct from their knowing (as we all do) what is best for the public? And if in fact the social esteem of Parliament were to become so high and the mechanism of selection so rational that everyone who felt himself to be of consequence and righteousness even wished to be in Parliament, it might depress leadership and standards all over industry, the professions, the unions and the schools far more than it would elevate Parliament. It is not merely a question of God protecting the common man from ever being governed by Wellsian 'intellectual Samurai'. There is no need even to regret the faded picture that the great Tory historian Sir Lewis Namier painted at the beginning of his famous study, *The Structure of Politics at the Accession of George III:* 'You will be of the House of Commons as soon as you are of age,' wrote Lord Chesterfield to his son, '. . . and you must make a figure there if you would make a figure in your country.' For the idea that Parliament was the natural show-place and prize-ring for any man of talent was only possible when to be an MP was for most a strictly part-time activity. The full-time professional MP cannot be regretted; he is a natural response to the volume and complexity of modern legislation and to the representation of Labour in Parliament, of men as financially dependent on their immediate job as most of their constituents are on theirs. The grumble about 'little men' in Parliament is still, at root, an irritable nostalgia for a Parliament of 'gentry'—in the full, technical sense of that term (even though they, of course, by their own self-understanding never needed to be 'particularly brainy').

The public is not let down by the kind of man who comes to Parliament, but it is let down by the use that is made of whoever comes. What is worrying is not that all 'the best men' do not go into Parliament, but that the talents that do, unless they hold office, are commonly so wasted (and it may be a realization of this, as much as faults in the mechanism for selection, which decides many good men not to become candidates). Some of the ways in which the Backbencher's talents are wasted or frustrated are in themselves extremely mundane, though in their consequences important, and would be easy to remedy. The point cannot be better put than by quoting at length from a speech of Mr Wedgwood Benn in that unusual debate of 31 January, 1958, specifically on the 'Procedure of Parliament':

> 'The conditions under which we are expected to work are a public scandal . . . I do not believe that people out-side have the slightest conception of the way in which members are required to do their work.
>
> Each of us has only one place private to ourselves, a locker which is so small it will not take the ordinary brief-case to be locked away. We have no access to a telephone unless we make the endless, senseless tramp around the corridors, waiting outside the kiosks, with our papers, wait-ing to telephone. No incoming telephone call can reach us, although every modern hospital has now devised the simple system of giving the doctors a tiny radio receiver which buzzes and from which they can pick up mes-sages . . .
>
> We cannot even communicate freely with each other. There is no general pigeon-hole where one can put mes-sages for a Member. To circulate Hon. Members for the debate today, my Hon. Friend had to pay 3d. postage for every member to whom he wrote . . . simply because the facilities were not available . . . it is a scandal and ought to be reconsidered. Unless Members are given the oppor-tunities to get greater help, this House cannot really be an efficient place.'

Mr Benn also regretted the lack of 'proper research facilities', which phrase might open up large vistas, but was at the time merely intended to point to the fact that MPs have not even got routine typing and clerical assistance by virtue of their office. An American Congressman, it is said, collapsed with shock on being shown the writing-rooms and the Library of the Commons full of men writing letters in longhand: Mem-bers of Parliament answering their constituency mail. For not merely does Congress supply from public funds at least rou-tine clerical assistance to its elected representatives, but so do nearly all the fifty States of the American Union (though this will not convince those so principled that to learn that Americans do a thing is sufficient reason for us not to). South Africa, Australia and Canada all provide free secretarial facilities during the session at least. The best that Parliament has done for its Members is to make a few rooms available to an *outside, private* secretarial agency, whose services MPs may then hire. How can people expect to find their local MP at all helpful when he may be in the position of having to deal with all his correspondence, the important to him and the routine which is important to anonymous others, unaided and by hand? Many Members, of course, though certainly less than half, have a secretary-typist. But this depends on a private income, on outside earnings or on facilities extended by some outside body—trade union, trade association or business firm—with whom the Member is intimately and usefully connected.

A few European legislatures are as badly off as Britain's: members of the French National Assembly, the Belgian Chamber of Representatives, and the Netherland's Second Chamber are all equally hard pressed for space and facilities. But Germany and Japan have not followed the Mother of Parliaments in this derogatory parsimony. And the Canadian, Australian and New Zealand Parliaments do not appear to have destroyed their traditions or threatened the powers of the Executive (if that is it) by having given their Members individual and well-equipped offices.[23] There are currently some two hundred desk spaces for MPs and seventy for their secretaries scattered around the Palace of Westminster; but all of them are open, none of them in any sense private rooms: a sensible graduate student in any decent library would not want to work on confidential materials in such a setting.

Improvements are planned. Agitation by the hard working Members who depend on Westminster, who are not able, or do not think it proper, to run their political and constituency business from some commercial or trades union office, has forced something out of the Government.[24] A new govern-

[23] See Alfred Junz, 'Accommodation at Westminster', *Parliamentary Affairs*, Winter 1959–60, pp. 100–13.

[24] See HC *Debates* (667), col. 1226 and HC *Debates* (682), 1 August, 1963, cols. 727–31, also pp. 65–66 below.

ment office site in Bridge Street, closely adjoining Westminster, is to provide some extra office space for the Opposition, and about 280 individual or shared rooms for Members and some extra shared rooms for their secretaries (if they have one). The site will be cleared during 1964. But the total position will still be bad. The existing desks are little used since they are so unsuitable; instead some 59 rooms will be constructed in roof and cloister space within the Palace of Westminster. So there will be in all about 339 rooms by 1966. Even if one subtracts the numbers of the Ministry and the PPSs, about 100, there will still be about 200 MPs without an individual office. Some say they do not want them anyway, or that they are quite content to work from their business office or London home. One respectfully wonders what these Members think they are doing. The public should insist that all MPs at least create the appearance of giving all or most of their time in conditions reasonably conducive to efficiency.

Barbara Castle spoke bitterly, in a debate of 15 March, 1963, on the new improvements:

> For years Hon. Members complained that we were in a straitjacket. There was inefficiency owing to physical difficulties. We were then told that there was to be an opportunity for us to expand and breathe again when the Government acquired the whole of the Bridge Street site, 230,000 square feet.
>
> But for what is that to be used?—Government offices. We on the Accommodation Committee, advisory to Mr Speaker, had a handout from the Government—the Government's *diktat*—that the House of Commons had finally been allocated 40,000 square feet. We were not asked if we thought it adequate. Nor were we asked how many square feet we thought were needed to give each Member his own office desk and space for a secretary. We were told that the Government needed more Government offices and they would make available to us 40,000 square feet out of 230,000 square feet. The balance was to be taken up by the Metropolitan Police, pubs, restaurants and shops. That is the rating in which the British House of Commons stands with the Executive.[25]

25 HC *Debates* (673), col. 1814.

The thorny question of MPs' salaries arises. Salaries are determined by the House itself, that is, of course, by the Government leading the House. Since 1957 Members have been paid £1,750 a year, of which the average sum reckoned to be acceptable as necessary expenses by the Income Tax authorities is £750. This later figure was calculated by the 1953 Select Committee on Members' Expenses and was, after much acrimony and confusion, the basis of their recommendation and the eventual salary increase agreed to by the Government from the previous figure of £1,000. Each increase from the original £400 granted in 1911 has similarly stirred up much Parliamentary and public dispute: the fate of any group having to determine its own salary.[26]

On the face of it, such a compounding of income and expenses might seem sensible. But in fact it has increased the ambiguity about who is paying who for what—as *The Times* warned in a leader headlined 'A Bad Business'.[27] For it thoroughly confused two quite separate issues: that of an MPs own proper 'take-home' salary, and that of what facilities he should be given to carry out his job efficiently. To be given a blanket expense allowance, like some commercial travellers, is surely not the best way either to help MPs or to ensure that public money is spent for proper purposes. The MP at the moment is given free railway travel only between his home or constituency and Parliament while in Session: free postage only to Government Departments; and free telephone only within the London area, and then only in Session. This parsimony seems out of keeping with the dignity of a great Parliament, and the theory behind it (the 'Executive mind' again) takes a far too narrow view of an MP's proper political duties if it restricts them to the actual Session, to the Member's Constituency and to his letters to Government Departments. Plainly it is in the public interest for him to travel, correspond and even—oh modern innovation!—*telephone* fairly widely within the United Kingdom both in and out of Session. And

[26] See Peter G. Richards, *Honourable Member: a Study of the British Backbencher* (Faber, 1959), Chapter 13, for an admirable account of these sad shuffles.
[27] *The Times*, 9 July 1954.

he does not have any secretarial assistance at all, nor yet an assured individual office. Even when the new Bridge Street site is completed, Parliament will be no nearer accepting the need for one man, one office and one secretary.

Such a system is not likely to be efficient. It does not give enough help to the (minority of) regularly attending and energetic Backbenchers, and it may be over-generous already to the (majority of) part-time MPs who regard their Parliamentary salary more as an honorarium or retaining fee than as a basic wage.[28] And lumping together two payments for different things makes the resulting sum seem larger in the eyes of the public and the press than it actually is, compared to other occupations where the craftsman's tools are, nowadays at least, almost universally provided by the employer. The actual difficulty about raising salaries has, however, not merely been fear of public criticism, but an at times quite violent aversion by many Conservative Members towards making it 'too easy' for 'the professional politician' (objections to 'excessive payments' are made at every belated move for an increase, presumably on the high constitutional principle of 'Damn you, Jack, we're all right'). And perhaps governments have not been entirely eager to strengthen the potential capabilities of Backbenchers even in this obvious respect.

The present sum is clearly inadequate for those who depend on it. It drives many into part-time jobs, though there are also those who unnecessarily restrict their Parliamentary activities so as to bolster an already adequate income by the pickings that an MP's status can gain them—in directorships and all kinds of consultative, public relations or plainly lobbying *jobs*. The public is rightly sceptical of this type of MP, who, under present arrangements, creates hardship for the other. The full-time Backbencher's ordinary postage bills can easily run to a hundred pounds a year, if he has even some small national reputation. Many MPs have two homes to keep up, unless they desert their normal home (or their constituency) for London entirely. Put it in such homely terms as this: it is well known in the House that those who live on their salary alone

28 See p. 86 below for some figures of attendance.

and pay proper attention to constituency and public duties, cannot regularly afford lunch or dinner in the dining room of the House of Commons and use only the tea room regularly. If the 'professional politician' did choose politics as a paying profession, then the miserable nature of the Member's (Pension) Fund would alone be a good reason for changing jobs again—or, better, emigrating to Canada.[29]

The Government has at last appointed an independent committee to make recommendations as to both MPs' and Ministers' salaries, so as to avoid what *The Times* called, 'the inhibiting embarrassment of members of Parliament sitting in judgement on their own pay claim'.[30] The Chairman and the Deputy-Chairman of the National Incomes Commission, together with Mr W. J. M. Mackenzie, Professor of Government at Manchester University, have been given this task, empowered to take evidence from whatever source they wish, but with an advisory committee of MPs to help them on 'Parliamentary matters'. The committee was not to report until after the General Election. Such a committee seems an essential and long overdue reform. It would be open to the committee, of course, to avoid embarrassing even themselves on future occasions: they could recommend a permanent solution by following the French example and tying salaries to some suitable scale in the Civil Service, thus surrendering responsibility to the Whitley Council.[31] But even if they did so, the point of the scale might not need to be spectacularly higher than the present £1,750 (so long as it moves with the cost of living) *if* the primary need were settled first: that of facilities. On all counts it is clear that a Member should be able to draw on public funds, or be reimbursed from them, for those essentials he needs to do his job properly: secretary, office, postage, telephone and travel. The public having elected Members, at

[29] See *Report of the Select Committee on Members' Expenses* (HC 72) 1953–54 for Commonwealth practices—almost invariably more generous and sensible.

[30] *The Times,* 20 December, 1963, report headed 'Independent Review of Pay for Ministers and MPs'.

[31] As suggested by my colleague Mr William Pickles in a letter to *The Times,* 28 May, 1954.

least in part to represent their particular interests, have a right
to demand that their MPs should be given the normal facilities
without which any managerial or professional man could not
be expected to function. Such minimum facilities are merely a
logical extension of the payment of MPs at all; it need raise
no new constitutional issue. From every aspect it seems incredible and negligent that the House should not have developed secretarial and office facilities for Members even in
their purely individual capacity, even to fulfil just their present
tasks—and if not for their own sakes, then for the sake of the
public which has an interest to demand an efficient MP in a
well-equipped Parliament building.[32]

Certainly, all this should be done before salaries are raised.
There would still be a case for raising them, but there would
be a better case for raising them selectively. As we will see,
the important work of Standing Committees, which meet in
the mornings, is poorly attended: only some 60–70 MPs in
the Session 1961–62 attended more than half the meetings to
which they had been summoned; over 100 did not play any
part in this work at all. One can assume that those who do not
attend are doing something else—lucrative. One need not deny
that *some* part-time MPs actually strengthen the House, such
as the lawyers (or some of the lawyers anyway); but it seems
hard to avoid the conclusion that it would be scandalous to
increase the 'honorarium' of part-time Members still more.
The solution might be to pay a *per diem* allowance for attendance at Standing Committees: this could be adjusted to some
notional proper salary in such a way that those attending, say,
more than half the morning meetings, gained that salary. Here
would actually be an element of incentive for that small and
dedicated band who attend most of the morning sessions: they
could actually exceed the norm.

The muddle over salaries and facilities will be as great as

[32] The Lawrence Committee reported in November 1964 in fa-
vor of a straight salary increase to £3,250 for all MPs; this was
accepted by the Government. The committee refused to be drawn
into any of the above considerations as 'outside our terms of reference'. See *Report of the Committee on the Remuneration of Ministers and Parliament*, Cmnd 2516 of 1964–65.

ever if the new committee cannot stretch its rather vague terms of reference to include facilities. One element of facilities, though, raises a special problem beyond their conceivable purview. *Office accommodation* is not merely a convenience for the MP himself, but would be a place where at least his secretary could be found, behind a door or on the phone, by both constituents and general public. Has no MP ever fully realized the disillusionment in the face of a constituent, lobbying him for the first time, when he may be expected to state his business in a corner of a crowded lobby which has all the *confusion*, the noise and, indeed, the *décor* of the entrance to one of the London railway stations, themselves equal victims with the House of Commons of the inconvenience of Victorian opulence? If MPs will not treat themselves well enough to have offices,[33] they should at least consider the public. Where could such accommodation be found within the Palace of Westminster?—even apart from cost, ancestral voices from nearby will protest.

But if anyone would bother to resurrect some of the evidence submitted to—but ignored by—the Select Committee on the Rebuilding of the Palace of Westminster, 1943–45, they would see that there is ample scope for adapting or rebuilding parts of the present site, if much of the phoney Gothic is treated with the respect it deserves. The whole of the new Bridge Street building could have been given over entirely to Parliament (and further sites need not have been ruled out, for it does not notably affect the dignity of US Senators to pass from desk to division on a delightful automatic underground railway). In fact the actual recommendations of the *Report* of the 1943–45 Select Committee sadly illustrates the

---

[33] Not even desks. See the *Report of the Select Committee on Accommodation* (HC 309) 1952–53, and HC 184, 1953–54, which, amid its report (or exposure) on the almost Pickwickian conflict of authorities within the Palace of Westminster, made the humble comment that sixty per cent of Members replied to an item in a questionnaire that they would welcome an individual, office-type desk. But the Lord Great Chamberlain, the Speaker, the Ministry of Works and the Sergeant-at-Arms were unable between them to find space, money or inclination for this simple task of bureaucratic joinery.

apathy and unimaginativeness of MPs themselves. The Report was dominated by three things: restaurant facilities, lavatory accommodation and the design of the present Chamber—making few concessions to its hallowed pseudo-Gothic inconveniences.[34] Only the facilities of the Press Gallery did well out of the rebuilding, though its size, like that of the slightly increased Public Gallery, is still ridiculously inadequate. It could be seriously argued that—the inconvenience of the present Chamber and its surroundings apart—the whole atmosphere of Westminster is dangerously that of a museum of a vanished order.

The Select Committee on House of Commons Accommodation of 1953 and 1954, the 'Stokes Committee', perhaps wisely gave most of its attention to the tangled question of the control of the Palace of Westminster and to the allocation of accommodation within the existing type of space available. Even the chairman, the late Richard Stokes, restrained his obvious inclination to advise that the whole building should be torn apart and rebuilt as something likely to serve its purpose and as a vindication of modern British industry and design, not as a monument to Pugin's theories about a non-existent Gothic race.[35] But it availed them little to concentrate on one main and simple recommendation, that 'some unified control of the whole Palace' should be created; that was ignored by the Government with nearly all the rest.[36]

[34] Of all the lost opportunities for Wren-like replanning presented by the Blitz, this is the worst: one is sad at heart to see what-little-happened at Westminster compared to the brilliant combination of tradition and modern convenience achieved in some of the German post-war *Länder* Parliaments—Hanover, for instance, an apt case.

[35] A new and functional Parliament building will only come when the Minister of Transport discovers that the Palace of Westminster is the sole obstacle to a Motor Way from Wandsworth Bridge to Blackfriars. One admires the spirit but recognizes the idealism of Mr William Proudfoot's, MP (Conservative), remark: 'Use the present building for State occasions and let's have a modern working building,' quoted in the *Observer,* 17 March, 1963, p. 13. If British businessmen can now abandon Bankers' Georgian, Statesman's Gothic might well follow after.

[36] And still is, see the debate on Parliamentary reform on Mr Charles Pannell's motion of 15 March, 1963, HC *Debates* (673), col. 1715–1820.

One significant characteristic of Parliament that emerges from all this is that it is cheap. It is both cheap by comparison with most other legislatures and by what is spent on even moderate sized Government Departments. This is shown in the following table:

COST OF HOUSE OF COMMONS COMPARED TO TREASURY AND HOME OFFICE

(Source: 1963–64 *Estimates*)

	House of Commons £	Treasury £	Home Office £
Amount carried on departmental vote	1,759,000	4,399,000	13,815,000
Less *Appropriations in Aid*	7,000	220,000	3,272,000
	1,752,000	4,179,000†	10,543,000‡
*Additional expenditure in connection with the service but carried on other votes**	934,000	1,445,000	1,762,000
	2,686,000	5,624,000	12,305,000

* Includes maintenance, furniture, fuel, light, stationery, printing, rates and Consolidated Fund expenditure (e.g. as carried on the Ministry of Works and Stationery Office votes).

† Includes the salaries of several Ministers, the Whips and the Royal Household appointments.

‡ Includes £9,670,000 spent on Law Services including Grants, and over £3,000,000 in fines as a grant-in-aid.

We get a House of Commons on the cheap. Money can hardly be added to time as one of the excuses why the Commons are not able to expand their facilities even to perform their minimal functions: partly, they do not want to, but anyway they are not allowed to by the Government.

The House of Commons also seems unduly modest and somewhat stick-in-the-mud about the Library it possesses. Until very recently it was little more than a gentlemen's private library with fairly complete runs of government publications, much on a level with the libraries of the political clubs.

Since the war it has improved greatly, but in stock and services to Members. In addition to the Librarian himself, there are now thirteen Library Clerks with university degrees of whom six are concerned primarily with research (three being Statisticians). As well as helping Members to books and reports, they will 'find things out for Members', will present short answers to fairly straightforward demands for statistics, will compile bibliographies or lists of references to a subject, and can often provide reports for Members, detailed and precise even by best Departmental standards; but there are obviously not enough of them to conduct any original research for Members, or even for Committees of the House, as the Library of Congress does, or the many American State Legislative Reference Libraries.

In the Debate on accommodation in the Commons of March 1960, some Members pressed for an extension of library services, and Mr Butler, as Leader of the House, asked the Library Committee of the House of Commons for tentative proposals for briefing Members. But the Library Committee came to a firm decision that the Library should not brief Members, but that instead the staff should be increased and efforts made towards 'enlarging the scope and depth of information available to Members' from existing services.[37]

In 1961 the Select Committee on Estimates published a report on the Library.[38] It showed an awareness of the issue, for it concluded:

[37] See *Report* of the sub-committee of the Select Committee on Estimates (HC 246) 1960–61, p. 8, para. 43.
[38] *Op. cit.* Several MPs, notably Mr Charles Pannell, challenged the Speaker about the propriety of the Select Committee in investi-

Effective control over Library expenditure will be impossible unless the House lays down a policy for the Library. In particular, the House should decide whether it requires a research service, in addition to an ordinary Reference Library.

It would then be necessary to decide whether such a research service should provide information only at the request of Members, whether it should prepare spontaneously background material and bibliographies on subjects likely to be debated in the House, and how far it could go in interpreting facts and figures for Members.

Neither of these two alternatives is being acted upon, although it is possible to imagine modest but significant steps in the latter direction coming up from within the Library without any formal decision being made. The continuing growth in demand by Members for the ordinary services of the Library may in itself create an increased sophistication among Members about what can be obtained and put together from existing sources, which might further stimulate the Library towards anticipation of such demands. Some recent innovations in the Library point towards its becoming a real research service rather than just a very good Reference Library. Visible strip indexes are now kept of references to Parliamentary papers of debates. There are selective indexes to press comments on both home and foreign affairs—and cuttings are filed of most of the material indexed. Major debates are documented by Reference Sheets compiled largely from these indexes, and each sheet is accompanied by copies of most of the material listed. But such innovations cannot go far without a great increase in skilled staff, which would involve policy decisions.

For the American Legislative Reference Libraries go far beyond anything known as a 'Reference Library' in Britain. They are centres of research for, and on behalf of, the Legislature. They are often the physical setting of the meetings of

_____

gating not a department of State, but a part of the House of Commons responsible to the Speaker himself. Their real worry was, however, not constitutional, but the somewhat cheeseparing attitude of the committee. See HC *Debates* (640), 18 May, 1961, cols. 1554–57, and also the strong plea of Mr Percy Daines for a better library with research officers, HC *Debates* (530), 22 July, 1954, col. 1669 ff.

the most important committees. They employ statisticians, economists, indeed social scientists and research workers of all kinds. They commonly provide assistants to work with investigatory committees. They are deliberately alternative—if often, of course, also complementary—sources of information to the great facilities of the Executive offices (as seen in Appendix C below).

The Library, though it is highly efficient within its limited budget and is a most lively-minded department, has far to go in extending obvious library services before it could provide a pool of expert staff and research workers for Select Committees of the House. There needs to be, for instance, an abstracting service for public documents and reports, a comprehensive press-clippings collection and a translation service for Members.[39] When the Select Committee on Nationalized Industries wondered whether to appoint—what it quaintly called—'a trained economist', one of the more sensible objections it made to this momentous step was that it would be difficult to attract a suitable person when the committee was only a Sessional one and when work might be spasmodic.[40] This practical difficulty of recruitment would be met if the Library of the House offered a career for a pool of research workers, some of whom might with mutual advantage regard such work as only an incident or stage in a career in the universities or public service. Perhaps the decline in the use of Select Committees[41] of the House of Commons and the vast increase in the use of Departmental and Inter-Departmental committees has been partly because the House cannot do justice, without such help, to the great complexity of many modern issues. Whenever such an expansion of the Library has been urged, arguments both political and allegedly constitutional have been advanced against the House's developing 'a counter bureaucracy' to Whitehall. Some MPs have such doubts but see the positive

[39] As urged by Sir Hugh Linstead, MP, in the debate on Accommodation of 1 August, 1963, HC *Debates* (160), cols. 752–60; he claimed that the cost of these three services would only be about £15,000 per annum.

[40] See pp. 95–96 below.

[41] See pp. 96–99 and 225–27 below.

advantages of expansion, though others seem all too satisfied and complacently content to rely upon the fruits of Departmental reports set on foot by the Government itself, and upon what other information can be gained from Whitehall by Parliamentary Questions. It does not impugn the honesty of civil servants to say that *all* factual information is inherently selective and is assembled in the light of certain prior purposes; all that needs to be insisted upon is that the critical functions of Parliament should not always coincide with the executive purposes of the Government.

Here is an example of a Parliamentary institution, practically unheard of to the general public, thought of as unimportant or parochial to most students, but which could gladly and easily develop in a way which could go very far indeed to restore the proper influence of Parliament. Most Backbenchers themselves show little understanding of the vital difference between a passive Reference Library and an active workshop of research. Perhaps, with instinctive defensiveness, the Executive does; so that even while such a development could not possibly threaten the Government's political control of Parliament, yet it is frowned upon because it would cut down some of the Government's exclusive advantages in reaching and influencing the public who become the electorate. Nothing should be done to hinder the former; something should be done to hinder the latter.

The Constituency Case

The general question of facilities for Parliamentary work also involves the efficiency of work outside Parliament. Clearly the first obligation of an MP in the British system of government is to support or to make things difficult for a particular government, according to the interests and the plans of a particular party. Let all this go with no more saying (except to reflect that most frontal attacks on the 'party system' in fact make more sense when recast as criticisms of the internal organization of the separate parties). But the MP has a secondary role to play in relation to his constituents—certainly secondary but

certainly necessary and important both politically and constitutionally.

Much of the work of the modern private Member is, some
have complained, that of a 'glorified welfare officer', someone
to whom complaints and inquiries come, often of a bewildering and ridiculous variety, about all sorts of inequities and
incomprehensions which the plain people find in dealing with
officialdom—often complaints about which the MP can do
nothing. Members receive precious little encouragement from
their leaders in this work. Lord Attlee has written:

> 'I think the present practice whereby many MPs spend
> the bulk of their week-ends dealing with constituency cases
> is a bad one. The MP ought to have leisure for recreation,
> home life, and possibly homework. Many MPs wear them-
> selves out doing work that ought to be left to others . . .
> in these days of legal aid and citizen's advice bureaux, he
> should not be troubled as he so often is today with a mass
> of detailed work which detracts from his work as an MP.
> It would be a good thing if there could be some kind of
> gentleman's agreement among all Parties on this, for as
> things are there is a tendency for competition in these mat-
> ters . . . Government Departments deal, I think, with cases
> on their merits, and intervention by an MP is often quite
> unnecessary.'[42]

But this is surely the very kind of attitude which creates as
well as reflects a sense of alienation between the public and
its Parliament. Everything is so geared towards the business
of carrying on central government that the public is actually
reprimanded for ignorantly wasting the time of MPs. Certainly the public is ignorant of the fact that an individual MP
can do little more in the great majority of cases than forward
his constituent's letter to the right Government Department
—on a standard form provided for that purpose, and then
send back to him a reply drafted and typed out in the Department. There is the occasional bigger fish to fry, of course
—a Crichel Down or a 'Thurso boy' case (and one such case
as either of these every so often goes a long way to making

Ministers and Departments careful and thorough in their answers to even apparently routine 'constituency' questions). But Lord Attlee would be the last to deny that Members should keep their ears open for that kind of thing, though not for 'work that ought to be left to others'. The mere fact that members of the public come to the MP's clinic (if he holds one at all),[43] whether they come to get legal advice, to complain about their house, their pension or their mother-in-law, shows that there is a need, shows that the Constituency MP can still be thought of as the person to turn to, even if he only posts one off to somebody else. Lord Attlee's laudable wish to find creative leisure for MPs should not be at the expense of that psychological level of representation without which the most efficient system of government can fall into the contempt of the governed.

There is a good case for saying that it is important not merely for MPs to receive no discouragement from their party leaders, but that the House of Commons as a whole should take 'the constituency case' more seriously. The leisure to think and read, which Lord Attlee rightly says is an urgent need of MPs, could be gained simply by giving them proper secretarial and office facilities: this would save far more time than abandoning work which, in fact, needs expanding. The public, when confronted with the bewildering diversity and, at times, remoteness of officialdom, needs to feel that it has an intermediary to whom it can turn for advice and help. Even if the help is purely a question of reassuring someone that the New Model Circumlocution Office is in fact dealing with him fair and fast, this reassurance is in itself a vital factor. Again, it would be overly abstract and endlessly debatable to say that

[43] A recent article by Robert E. Dowse, 'The MP and his Surgery', *Political Studies,* October 1963, pp. 333–41, has attempted to study this by means of a questionnaire posted to a random sample of 100 MPs. Of the 69 who replied, a fifth held no surgery at all (Labour MPs showing themselves *slightly* more involved in this work than Conservatives). But about a third of those who did hold 'surgery' did so only once a month, only 8 Members out of the 69 claimed to do so weekly—and one assumes that those who replied to the questionnaire are more likely to be interested in such work than those who did not reply.

the public has a *right* of access to and advice from their Member; it is rather the question that at times people feel the *need* (whether rightly or wrongly in administrative terms is *not* the question) to put their troubles, administrative and personal, before their Member.[44] If such needs are not met, who is to blame that the public is cynical about Parliament? One can go further and say—shuddering at the shaking of heads which such a wild suggestion will cause—that it would be wholly a good thing if each MP had a local secretary who was in fact a trained social worker, paid for out of local rates and with a known office in some local public building, not in the party offices, where many people—again rightly or wrongly is not the question—are probably reluctant to go.[45] The reasons are obvious why the life of an MP should not become dominated by 'constituency case work', but it would be an act of great wisdom, understanding and compassion for the small man in the big world—not a regrettable 'tendency for competition in these matters'—if some party leader were even to devote two minutes of a political broadcast to reminding the public that they have an MP who is somewhat there to help them.

Disquiet Among MPs

It becomes clearer and clearer that the traditional account of Parliament's role, however much one tries even to outdo Bagehot in realism, is simply not being fulfilled. We will examine later the few collective attempts of MPs to do something about it. But it will be useful to consider the general views of MPs on the working of Parliament today. Appendix B reprints in full a most useful and revealing survey by Mr Rudolf Klein

[44] The helping and expansion of this existing institution might go better with British law and practice than the importation of something like the Scandinavian *Ombudsman*—the official investigator of grievances. But if MPs do not become far more effective intermediaries between the public and The Executive, then the *Ombudsman* is worth turning to—see articles and editorial in the *Observer*, 31 May and 7 June, 1959, which started the *Ombudsman* boom. See Chapter 8 below for a full discussion of the issue.

[45] *Ibid.*, p. 335.

of the *Observer* from which these following assertions are taken.[46]

On salaries, 64 per cent of Conservative MPs and 94 per cent of Labour MPs thought their salaries 'inadequate'.

On Backbench influence, Members divided equally that they had 'enough influence' or 'too little influence' (a significant Party difference: 59 per cent of Labour as against 32 per cent of Conservatives backed the latter statement, but then the Party in opposition is likely to feel more strongly on this).

On Party discipline, 70 per cent of all Members thought that it was 'just about right' and only 20 per cent 'too strict'.

On professionalism, 78 per cent of Conservatives thought that 'the trend towards MPs becoming full-time politicians' was 'regrettable' (as against 26 per cent of Labour), whereas 68 per cent of Labour thought it either 'desirable' or 'inevitable' (as against 8 per cent of Conservatives).

On time spent how, 60 per cent of all MPs thought that 'the House of Commons spend too much time' on 'debating details of legislation' (no one thought that it spent too much time 'discussing broad issues of policy'); 54 per cent thought that some work could be delegated to specialized committees, Defence and Agriculture being the most often mentioned.

On financial control, 61 per cent of all MPs (the Parties agreeing almost equally) thought that the 'House of Commons' control over the Government's expenditure' was 'too loose'.

On Parliamentary power, 63 per cent of all MPs thought that 'the balance of power within the House of Commons since 1945 has shifted towards' the 'executive' (56 per cent of Conservatives, but 71 per cent of Labour), and 23 per cent of all MPs thought that it had 'remained the same' (with an interest-

[46] Rudolf Klein, 'What MPs Think of their Jobs', *Observer,* 17 March, 1963, and Appendix B below. The *precise* figures must be handled with caution, for they are based on 162 replies received from a form sent to all MPs. There is obviously a bias towards Backbenchers in the figures, which is not important for our argument, but also probably a much bigger bias towards those interested in the problem at all. However, the closeness of the responses when identified by Party at least show that if the opinions now reported may be in advance of those of the House as a whole, yet they are amazingly cross-bench.

ing 12 per cent of Conservatives, as against 1½ per cent of
Labour, who thought that it had actually 'shifted towards the
Backbench members'—which probably reflects both a greater
real degree of influence from Conservative Backbenchers on
their Leaders, and also the situation of a Party long in office
with a large majority, discipline becoming less rigid).

The last two significant questions put must be quoted in full
to appreciate the greater division of opinion about the basic
questions of Parliament's efficiency and prestige—at the best,
great uncertainty is revealed:

*Do you think, on balance, the House of Commons does its
work:*

	Percentage of Total	Percentage of Conservatives	Percentage of Labour
Efficiently?	15	20	8
Adequately?	44	42	45
Inefficiently?	33	27	41
Mixed views or none	8	11	6

The division of opinion is interesting here and also the small
numbers in the first category.

*Do you think the prestige of the House of Commons, in the
eyes of the public as a whole, is:*

	Percentage of Total	Percentage of Conservatives	Percentage of Labour
Rising?	6	4	9
Static?	48	46	50
Falling?	36	37	36
Mixed views or none	10	13	5

The number in the first category is again fascinating, and the number in the third, much the same as in the third category of the previous table, suggests that MPs are more aware of public disquiet than the collective actions of the House imply, or than the views of many commentators about the thickness of the walls at Westminster would suggest.

So however narrowly and realistically one defines the functions of the House of Commons—say, to scrutinize, to uncover, to publicize and to criticize as well as to *support* a Government and to *pass* the Government's legislation—it seems highly doubtful whether the methods Parliament has at hand are adequate, or adequately developed, to fulfil these functions in face of the changing nature of executive power. This chapter set out to be an objective account of how Parliament works in relation to the Private Member: to show the meaning of Bagehot's concepts, as slightly amended, in practice. But it is not possible to ride on such a tight and dispassionate leash simply because Parliament is not fulfilling its function. Could this not just mean that the account of the functions is idealistic and factually wrong, that we must look still more realistically at what it actually does? We could, but the minimal functions we have been talking about are, after all, not just the working of Parliament, but of Parliament as part of the wider system of British Government. That wider system of government itself depends upon these functions of Parliament working properly, both for restraint and advice. It could be, of course, that we must recognize that the system has changed: that we have Presidential government. This conclusion may become true. But it is too radical a solution until the possibilities of Parliamentary reform in order to preserve the customary British system of government and politics have been exhausted.

CHAPTER IV

WHAT THE COMMONS DO
COLLECTIVELY

The Concept of Control

Politics, not Law, must explain the concept and practice of Parliamentary control of the Executive. In modern conditions any such control can only be something that does not threaten the day-to-day political control of Parliament by the Executive. The hope for any worth-while function of control by Parliament would be grim indeed if it depended on the ultimate deterrent of the vote: the undoubted Constitutional right of Parliament to vote against the Queen's Ministers and the Convention by which they would then resign. But control, on both sides, is indeed political. Governments respond to proceedings in Parliament if the publicity given to them is likely to affect public confidence in the Government, or even if the weakness with which the Government puts up its case, even in purely Parliamentary terms, begins to affect the morale of its own supporters (though it takes a very long succession of bleak days for the Government in the House before the country begins to be affected).

The only meanings of Parliamentary control worth considering, and worth the House spending much of its time on, are those which do *not* threaten the Parliamentary defeat of a Government, but which help to keep it responsive to the underlying currents and the more important drifts of public opinion. All others are purely antiquarian shufflings. It is wholly legitimate for any modern Government to do what it needs to guard against Parliamentary defeat; but it is not legitimate for it to hinder Parliament, particularly the Opposition, from reaching the public ear as effectively as it can. Governments must govern in the expectation that they can serve out their statutory period of office, that they can plan—if they choose—at least that far ahead, but that everything they do may be exposed to the light of day and that everything they say may be challenged in circumstances designed to make criticism as authoritative, informed and as public as possible.

Thus the phrase 'Parliamentary control', and talk about the 'decline of Parliamentary control', should not mislead anyone into asking for a situation in which Governments can have their legislation changed or defeated, or their life terminated (except in the most desperate emergency when normal politics will in any case break down, as in Chamberlain's 'defeat' in 1940). Control means *influence,* not direct power; *advice,* not command; *criticism,* not obstruction; *scrutiny,* not initiation; and *publicity,* not secrecy. Here is a very realistic sense of Parliamentary control which *does* affect any Government. The Government will make decisions, whether by existing powers or by bringing in new legislation, in the knowledge that these decisions, sooner or later, will find their way to debate on the Floor of one of the Houses of Parliament. The type of scrutiny they will get will obviously affect, in purely political terms, the type of actions undertaken. And the Civil Service will administer with the knowledge that it too may be called upon to justify perhaps even the most minute actions.

Governments are virile and adult; they are beyond the strict parental control of Parliament. But they are likely to be deeply influenced by well put home truths from the family, if only (or above all) because this may be some sort of clue to their public reputation; and also because, after all, they have to share the same overcrowded house. Defeating the Government or having the whips withdrawn represent, like calling in the police, the breakdown, not the assertion, of normal control.

Governments deserve praise in so far as they expose themselves, willingly and helpfully, to influence, advice, criticism, scrutiny and publicity; and they deserve blame in so far as they try to hide from unpleasant discussions and to keep their reasons and actions secret. Parliaments deserve praise or blame as to whether or not they can develop institutions whose control is powerful in terms of General Elections and not of Governmental instability. This 'praise' and 'blame' is not moralistic: it is prudential. A Government subject to such controls is not likely to get too far out of touch with public opinion; it may not, even in Bagehot's sense, attempt to 'teach' public opinion, but it will not destroy it. So Parliamentary control is not the stop switch, it is the tuning, the tone and the amplifier of a system of communication which tells governments what the electorate want (rightly or wrongly) and what they will stand for (rightly or wrongly), and tells the electorate what is possible within the resources available (however much opinions will vary on what is possible).

It is in this sense of control that we must now examine the main ways by which Parliament attempts to control (influence, advise, criticize, scrutinize and publicize) the Executive. But one preliminary comment: it follows from this that it is possible to exaggerate what many see as the 'all-important' aspect of financial control. Certainly the history of Parliament was the history of the power of the purse over the Crown. But now that 'the Crown' is a Party Ministry, control is nothing if it is not influence over the policy of Governments. It is politically impossible to separate out economic from political factors.[1] It is procedurally worthless to look at the form of legislation or of estimates without being able to consider the content. And the fact that Parliament scrutinizes financial legislation in a less and less detailed manner is not the cause of the general decline of Parliamentary influence, but is the effect; therefore it cannot sensibly be regarded as the unique lever, or even the first priority, in any attempt to restore or create a true reciprocity between government and consent. The problem is of a general lack of development, or in some cases of the decline, of devices for informing and communicating authoritatively.

The dogged novels of Sir Charles Snow, Professor Parkinson's *Law* and Professor K. C. Wheare's *Government by Committee* are all, in their different ways, testimonies to the truth

[1] Even, ultimately, theoretically impossible to separate out economics from politics; see my *In Defence of Politics*, revised edition (Penguin, 1964), Chapter 1 and the 'Footnote to Rally the Academic Professors of Politics'.

that the most important work of central government is conducted not by civil servants or MPs working as individuals,
but by committees. To say this is not to underestimate the
great importance of the general debates on the floor of the
Commons—or even those in the House of Lords. These debates
on the floor are invaluable as occasions on which the Government is forced to explain its actions or intentions before a
partly hostile audience which can gain the maximum of publicity. And generally the House is at its best in the conduct of
general debates; there seems little cause for public concern
here—if the giants of yester-year are mourned by some, so
have they always been. In the days of Gladstone and Disraeli
there were old hands who yawned in their faces at the memory
of Peel and Russell. Members themselves feel strongly that
there is never enough time for as many as want to speak in
debates to speak. But the public may perhaps be justified in
regarding this as a purely domestic matter of the House when
all experience suggests that the eager expectation of novelty
in the umpteenth speech of a major debate is usually only a
function of having forgotten the content of the first dozen. It
is rather depressing to find that most MPs view the whole
topic of Parliamentary reform as simply meaning suggestions
as to how to find time for more Members to speak more often
on the Floor of the House, rather than as how to equip themselves to speak with more authority when they do.

But the scrutiny of legislation and Parliamentary control of
the actions of the Executive, particularly in its lower reaches,
give cause for greater disquiet. Proposals for legislation, or
even for changes in departmental or administrative policy, are
usually the product of a network of departmental and inter-
departmental committees. These bring together the departments affected and expert opinion—both inside and outside
government service—and, far more than is commonly realized,
consult with interested parties, outside interests and the whole
range of legitimate pressure groups. Thus a Minister when he
rises from his seat to face the House is as well prepared as
the resources of what is still one of the most efficient and
highly qualified civil services in the world can make him. It is
not uncommon for a major Bill to make fifteen or more jour-

neys for redrafting back and forwards from the Ministry to the Parliamentary Counsel. It is common to speak of the process of a Bill through Parliament as being but the exposed tenth of the mass of an iceberg. So much skilled staff work goes into the drafting of modern legislation and the formulation of policy that it is hard to see how criticism from the Floor can hope to be informed and even modestly effective unless MPs have some, even remotely, equivalent source of knowledge, or way of getting it. The reliance of the ordinary MP on Government sources is flattering but extreme. The ordinary MP may have his 'speciality' as the fruit of past experience, but he is simply not equipped and assisted to break new ground. The conscientious MP spends most of his working life in committees: some have brains, some have teeth, but none—except Committee of Public Accounts—have hands and feet to work for them.

Any complex matter put before any large association of men is commonly dealt with in four ways: by appointing a small committee; by giving that committee as precise a definition of its function as possible; by giving the committee as much time as possible; and by including among the committee technical experts or giving it access to such experts. Few of the activities of the House, as we will now see, measure up to such a standard.

Committees of the Whole House

Paradoxically, the most common type of committee of the House is not really a committee at all. The House, as is well known, sits as a whole as the Committee of Supply or the Committee of Ways and Means, when discussing the Finance Bill and the Budget as it does, indeed, on any Money Resolution or Supplementary Estimate relating to the Consolidated Fund. Commonly Bills of exceptional importance are given in their committee stage to the House as a whole, rather than being sent 'upstairs' to a Standing Committee; and uncontested Bills of a minor nature are almost certain to be 'passed on the nod'. Thus, the finance Bills apart, there are two occasions when time can actually be saved by the ordinarily more cumbersome device of 'Committee of the Whole': when the matter is not going to be discussed anyway, and when the matter is felt by Members to be so important that the Report Stage on the floor of the House would probably want to cover again all the ground already covered by the normal Standing Committee upstairs.

But if the Government is in a hurry, then the Committee Stage may be taken on the Floor, since the Standing Committees then take too long.[2]

A Committee of the Whole on the Finance Bill and on Money Resolutions, although it has some greater procedural flexibility over a normal session of the House when the Speaker is in the Chair, is at best a cumbersome, and at worst an extremely time-wasting device. It is justified not in terms of efficiency but in terms of alleged constitutional principle: that all MPs should be able to contribute to every level of the discussion on granting Supply. But this is one of those 'principles' which if rigidly adhered to, irrespective of changing circumstances, are self-defeating. And the Executive is now probably happy that it is. Control by sixty men, say, would obviously be more influential than by six hundred. Supply days are now, of course, occasions for general debates about Government policy on topics chosen by the Opposition (some twenty-six days in the Session 1957–58, for instance). This has been a practical response over a long period of time by Parliament both to the impossibility that the whole House should control finance and to the greater need to debate the wood rather than the trees.[3] One would expect this process

[2] And also perhaps because, as Sir Edward Fellowes, the former Clerk of the House of Commons, has put it: 'Governments have a slight bias against Standing Committees where their hold is not so strong and prefer the House to be occupied by legislation.' 'Parliament and the Executive', *Journal of the Parliaments of the Commonwealth*, October 1962, p. 337.

[3] Though some still protest that the House does not examine estimates in depth, see the excellent account of the Backbench revolt against granting Supply 'on the nod' of February–March 1960 in A. H. Hanson and H. V. Wiseman, *Parliament at Work* (Stevens, 1962), pp. 271–78. See also Sir Edward Fellowes 'Financial Con-

to be completed by taking the committee stage of the Finance Bill upstairs in a genuine committee. Even the very cautious *Select Committee on Procedure, 1959,* thought seriously of ways and means by which this could be done. But the Government, after dallying a while, have now repeatedly frowned on the idea, claiming—sheer nonsense or hypocrisy—to be concerned with the traditional rights of the Private Member. In one way or another over the last ten years, according to evidence put before the *Select Committee on Procedure,* the House has spent about a fifth of its entire working hours in Committee of the Whole.

General Standing Committees

All legislation in its Committee Stage is automatically considered by a Standing Committee unless it is claimed for the Floor of the House or sent—as very occasionally happens—to a Select Committee, or else (if it exclusively concerns Scotland) to the Scottish Standing Committee.[4] Currently, there are seven such committees appointed, though the number can be varied at need; one committee is reserved for Private Members' Bills, but otherwise there is no specialization on different topics. Bills come to them quite arbitrarily, according to their order on a calendar and according to which committee finishes its work first. These Standing Committees are thought of as the House of Commons in miniature and not as a gathering of specialists or special interests. Until 1960 each committee was composed of a core of twenty Members appointed for the Session by the Committee of Selection, but then up to thirty Members could be appointed for each Bill. Many of these Members would be chosen for their special knowledge. Since 1960 the composition has been made more flexible. The core has been abolished, the Speaker appoints a Chairman and then anything from twenty to fifty Members as required. This has strengthened the possibility of specialization of Mem-

---

trol of the House of Commons', *Journal of the Parliaments of the Commonwealth,* July 1962, pp. 225–26.

[4] See J. H. Burn, 'Scottish Committees of the House of Commons', *Political Studies,* October 1960, pp. 272–96.

bers to each Bill, but avoided still, like the plague, any gathering together for a whole Session of cross-bench opinion on definite subjects: anything like the Standing Committees of the American Congress or the French Assembly. And these British committees, of course, have no vestige of executive power; they cannot summon persons and papers before them; they cannot debate or discuss matters irrelevant to the actual text of the Bill before them; their proceedings are reported in the 'Committee' *Hansard* and there are clerks at the table to assist the chairman with procedural matters, but they have no research staff on call to examine the evidence behind the legislation before them.

When Standing Committees were first established by Gladstone in 1882 (though they fell into abeyance after one Session and were not revived as a regular device until 1888), they were specialized: two large committees dealing with Law and Commerce respectively, though both construed very broadly. The presumption was, however, that Standing Committees would only deal with more or less non-political matters. This presumption was reversed in the reforms of 1906; they became the normal way of doing business, but when the number was consequently increased, the specialization was abolished.[5]

The change in the composition of the Standing Committees in 1960 towards greater specialism was more apparent than real. The real reason for the change was the difficulty of finding enough Members to work the committees. They sit for about 2½ hours in the morning twice a week and before 1960 they needed something like 250 Members to work them at full strength. And though there was no precise evidence put forward, a figure as low as 200 was frequently mentioned in the proceedings of the Select Committee on Procedure, 1959

[5] See Josef Redlich, *The Procedure of the House of Commons: a study of its history and present form* (London, 1908), Vol. I, p. 174, II, 182–84 and III, 208 ff. Sir Erskine May first suggested the device of Standing Committees to the *Select Committee on the Business of the House* of 1854: his thirty-year campaign had some fruit.

as being the number of Members who 'fairly regularly' attend this important morning work.[6]

The Table of Attendance of MPs at Standing Committees for 1961–62 which we have compiled does not bear this out. It depends what one means by 'fairly regularly', since Members now come on and go off committees much more fre-

FREQUENCY OF ATTENDANCE OF MEMBERS AT
STANDING COMMITTEES, SESSION 1961–62

(Source: *Return of Standing Committees*)

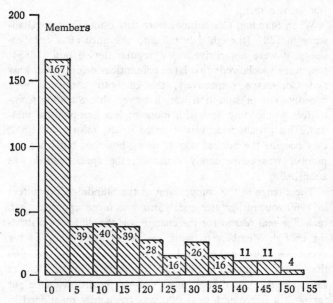

Frequency of Attendance

In addition 65 members who were appointed did not attend, and 2 members attended 64 and 78 times respectively, making a total of 464, of whom 247 were appointed to more than one Committee.

[6] Sir Edward Fellowes, 'Parliament and the Executive', *op. cit.*, has referred to the difficulty in manning the Standing Committees and reminded the House that they have the power to adjourn to

quently according to the topic, perhaps working hard in committee for some days and then retiring to do something else. And since Members will commonly serve on more than one committee, a maximum attendance figure is not meaningful —though one dedicated man notched up 78 attendances, as against 65 Members appointed who did not attend at all and about 100 Members (excluding those in the Ministry, of course) who were not even summoned. But only 112 Members attended more than twenty times; the figure of 200, or very nearly, is only reached if one goes down to the total attending more than ten times. If one took 'fairly regularly' to mean no more than once a week in the thirty weeks of a normal Session, then the number would only be a devoted band of about 70 Members.

There are, of course, as we will now see, other committees meeting in the mornings which can claim a Member. But it does seem clear that the regular committee work of the House involves an astonishingly small proportion of Members. If there were to be any radical expansion of committee work, clearly either some pressures would have to be found to make more MPs full-time MPs, or else an acceptance of even smaller quorums for committees coupled with far greater facilities for them. But it might depend what the committees are considering. Certainly service on Standing Committees is most unpopular among Members, and is felt to be thankless, simply because there is so little real chance of influencing legislation, and no compensatory possibility of discussing the broad subject.

There are also two special Standing Committees which are much better attended and which are also peculiar in that they represent some kind of specialism—if geography can be said to determine knowledge: the Scottish Grand Committee and the Scottish Standing Committee. The Scottish Grand Committee consists of all Members for Scottish constituencies together with ten to fifteen other Members to maintain the bal-

---

facilitate the work of committees (under SO 10), but they never make use of it; he suggests that an occasional Wednesday afternoon in committees would enable the House to double its business.

ance of Parties. They have three functions: to discuss for two days of each session matters of exclusively Scottish concern; to consider for six days such Estimates as refer exclusively to Scotland; and also to consider the principles of any Bill which the Speaker certifies as relating exclusively to Scotland—which is the Second Reading debate for that Bill in fact, if not in name. Such a Bill can then, on the motion of a Minister, be referred for its Committee Stage to a Scottish Standing Committee which consists of thirty Scottish Members nominated for each Bill and not more than twenty other Members (either from Scottish or other seats) nominated in respect of their qualifications and the demands of the balance of the Parties.[7] This peculiar dispensation to the Scots is not without its wider interest since it shows the quite elaborate exceptions the Government and the House will allow when they have the mind.

Specialized Standing Committees

Select Committees are normally those appointed by the House from time to time to deal with particular matters as they arise; but there are some Select Committees which are in practice perennial and are most readily understood if described as 'specialized standing committees'. The Select Committee on Kitchen and Refreshment Rooms has actually been given (strange anomaly) executive powers—in its rather narrow field. The examples of the Select Committee of Privileges and the Selection Committee, however, show that many of these 'specialisms' are in fact procedural or domestic to the House. But there are certain great exceptions. The Committee of Public Accounts and the Select Committee on Estimates are radically different in character from the Standing Committees or from ordinary Select Committees; and so is the Select Committee on Statutory Instruments. And recently the originally somewhat experimental Select Committee on Nationalized Industries has been made sessional and is now an established institution.

The great esteem and effectiveness of the Committee of

[7] See Burn, 'The Scottish Committees . . .', *op. cit.*

Public Accounts, whose duty it is to ascertain whether money is spent for the purpose for which it was voted, is bound up with the fact that the reports and the independent status of the Comptroller and Auditor General furnish them with an un-rivalled extra-governmental source of advice. The committee has no executive power and few of its reports ever get debated on the Floor of the House, but the fear that its criticisms in-spire in Whitehall, the reputations which are furthered or ruined when civil servants appear before the committee to explain, or explain away, sections of the Comptroller General's report, makes it a real example of effective Parliamentary control of the Executive. The Comptroller General has, of course, an expert and a very large staff, some 580 people, of whom 560 are on audit duties—virtually a Department of State. The Committee has existed with broadly its present role for about forty years, but it has widened the range of its oper-ations so that it now looks at nearly all Government accounts. Modern accounting methods leave little room for great mis-takes or malpractices, so the Committee tries more and more to get beyond mere auditing to study the efficiency of the methods by which policy decisions are implemented and their financial effects. That the chairman of this committee is always a member of the Opposition is well known and still important.

The Select Committee on Estimates, on the other hand, has had a much more chequered and at times dispiriting career. Between the wars it met as a single committee, was cumber-some, always in disputes with both Government and House for interfering with policy matters, and it suffered under the reputation of pedantically doing over again something already well done by the Treasury. Part of its difficulties arose, and still do, from the fact that, unlike the Public Accounts Com-mittee, it is concerned with scrutinizing and suggesting econo-mies on *current* estimates, while being, of course, precluded from challenging the policies themselves. It was easy to con-strue the slightest suggestion of an economy as a challenge to Government policy, so the Committee often used to take ref-uge in trivialities which gave the whole field a bad name among the younger and the more ambitious Members. But since the war, as a result of wartime experience in the National Expenditure Committee, the Committee has worked through five sub-committees and has proved more adept at challenging at least the policies of how to implement the basic policies.[8] Reports of the Select Committee have been much more often in the news. They have much better working arrangements with the Public Accounts Committee, so that some matters on which Government Departments stone-wall at the estimates stage can be nagged at again at the expenditure stage. The sub-committees have proved particularly effective of late in identifying, and thus forcing the whole case to be argued out publicly, those apparently innocent 'once-and-for-all' expenditures which in fact—especially in Defence—pave the way for recurrent and increasing expenditure. It is usually better to write-off a mistake or an unexpected failure, however politically unpopular, rather than to keep on pouring in good money to bail out bad.

The Committee suffers from having no specialized staff to do the kind of work done for the Public Accounts Committee by the staff of the Comptroller General. Both Comptroller Generals and Governments have steadily refused requests from the Estimates Committee for such assistance: the Comptroller General being rightly loath to get his department involved in policy matters, and Governments being, as usual, more interested in patting paper tigers than in riding real ones. A number of clerks from the Clerk of the House's Department serve the committees, but none of them can devote their full time to it and none of them are really expert, though some of them gained valuable experience on the wartime National Expenditure Committee. Sir Edward Fellowes puts it: 'Though not experts in accounting or finance, the staff who serve the Estimates Committee can claim to be intelligent laymen with the necessary knowledge of where the information sought by the Committee can be obtained, and the experience to know

---

[8] The difficulties are amusingly seen in a violent onslaught against the committee by Professor Bruce Miller *for* dabbling in policy matters and riding their own hobby horses. See his 'The Colonial Office and the Estimates Committee', *Public Administration*, Summer 1961, and the give-as-good-as-he-got reply of the chairman, Sir Godfrey Nicholson, in *Public Administration*, Summer 1962.

what to look for when the facts and figures are put before the Committee.'[9] This is not whitewash. His clerks did the job as well as any laymen could, and possibly better than some experts, being more attuned to what the Members really want. But why just laymen? Why the stupid parsimony of only part-time assistants to such a committee? And is the department of the House concerned with procedure necessarily the best place from which to recruit or borrow assistance for such a technical task? Such committees need both procedural and expert help. It is curious that Parliament-on-the-cheap and amateurishness are allowed to go together at this point of all points. But, once again, the issue is of control in the sense of publicity, not of restriction. Any idea of reviving Parliament's 'power of the purse' is misconceived: no modern government would allow itself to be overruled on finance for a farthing or a minute. Only the electorate can *enforce* economy. But the evidence put before it is sadly incomplete.

The Select Committee on Statutory Instruments—known as the 'Scrutiny Committee'—is also of some interest, not so much for what it does, but for what it could do and for the grudging recognition it represents that in some areas at least specialized scrutiny by the House of acts of the Executive is necessary. The committee was established in 1944 in partial fulfilment of one of the recommendations of the Donoughmore Committee on Ministers' Powers of 1932. It has the task of scrutinizing every instrument made by a Minister under some powers of delegation on which the House may or must move a resolution. But its terms of reference are limited to drawing the attention of the House, without explanation, to any instruments which appear to make unusual or unexpected use of the powers conferred by the enabling statute. It cannot consider the merits of such instruments, nor grievances arising out of those instruments already in operation. And, in any case, only about half the Statutory Instruments made have to be laid before Parliament in any manner.[10] The Committee has the assistance of the Counsel to the Speaker, yet it is doubtful in

[9] See Fellowes, 'Financial Control . . .', *op. cit.*, p. 227.
[10] See John E. Kersell, *Parliamentary Supervision of Delegated Legislation* (Stevens, 1960), p. 159.

the extreme whether they do a thorough job—largely due to their lack of staff. *The Report of the Select Committee on Delegated Legislation,* 1953 (HC 310), rejected a proposal to make this sessional committee a Standing Committee with greater powers and wider terms of reference—as, indeed, with famous and ludicrous consistency, it rejected all other proposals for reform in this field: the final burial of the much re-buried Donoughmore Report. The Select Committee evidently regarded the fact that the Scrutiny Committee had brought to the special attention of the House only 56 Statutory Instruments out of a total of 5,496 considered between 1947 and 1953 as evidence that there was nothing worth worrying about. Thus if only one instrument of delegated legislation out of a hundred ever even raises the suspicion of having gone beyond the Statute or of containing unusual provisions, then we are all indeed fortunate that Whitehall has gained so much power at the expense of Westminster. Otherwise one might think that the Scrutiny Committee as a watch-dog is toothless,[11] blind or a bit too slow to anger.

Certainly, if there is any radical attempt—and it may become necessary—to lessen the burden of legislative detail by *increasing* the amount of delegated legislation, the Statutory Instruments Committee will be found both ill-equipped and lacking in adequately wide terms of reference to give proper Parliamentary control. Sir Edward Fellowes made this suggestion in his evidence to the Select Committee on Procedure of 1959. It was almost ignored by the Committee, but their greater willingness to contemplate more devolution to committees of the Finance Bill may well have been because the existing Select Committee on Estimates is, after all, fairly effective and is readily capable of expansion and strengthening.

The most interesting exception to the prejudice against specialized Standing committees is, however, the Select Committee on Nationalized Industries. It may well prove the pattern

---

[11] The House of Lords Special Orders Committee considers a narrower range of instruments, but may report on any which appear to raise issues of policy or principle: the whole field is a thorough muddle of anomalies. See Kersell, *ibid.,* p. 159 *et passim.*

of future reform. The circumstances of its origin are significant.

The principle of Public Corporations is accepted, perhaps too readily, by both Parties. There was violent disagreement between the Parties in the 1945–50 Parliament about nationalization, but there was agreement that the pre-war form of the Public Corporation was the correct form to adopt, and not administration by Government departments. A Statute would lay down in each case the respective responsibilities of a Minister and an appointed Board, but in each case they were broadly similar: the Minister was not to be responsible for, nor to intervene in, the day to day running of the Boards, but only responsible for broad issues of public policy. Their semi-independence from both Whitehall and Westminster was to be genuine. This led to great difficulties in the framing of Questions to Ministers.[12] The Speaker was put in an almost impossible position of trying to interpret the Minister's legal responsibility under each separate Statute, trying to satisfy the House and trying to avoid gross inconsistencies between the type of Questions allowable on different Nationalized Boards.

When the Government changed in 1951 it became clear that, Steel apart, the Nationalized Industries were here to stay. Conservative Backbenchers continued to be unhappy at the lack of clear-cut Parliamentary responsibility, and they were joined by many more Labour MPs once Labour was in Opposition. In an article in *The Times* of 8 September, 1949, Mr Hugh Molson, MP (Conservative), had proposed the setting up of a Select Committee to inform and advise the House on the affairs of the Nationalized Industries. The Government yielded to Backbench pressure, particularly from its own supporters, and set up a Select Committee to examine the matter, which reported in favour of a Select Committee on Nationalized Industries.[13] But not until 1955 did the Government

[12] See Hanson and Wiseman, *Parliament at Work*, pp. 309–14; also Chester and Bowring, *Questions in Parliament*, pp. 301–5; A. H. Hanson, *Parliament and Public Ownership* (Cassell, 1961), and W. A. Robson, *Nationalized Industry and Public Ownership* (Allen and Unwin, 1960), *passim*.

[13] See HC (235), 1953.

allow such a committee to be set up. It was instructed 'to examine the Reports and Accounts of the Nationalized Industries' and to 'obtain further information about their current policy and practices'; but it was specifically debarred from considering matters which '(a) have been decided by or clearly engage the responsibility of any Ministers; (b) concern wages and conditions of employment and other questions normally decided by collective bargaining arrangement; (c) fail to be considered by formal machinery established by the relevant Statutes; or (d) are matters of day-to-day administration.'[14]

The committee met, but then decided unanimously that it had 'insufficient scope to make inquiries or to obtain further information which would be of any real use to the House'. This rare collective firmness touched off something like a revolt in Conservative Private Members' committees. The Government yielded, indeed changed its mind remarkably, for the next year it set up a committee of thirteen Members with powers as wide as the first committee's powers had been narrow. It was given instructions to examine: 'the Reports and Accounts of the Nationalized Industries established by Statute whose controlling Boards are appointed by Ministers of the Crown and whose annual receipts are not wholly or mainly derived from moneys provided by Parliament or advanced from the Exchequer'—practically a free rein, though with heavy verbal warnings that the existence and powers of the committee would be subject to review.[15]

So they began cautiously by examining—actually visiting and hearing evidence from interested parties—the North and then the South of Scotland Hydro-Electric Boards, bodies whose affairs Parliament had never found time to debate. The committee made several useful recommendations, some of which were accepted by the Minister. It was a workmanlike

[14] See Hanson and Wiseman *Parliament at Work,* p. 309.

[15] The whole incident is instructive of what MPs can do collectively, working both the Lobbies and the Floor, when they know that they are not threatening the Government's political control, or even their reputation in the country, but are just stopping the Government from being too cautious or too really pig-headed.

sprat to begin on, and the second report made a seeming placatory noise which was in fact a promise to go out after bigger mackerel: 'Your committee have looked so far at two of the eight Nationalized Boards which lie within its terms of reference, are not yet able to say whether there are any grounds for thinking that the influence of the Treasury has in any way hampered or is hampering the initiative of the Board.'[16]

It is worth appreciating the kind of questions that such a committee can handle, and what has happened to their recommendations: Appendix D of this book summarizes the Reports and the reactions to them when the committee went on to fry the far bigger fish of the Coal Board, the Air Corporations, British Railways and the Gas Industry. There can be little doubt from this that the Committee's work had led to significant changes in administration, even in policy, and to a far greater knowledge of the subjects in question among MPs. The Committee is now a permanent feature of Parliament. Admittedly this has taken place in a unique area where the Government does *not* want to take full responsibility and where cross-bench opinion about such investigations has been remarkably unanimous. But it does show what can be done and is a precedent that will surely in time, though that time may be too long, impress even the most traditionally-minded that specialization threatens neither the Government's control of the House nor the basic character of the House itself.

The Committee, however, has proved much less enlightened and hesitant about asking for special or expert assistance. It devoted a special report to the subject.[17] They accepted as a general principle that any staff working for them should be servants of Parliament and not of the Executive, and also that any increase in staff should not lead to interference in the working of the Nationalized Industries. A proposal for an officer of the stature of the Comptroller and Auditor General was discussed but not advocated as it would seem to violate the second principle and lead to a 'Grand Inquisition' of the Nationalized Industries. Proposals for less exalted experts or specialists, something like research officers, were turned down

16 HC (304), 1956–57.
17 HC (276), 1958–59.

on grounds of practicability, the difficulty of recruiting suitable
people for a spasmodic job, and because of fears among
some Members that the experts might come out on top, not
just on tap. This argues for a certain uncertainty still in the
minds of the Committee about their task: no one who knows
what he wants is dominated by his expert assistants or
specialized advisers. They finally recommended that they
should have the services of an additional clerk and that the
senior of their two clerks should stay with the Committee for
a number of years. This has since been adopted. But the clerks,
able men all, yet are expert only in procedure; they specialize
in particular aspects of the House's work, but they are not, for
instance, trained research workers.

Select Committees

Most Select Committees are simply small committees of Members appointed by the House to examine, investigate and to
make a report on a particular subject or problem on a particular occasion. They perform a kind of task for which the House
itself is not suited: the examination of witnesses, the sifting of
evidence, the production of a reasoned and concise report and
usually proposals. Select Committees, of course, simply publish their reports and the House may or may not find time
even to debate them; and the Government may or may not
take any action in line with the proposals put forward. These
committees have no executive power. But they are usually
given power 'to send for persons, papers and records'; they
can then enforce attendance and require answers from any
British subject except a Peer or an MP. They are assisted in a
procedural manner by clerks of the House, but they rarely, if
ever, have funds or facilities to sponsor original research.

In the nineteenth century much important legislation was the
direct result of the reports of Select Committees; they were
major instruments of reform. But in this century there has
been a steady decline in the numbers of Select Committees
and, with a few notable exceptions, in their importance and
influence. More ponderous Royal Commissions and more mal-

leable Departmental Committees have largely replaced them
as investigatory bodies; and since the Tribunals of Inquiry
(Evidence) Act, 1921, the more sensitive political scandals
have been shuffled off into judicial hands. Indeed, from 1945
to the present day only a handful of such committees have
considered matters of public policy, as distinct from the domestic affairs of the House.[18] For one thing, Select Committees on matters of public policy are thoroughly distrusted and
disliked by the Whips; despite Government majorities on
them, they have an awkward tendency to develop cross-bench
sentiment, a shocking habit of regarding the Executive as
guilty until it is proved innocent.

Obviously, Select Committees have the great advantages
over Royal Commissions, of speed and tighter control, except
in the most complex and wide-flung matters. Their real enemy
is the Departmental Committee—as well as the general shortage of time to serve on them among *the minority* of Members
who do the real work of the House. They can be an effective
and indirect instrument of control over the Executive, without
in any way being able to dictate to the Executive. The House
of Commons could and should make more use of Select Committee procedure on matters of public policy on which there is
simply a lack of information. Obviously, a Select Committee
cannot usefully be employed when it is considering a matter on
which there is a predictable party split and rival line already
well known. It will be most useful on matters which can be regarded as non-partisan (or, more often, which cut party lines
badly), or on matters on which the government has no clear
policy and is willing to surrender some responsibility to the
House. Recent examples are the Select Committees to revise
the Army Act in 1952; to revise the Naval Discipline Act in
1955; to consider the Obscene Publications Bill in 1956, and,
of course, in 1958 yet another Select Committee on Procedure
—all these in addition to those so-called Select Committees,
mentioned above, which are now really standing committees.

It has been calculated[19] that from 1867 to the end of the
century there were—on a rough average—something like 33

[18] See Appendix A, pp. 225–27.
[19] *Loc. cit.*

Select Committees sitting each session, on which about 250 members a session would serve, and of which about three-fifths sat to consider matters of general public interest. But a similar count from 1945–61 shows an average of only 15 Select Committees a year, involving about 150 Members a session, and of which only six, or seven at the best, could be said to have been of public interest and not simply concerned with the domestic affairs of the House. There can be little doubt that this decline is unfortunate, a symptom not of any real threat to the Executive, but of the Ministerial willingness to be advised on policy by Whitehall a hundred times more gladly than by the House. Many Departmental Committees inevitably usurp a function which is more properly that of the Executive, or, if the Executive is in doubt, open-minded or even anxious to avoid responsibility, the House. Better by far for a Government Department to produce evidence for a Select Committee, which then appears, argument and all, in the Minutes of Evidence of that Committee, rather than for Parliamentary control of the Executive—and Parliament's ability to make up its own mind—to continue to decline.

Thus, to summarize, there can be little doubt that the present committee system of the House is a ramshackle compound of conflicting elements. In a purely procedural sense, the difficulty is that the desire of MPs to keep all legislation of any importance on the Floor of the House conflicts with their desire or need to have more time on the Floor to discuss really important general issues. And in a more political sense, the difficulty is that the Party leaders have not caught up with the fact of *how much already* the House has been forced to specialize in committee work; and neither MPs nor public are fully aware of how much more important and effective, on a vast range of matters, committees prove than the Floor. There is need quite simply to stop thinking of the 'essential' House of Commons as just the Floor, but rather as a dynamic relationship between the general-Floor and the specific Committees—committees which nevertheless have to report to the whole House and whose reports have to be acceptable to the whole House. The theory of Parliamentary procedure is still anti-specialist; the practice of the House is becoming more and more specialist;

there is need for the theory to catch up with the practice and then to go beyond the existing practice, both to extend and simplify the present un-system of committees, to systematize them and to give them greater facilities.

Party Committees

The House has something to learn from the maligned parties which compose it in the matter of intelligent organization. Public interest in the affairs of the two Parliamentary Parties is all too much absorbed in the issue of 'party discipline'. This, as such, is not directly relevant to the concern of this tract, though three points deserve to be made in passing. Firstly, both the Bevanist rebellions in the Labour Party of 1952–55 and the Suez rebels in the Conservative Party in 1956 demonstrate that 'if a minority group is sufficiently large and determined, sanctions for indiscipline become ineffective': they tend to form the focal points of systematic dissent both within the Government, and the Opposition Party.[20] Secondly, critics of party discipline often ignore the fact that the problem of the rebel and the leader is, to put it mildly, an endemic one in any kind of large organization or association. And thirdly, it is not commonly appreciated how elaborate is the organization of the two Parliamentary parties, and how influential their sub-groups can be.[21]

[20] Peter G. Richards, *Honorable Members* (London, 1959), p. 150; his whole chapter on 'Party Discipline' is admirably sensible; see also W. L. Guttsman, 'The Labour Rebels: an analysis of divisions', *Guardian*, 14 April, 1955, and S. E. Finer, H. Berrington *et al., Backbench Opinion in the House of Commons* (Pergamon Press, 1961).

[21] This subject, despite its inherent difficulty, cries out for systematic study. Dr Eric Taylor, in his *House of Commons at Work* (Pelican; London, 1958), p. 167, dismisses consideration of them because they are not really 'committees' within the meaning of Parliamentary procedure and because they have no 'powers' apart from 'persuasion'!—but who indeed ever does? But he is one better than his fellow Clerk, Kenneth Mackenzie, who, in his *The English Parliament* (Pelican; London, 1950), does not mention them at all. This is too narrow-minded: these Party groups are, after all, cov-

Much of an MP's time is spent in unofficial party groups and committees. And there is no nonsense about these groups not being specialized. Let us look first at the Conservative Party organization. All Conservative MPs who receive the Whip can meet weekly as the Conservative and Unionist Private Members Committee (the so-called '1922 Committee'), Ministers only attend (if they wish) to discuss policies for which they are responsible and they are not eligible for election to the executive committee of the group. A senior whip always attends; resolutions are not moved, nor are votes taken, but the 'sense of the meeting' usually emerges and is reported back by the Whip to the Conservative leaders. The 1922 Committee does not challenge the right of their party leader alone to determine policy, but it is a most effective sounding-board as to whether he is likely to be followed if he leads, or does not lead, in a particular direction. But subsidiary to this Grand Committee of the Conservative Party, there are other committees. Their structure is flexible, they come and go—particularly the sub-committees—as problems rise and fall; their membership is open to any Conservative MP who cares to attend. It is worth listing those in existence in the session 1962–63 together with their sub-committees:

CONSERVATIVE PARTY COMMITTEES

(House of Commons, 1962–63)

Defence
  Navy
  Army
  Air
Finance
Trade and Industry
Foreign Affairs
Commonwealth Affairs
  East and Central Africa
  West Africa

Mediterranean
West Indies
Far East
Commonwealth Development and Economic
Commonwealth Relations
Labour
Agriculture, Fisheries and Food

ered by Parliamentary privilege in their proceedings—as Garry Allighan once found to his cost in reporting them.

Horticulture	Education
Fisheries	Transport
Forestry	Shipping and Shipbuilding
Home Office Affairs	Power
Science and Technology	Aviation
Health and Social Security	Space
Housing, Local Government and Works	Arts and Amenities
New Towns	Broadcasting and Communications

These committees can raise issues before the 1922 Committee, though, as already noted, there will be no vote. Conservative Ministers on the whole appear to view these committees as useful places to explain departmental policy and to gain support for such policies, rather than annoying sources of inter-party opposition.

The Parliamentary Labour Party has a more formal organization. When the Party is in Opposition its leader is elected annually; he is then chairman of the Parliamentary Committee of the Party, a committee of 18 which is itself elected. At a full Party meeting, then, the Party leaders, unlike in the 1922 Committee, sit facing their followers and formal resolutions are considered which are often put to the vote and are then held to express the policy of the Parliamentary Party. However, it is hard in the extreme to say whether the Backbencher has more influence over his chiefs amid the informality of the open-eared Conservative oligarchy or amid the democratically voting, but hence more deliberately managed and fiercely contested, Labour meetings. The Conservative Party usually wash their linen behind closed doors, the Labour Party virtually in the streets. The public has the advantage of usually knowing what is going on in the Labour Party—the voting and thus the rancour in Party meetings is almost impossible to keep from the press; but the Conservatives have the disadvantage that in their conciliatory-informal style of politics the best way to hide differences is often an agreement to let the whole thing drop. If the Parliamentary Labour Party seems adept at rocking its own boat, the Conservatives, when faced with disagreements about where they are going, are apt to agree just to drift with the tide.

The Labour Subject Groups also have a more official flavour: when Labour is in Opposition the 'Shadow Cabinet' spokesman for a particular topic presides over the group. In the session 1962–63 they were:

LABOUR PARTY COMMITTEES

(*House of Commons, 1962–63*)

Agriculture, Fisheries and Food	Fuel and Power
Arts and Amenities	Health Services
Aviation	Home Office Affairs
Commonwealth and Colonies	Housing and Local Government
Consumer Protection	Public Information
Defence and Services	Science
Economic	Social Insurance
Education	Transport
Foreign Affairs	

Trade Union MPs also meet together regularly, as do the Cooperative MPs. In addition, the Parliamentary Labour Party has the habit of forming special working parties to consider each major item of legislation—these can be important bodies. And there are also ten Area Groups, but they are relatively unimportant, fulfilling no real function which is not better served by the Subject Groups, except perhaps the Welsh and Scottish groups. These area groups were an attempt to mitigate what was felt at one time to be the extremism of some of the specialist groups. But within a Party, if there are to be subgroups at all, the logic of specialism is hard to avoid; and, though a group may come to a meeting of the Parliamentary Labour Party with resolutions, it is for the Parliamentary Party as a whole to accept these resolutions or not—just as it is for the House of Commons itself to take action or not on the report of a Select Committee. The leadership of neither Party allows itself to be dominated by their specialized committees, but their existence does help issues to be presented in an informed and well-considered manner.

Thus there is good ground for saying that the Parties organize themselves to discuss the business of Parliament far more sensibly than does the House of Commons itself; and if the Parties are not dominated, but only advised and thus indirectly controlled by their committees, there seems little reason to think that the House could be dominated by its committees if they grew more openly and rationally specialized, indeed less reason when all the massive bonds of party unity in face of opponents are considered.

CHAPTER V

WHY THE HOUSE OF LORDS ENDURETH

Powers and Composition

It depends which concept one has in mind. The 'Second Chamber' endures because the work it does is extremely useful to the House of Commons. The 'House of Lords' endures because the Conservative Party has a political interest in retaining a connection between the Order of Peerage and the membership of the House of Lords, and because the Labour Party has no better idea of how to find enough people to do the work.

No real progress can be made in clarifying or reforming the relationship between the Executive and Parliament until Parliament is looked at as a whole, not just the House of Commons. Many of the present things the House of Commons does not find enough time for are already touched on or completed by the Lords; many things the House of Commons might like to do, but is prevented by lack of time or personnel, could be done in the Second Chamber.

It is essential to examine in some detail what the present House does do, even in the period when it was predominantly hostile to the Government of the day. For the key to any worth-while reform of the Lords is no longer the question of its powers, even of its composition, but primarily of its true function. Argument about powers, we will show, is over; and argument about composition can only be fruitful if it is first made clear what is the nature of the task for which people are needed.

The analysis which follows will seem singularly bereft of 'principle'. This is deliberate. For until one sees why the institution is so useful, one cannot begin to sort out arguments 'on principle' against the giving of special political influence to an

Order of Peerage, from those aimed at any form of Second Chamber. Many recent arguments have been misleading, being aimed at out-dated views of the actual functions and powers of the Lords, confusing their indefensible though charming peculiarities with the more general questions of the role of a Second Chamber and, in their desire to relive old battles, largely ignoring the experience of the period since 1945. Not merely in Great Britain, but in other countries with Second Chambers, the growth in complexity—more than just in volume—of legislation in this period, while often making the original functions and the justifications of them irrelevant, yet have added new reasons to ensure the survival of revising, scrutinizing, amending and advising Second Chambers in some form. Everything we said about the real meaning of 'control of the Executive' in relation to the House of Commons is relevant to the work of Parliament as a whole.[1]

The present power of the Lords to reject or delay, in whole or in part, Bills coming from the Commons, can be stated briefly. The Parliament Act of 1949 enacts that if the Lords refuse in two successive Sessions of Parliament to pass a Bill, so long as a year elapses between the date when it receives the Second Reading in the first Session and the Third Reading in the second Session, the Bill shall become law notwithstanding its rejection by the House of Lords. Previously, under the bitterly contested Parliament Act of 1911, three Sessions and two years were the suspensory period.

The Act of 1949 left unchanged the other vital provision of the Act of 1911, namely, that any Bill purely on financial matters and certified by the Speaker of the Commons as a 'Money Bill', cannot be rejected, or discussed by the Lords for longer than one month.

The Parliament Act of 1949 was passed under the provisions of the 1911 Act, being introduced in 1947 and twice rejected by the Lords following a breakdown of a Conference of Party Leaders of both Houses on the reform of the Lords. The Parliament Act of 1911 was passed under the threat of asking

[1] So this chapter and the following will be limited to those aspects of the Lords which do effect the work of Parliament as a whole. The best general treatment is P. A. Bromhead, *The House of Lords and Contemporary Politics* (Routledge, 1958).

the King to create sufficient Liberal Peers to ensure its passage. This threat of 'swamping' could still apply, although if the Act of 1949 remains on the Statute Book, it is almost impossible to conceive circumstances when it would be necessary.

So the most the Lords can do is to delay a Bill for approximately one year. And since all the Bills to raise the financial requirements of Government and to implement Budget policy are certified as 'Money Bills', the power of the Lords now to obstruct the actual processes of Government is negligible. The year's delay the Lords can inflict on ordinary legislation is only, on the average, five or six months longer than the normal passage of major legislation.

Any Bill to extend the life of Parliament is exempted from both Parliament Acts. Thus the Lords could reject outright, and not merely delay, any proposal by the Commons to extend their life beyond the statutory five years. But since they could only delay for one year any Bill to abolish themselves (or less if swamped by new creations), this only means that they would have to be abolished before Parliament could thus break the Constitution.[2]

The formal composition of the Lords at the end of the Session 1961–62 was as follows:

ROLL OF THE HOUSE OF LORDS, 1961–62

Peers of the Royal Blood	4
Archbishops and Bishops	26
Dukes	23
Marquesses	26
Earls	144
Viscounts	112
Barons	
Created under Appellate Jurisdiction Acts (i.e. Law Lords)	16

[2] This is the ultimate example of the political limitations upon any possible attempts at legal limitation of the Sovereignty of Parliament.

Created under Life Peerages Act 1958 (including 7 Baronesses)	42	
Other Barons	539	
Total Barons		597
Total Lords		932

This, of course, has little relation to the actual attendance of Peers. For most of them do not ever turn up anyway. And, under recent changes in the Standing Orders of the House, those who do not respond to the Writ of Summons are deemed to have 'leave of absence' for the Parliament or the Session—which prevents them from returning to vote without serving notice and some delay.[3] At the beginning of the above Session of 1961–62, 153 Lords had leave of absence for the Parliament—at the end 141; and at the beginning of the Session 61 had leave of absence for the Session—at the end 62. In that Session 549 Peers attended at least once (though only 120 attended more than half the possible days),[4] which leaves only 80 Peers who did not turn up but could have done so without giving notice.

The political dominance of the Chamber, of course, throughout the entire modern period has been overwhelmingly Conservative. There are no official figures of Party allegiance in the Lords, but some very rough figures calculated for the whole Peerage came out as shown on the following page.[5]

When Labour was in office it was never interested in creating more than the necessary minimum of Peers to introduce Government business (relying not on numbers but on the threat of abolition or radical reform if regular obstruction had been attempted). And the post-war Conservative administra-

[3] See pp. 135–36 below.
[4] See p. 137 below for a table of Frequency of Attendance of Peers Attending At Least Once, Session 1961–62.
[5] See Lord Chorley, Bernard Crick and Donald Chapman, MP, *Reform of the Lords*, Fabian Research Series, No. 169 (London, 1954), p. 9.

PARTY AFFILIATIONS OF PEERS

	Labour	Liberal	Con-servative	National Liberals, etc.	No Informa-tion
1939	16	56	517	31	126
1954	60	43	465	16	249

tions seem to have been restrained from any thought of diversifying the Chamber in order to forestall future criticism either by the difficulty of finding Socialists willing to become Peers, or by their own quite unprecedented hunger and thirst after patronage.[6]

This chapter will now consider the work of the Lords, but with examples drawn mainly from the period of the Labour Government. For there, if anywhere, would evidence be found for any case for abolition; and, even short of finding open obstruction of a Labour Government, any non-Conservative rightly asks for much evidence that the natural conservatism of any Second Chamber does not colour too greatly anything they touch. It is the behaviour and work of the Lords in this period which both explains why they have escaped fundamental reform and also points to the directions in which they *should* be reformed if they are to play a part in a sensible total pattern of Parliamentary control.

Some idea of maximum attendances in the period before the Life Peerages Act of 1958 can be gained if we look at the three divisions on the Parliament Bill of 1948 itself—which naturally aroused some interest:

9 June, 1948 288 (For the Bill – 81, against – 177)
23 September, 1948 256 (For the Bill – 34, against – 204)
29 November, 1949 166 (For the Bill – 37, against – 110)

[6] See Peter G. Richards, *Patronage* (Allen and Unwin, 1963), pp. 215–21.

Of these, 91 voted in all three divisions, 108 in two and 154 in one only; 354 individual Peers voted at least once.[7] For the whole period from 1919 the average number voting in divisions has been 'around eighty'.[8] The most heavily attended divisions since 1945 have been, in addition to the Parliament Bill divisions, a motion against Commercial Television in November 1953—244 Peers voting, and when the Lords twice rejected Bills passed by the Commons to abolish the death penalty, 209 voted in 1948 and 333 in 1956. Thus the number of 'casuals', who are attracted by such sensational or macabre occasions to make one of their infrequent visits on those days, is about 150, that is roughly half the numbers voting in these abnormally large divisions.

This needs to be shown in detail, for whatever is done to reform the Second Chamber, though there is little truth in the old Left Wing picture of Mongol hordes of backwoodsmen riding in to axe reform, yet the things that do attract the casuals scarcely seem to justify their continued right to attend. Perhaps it is more revealing to examine the number of times which those attending the more normal size vote of 29 November, 1949 (thus those who can reasonably be supposed to be normally active members) attended over the whole three Sessions during which the Parliament Bill was before the Lords. For these three Sessions the maximum attendance was 242.

Times Attended	242	200	160	120	80	40	0
No. of Peers	9	23	31	30	24	23	

Thus the work of the House at this time depended on about 60 Lords who attended regularly (that is more than half the sittings), with about another 50 who turned up when their special interest was being discussed, and (if our assumption is correct) with only a small tail of casuals just 'dropping in'. This number of 'fairly regulars' appears to have doubled in the recent Session 1961–62.[9] But the two figures when taken

[7] See Chorley, Crick and Chapman, *Reform of the Lords*, pp. 9–10.

[8] See Bromhead, *House of Lords*, p. 32.

[9] See p. 137 below.

together are some guide to a possible optimum size for a
British Second Chamber. Peers of first creation seem to have
composed about half those attending.[10] This became an obvious pointer to the need for Life Peers.

Functions and Work

The great statement of the general functions of the House of
Lords, indeed in terms relevant to any possible British Second
Chamber, was made by Lord Bryce in 1918:[11]

(i) 'The examination and revision of Bills brought from the
House of Commons, a function which has become more
needed since, on many occasions, during the last thirty
years, the House of Commons has been obliged to act under
special rules limiting debate.

(ii) The initiation of Bills dealing with subjects of comparatively non-controversial character, which may have an
easier passage through the House of Commons, if they have
been fully discussed and put into a well-considered shape before being submitted to it.

(iii) The interposition of so much delay (and no more) in
the passing of a Bill into law as may enable the opinion of the
nation to be adequately expressed upon it. This would be
specially needed as regards Bills which affect the fundamentals
of the Constitution or introduce new principles of legislation,
or which raise issues whereon the opinion of the country may
appear to be almost equally divided.

(iv) Full and free discussion of the large and important
questions, such as those of foreign policy, at moments when
the House of Commons may happen to be so much occupied
that it cannot find sufficient time for them. Such discussion
may often be all the more useful if conducted in an Assembly
whose debates and divisions do not involve the fate of the
Executive Government.'

[10] Chorley, Crick and Chapman, *Reform of the Lords,* p. 10.
[11] *Conference on the Reform of the Second Chamber: Letter
from Viscount Bryce to the Prime Minister,* Cmnd 9038 of 1918.

The force of the first two points is now much stronger than when Bryce wrote, with the increase in the amount of Government business and of delegated legislation. The rules limiting debate in the House of Commons have been vastly increased since 1918 by the 'guillotine' procedure. By resolution of the House, periods of time can be fixed for each stage of a Bill, at the end of which time a vote is taken even if clauses are undiscussed or the general discussion is still taking place. In 1945 this procedure was extended to the vital Standing Committees with the result that in 1947 much of the Transport and the Town and Country Planning Bills were not considered at all, even in Committee. This resulted in the Government as well as the Opposition tabling very many amendments in the Lords.

Bryce's third point may seem more unreal now that the Parliament Act of 1949 has been passed limiting the power of delay to less than one year. The presumption is now, at least amongst Labour and Liberal consitutional writers, that the Lords or indeed any Second Chamber are not a proper body to set themselves up as interpreters of the Nation's will over the Commons. The power of amendment and of slight delay is to give the Commons a chance to reconsider the implication and drafting of a Bill, not its fundamental object: to influence, but not to determine, the course of legislation; and to be a Chamber concerned with administrative implication and method rather than the making of political decisions.

By far the most important work of the Lords is the examination and revision of Government Bills coming from the Commons. For Private Bills or Consolidation Bills there is a slightly different procedure, but for normal measures, the House sits as a whole in Committee and Bills are carefully examined clause by clause. This Committee stage follows the Second Reading which is on the general issues of a Bill, and there is a still further opportunity to move amendments on the Report Stage, before the Third Reading.

The Committee stage in the Lords is far from a mere formality. For any moderately important measure there will be many Government amendments moved to meet points agreed to during the Commons debate, or amendments that had not time to be introduced there, and to clear up flaws in drafting consequent upon other amendments, or noticed during the Bill's progress. The pressure at which the Parliamentary Counsel's Office—those responsible for the drafting of Bills—has to work makes drafting amendments more and more prevalent as flaws or ambiguities are noticed during a Bill's progress through Parliament; most of these are dealt with in the Lords. As an illustration, the Companies Bill of 1946–47 may be mentioned. This purely technical measure was actually introduced in the Lords, and yet over 400 amendments were dealt with at the committee stage, much the largest part of which were purely drafting amendments.

The Transport Act of 1947 is a good example of the work of the Lords and a case where one might expect abuse of their powers. This large and complex Bill, however justified in outline and intent, was admittedly badly drafted, due to the extreme pressure of Parliamentary business with the monster Town and Country Planning Bill following close behind it. The Bill left the Commons with much of it undiscussed even in Committee: 31 Clauses and 5 schedules received no consideration at all, with upwards of 200 Government amendments being made with no time for discussion allowed. The Bill was before the Lords nine whole days in Committee and two on the Report Stage; perhaps never before had such a quantity of work fallen on the House, not merely in the Opposition's attempts to decentralize the administration envisaged in the Bill and to limit the extent of Road Haulage nationalization, but also in the multitude of Government amendments. *The Times*, devoting four leading articles to this work, commented:

> Seldom if ever have the surviving functions of the Upper House been more important. The most casual glance at the Bill as it leaves the Commons suggests that if a revising Chamber did not exist it would have to be invented. The Bill will no doubt pass into law. There is no question of the Lords frustrating the will of the Commons. But it is vitally important that, before it is passed, those sections and clauses which have so far been discussed inadequately or not at all should be subjected to the impartial, practical

and expert examination of which the Upper House is capable.[12]

There was a real endeavour by the Conservative Opposition, as well as by the Government Peers, to make constructive amendments. The Opposition sharply criticized the detail but admitted that the mandate to nationalize Transport in some form was definite. Much give and take took place on valuable details: in particular a series of amendments by Lord Beveridge was accepted. When the Bill was returned to the Commons, 242 amendments had been made, 200 of which were purely drafting or agreed amendments, mostly Government sponsored, but of which 42, involving 10 major issues, had in 10 divisions been passed and won against the Government. The Commons rejected these 42 disputed amendments en bloc, and the Lords protested but accepted the Commons' rejection. Thus the ultimate power of the Commons and the Lords' compliance to it is clearly shown even in such matters. Yet the importance of the give and take in Committee on the drafting and minor points of the Bill should not be underestimated. Thus for many reasons, not least of Parliamentary time, the passage of the Bill in an efficient form would have been impossible but for the existence of a revising body.[13]

[12] *The Times,* 6 May, 1947.
[13] It is worth adding a word on the less complicated de-nationalization of Road Haulage (a section of the 1947 Act) in the 1952–53 Session. In this case there were 71 Lords amendments. On the Third Reading in the Lords, Lord Leathers (Secretary of State for the Co-ordination of Transport, Fuel and Power) said: 'I am told that nearly a hundred amendments out of a total of 211 on the Order Paper will have been incorporated in the Bill during its passage through your Lordships' House and, of these, over thirty must rank as major or important items.'
Mr Crookshank, Lord Privy Seal, said on 27 April, 1953, in the Commons debate on the Guillotine Motion: 'Of these 71 Lords amendments 24 are consequential or drafting: of the rest seven were put forward as a result of representations by the British Transport Commission and some of them are known to have Opposition support, at any rate, in principle; five were put forward to meet Opposition criticism; three more went some way to meet the Opposition point of view; and others are either non-controversial or merely clarify the existing provisions of the Bill.'

Tables (i) and (ii) in Appendix E[14] show the total list of
Government Bills, initiated in either House, before the Lords
in the Sessions 1948–49 and 1961–62. An idea of the extent
of the work done can be gained by seeing the number of
amendments accepted, rejected or withdrawn in the Lords.
Even where no emendation has taken place, the process of
close scrutiny still continued. Where an amendment is rejected,
a division has occurred: the total number of divisions is set out
and analysed in Table (iii) of Appendix E. The vast number
of withdrawn amendments are those moved by the Opposition in the hope that the Government will accept them. Most
of the amendments try to be helpful and consistent with the
general aim of the Bill under discussion, and are withdrawn
if not accepted, a division very rarely being pressed. The
Government Frontbench usually try to meet good criticism of
a Bill's structure, and often such points will be incorporated
into the Government's amendments in the Commons or in the
Report Stage in the Lords. Obviously if the Opposition pressed
every one of their amendments to a division Parliamentary
business would be much obstructed; but in fact this is not done,
or so rarely that it is worth setting out and considering all the
divisions of the same two Sessions in detail.[15]

There are a number of reasons why the work on the committee stage of legislation is often better done in the Lords
than in the Commons. There is less scoring of purely party
points, hence more talking to the text of the Bill and less to
the public. There is the strong cross-bench element in the
Lords. Peers from the armed services, Law Lords, and former
diplomats and colonial civil servants tend to sit on the cross-
benches, and valuable suggestions often come from them in
respect of non-controversial, or partly controversial measures.
For example, a Bill to destroy the old legal doctrine of the restraint on anticipation which was introduced under the Labour
Government, was strongly opposed from the Opposition Frontbench, particularly by Viscount Simon, an ex-Lord Chancellor. The intervention of Lord Simonds, who has since become
Lord Chancellor in the Conservative Government, in support

[14] See below, pp. 255–66.
[15] See below, pp. 267–74.

of the measure was decisive in securing its successful passage. Lord Simonds who had been leader of the Chancery bar, spoke on such matters as restraint on anticipation with greater knowledge than did Viscount Simon, a common lawyer. The value of the cross-bench element is not, of course, restricted to the Committee Stage of Bills.

The more informal atmosphere which exists in the Lords made it possible during the 1945–50 Parliament to hold a number of private all-party conferences of leading Peers. These were to thrash out some agreement on a number of substantial measures which, while predominantly of a non-partisan character, yet involved issues which many Opposition Peers wished to resist. The differences were then narrowed to a matter of tabling one or two amendments and reaching a compromise over them.

The most notable example of this was the Companies Act, 1947, the whole structure of which was radically changed in respect of its accountancy provisions as a result of a series of such informal conferences, attended by two Peers representing each Party together with their technical advisers. This was the most successful example of a new technique which was afterwards employed on a number of occasions, and which might with advantage be extended and developed.

As has already been seen, the majority of this routine work is done by a hard core of about 60–80 members, with about another 50 who attend when their speciality is being discussed. Agricultural Bills are a good example; and Company Law or Patents legislation will give expert technical debates of a high standard. General legal matters and the legal minutiae of drafting any legislation is a continual watching brief for the Law Lords and several other legal figures who sit as Lords in their own right.

Consolidation Bills—these are Bills bringing into one Statute a branch of law previously scattered throughout many old measures and judicial rulings—whether coming from the Commons, or initiated in the Lords, are examined not by the whole House in Committee but by the small and hard working 'Joint Standing Committee on Consolidated Bills' whose membership is drawn from both Houses. Their conclusions are reported to the Lords and rarely challenged or discussed. These welcome measures for making the law more compact and comprehensible have increased markedly in volume over the last ten years. The brunt of the similar work of repealing obsolete Acts of Parliament and tidying up the body of Statute Law has fallen upon the House of Lords, in particular on the Lord Chancellor.

Table (ii) in Appendix E[16] shows Bills which were initiated in the Lords in the Sessions 1948–49 and 1961–62. The volume of this business varies, but in any Parliament it is a great time-saver for the Commons. Such work is fairly typical of the usually dull, almost always unsensational routine work, in some sense scarcely political at all, which is performed by the Lords and is of the very stuff of central government.

As has been seen, many Consolidation Bills start life in the Lords; so do about half the Private Bills, which are mostly sponsored by Local Government Authorities or other Public Bodies to give them powers for a specific purpose not in their own legal competence to perform. These Bills pass through an elaborate procedure which gives plenty of opportunity for local and other interested parties to state their case before a Select Committee of the House; such a committee consists of members—the quorum is four—who meet to consider each clause of the Bills and to hear and question representatives, usually legal counsel, of the sponsors and other interests concerned. This is probably the most dull and thankless of Parliamentary work, albeit very necessary—to enable the Local Authority to close the river so as to build the bridge; the racecourse to enclose public land for a car-park; the university to alter its chartered Constitution to raise some more money from new sources.

While Bills originating from a Private member of the House are not unknown, they are certainly even more rare than in the Commons. The mass of the work is Government-sponsored legislation. This is often routine and non-contentious in a Party sense, although often it includes such important measures as a Coast Protection Bill, or a Justices of the Peace

[16] See pp. 259–66 below.

Bill, which have many problems and need much detailed discussion for which adequate time could not be found in the House of Commons. On such measures the Lords are usually at their best; the legislation introduced by their own Chamber shows them exhibiting some of the outlook proper to the composition of the Second Chamber that Bryce described as:

A certain proportion of persons who are not extreme partisans, but of a cast of mind which enables them to judge political questions with calmness and comparative freedom from prejudice or bias. No assembly can be expected to escape party spirit, but the excess of that spirit can usually be modified by the presence of a good many who do not yield to it.

The enormous volume of work summarized in Appendix E on 'The Work of the Lords' is not exciting even to glance at. But such is the typical work of the Second Chamber, something obviously necessary to the functioning of Parliament at the moment in any reasonable manner at all. Someone must do this work whatever are the objections to the present constitution of the Lords. The work they do is, on the whole, well done. The rareness of divisions against the Government marks the responsibility of the Lords, or, more certainly, their fairly clear knowledge of what will be politically tolerated if they are not to endanger the connection between the Peerage and the Second Chamber.

A division against the Government is the process whereby the majority in the Lords force the Government to reconsider parts of a Bill. Almost always, if the Government sticks to its guns, the Lords will withdraw their objections; only in the Parliament Bill and the Steel Bill during Mr Attlee's Administration was opposition in the Lords pressed to the limit, and then on the two occasions when Bills from the Commons would have abolished Capital Punishment.

If Bills are to be reconsidered by the Commons at all, a Second Chamber must have some powers of reference back— which inevitably involves some slight delay. But it might be that the present Chamber, by its rather grotesque composition, misuses this power in an obstructive manner. To assess properly the balance of obstruction to genuine revisatory work, each division of the two Sessions must be looked at in detail. Table (iii) in Appendix E lists and describes the occasion of each division in the Sessions 1948–49 and 1961–62. Given the nature and circumstances of the Bills involved, it does not in general appear that this power is abused (or more than very occasionally indeed).

These Tables of Divisions include some divisions on resolutions, not on items of legislation at all. These, even if carried against the Government, have no legal force and may not even engage the attention of the Commons; but they do occasionally mark the use of the Lords as a vehicle for catching the public ear on policy matters, going above the heads, as it were, of the Government and the House of Commons—particularly a Labour Government. But the kind of debate and vote on, for instance, the ill-fated Groundnuts Scheme might seem a small price to pay for the dull, good work their Lordships do; or it might seem a quite unnecessary nuisance that they should actually record votes when they are so completely unrepresentative.

General discussions do play an important part in the life of the Lords—as in Bryce's fourth point. (The topics for debate in the same two Sessions are set out in Table (iv) of Appendix E.) The usual procedure is for the Government to grant an afternoon, by arrangement, and then for an Opposition Lord to 'move for papers' on a subject and then, after a full and critical discussion, to withdraw his motion. This is simply a procedural device to get a debate and only rarely is the motion pressed to a division. Many matters of public importance are debated with much specialized knowledge and in a very flexible manner. (It may be hard to find similar time in the Commons apart from some of the debates on going into Committee of Supply, and occasional Friday motions: the chance of raising a topic on 'the motion for the adjournment' is small and, in any event, for normally only half an hour). Good examples from the 1948–49 Session are the debates on Afforestation, with many speeches from active members of Forestry Commissions or landlords practising afforestation; Human Slaughter of Cattle, a debate informed by much lobbying by the

RSPCA and farmers' interests; Artificial Insemination and Legitimacy, a technical and legal discussion on a very high level concerning the anomalies in the laws regarding adultery, legitimacy and divorce that have arisen from Court decisions in cases involving artificial insemination; Teachers for Technical Colleges, etc. The experts may not be more expert than in the Commons, but they are listened to with greater attention and, on the whole, the non-experts hold their peace in technical legislation. Both here and in the revision of legislation, the Lords are fortunate in having the 'cross-bench' members who can afford to take a line more independent of their Party's policy than can a member of the Commons.

In the relatively technical debates, the level is often admirable, but there is perhaps a tendency to overrate the exceptional discussions. There are certainly some obversely exceptional discussions. Despite (or because of) the stiffening of former diplomats, soldiers and colonial civil servants, debates on Defence, Foreign Affairs and Colonial matters tend to be rather depressing affairs, usually containing little that has not been said in the correspondence columns of *The Times,* the *Telegraph* or even the *Guardian.* These occasions put one in mind of what Bagehot meant when he said that the cure for admiring the House of Lords was to go and look at it, or of the Noble Lord who said that he would, indeed 'speak up', if he thought that anyone was really listening. The House shines in dealing with matters that the Commons can give little time to; it is mostly dull and often downright embarrassing, though probably fairly harmless, on the 'great issues' which constantly engage the Commons.

Two more functions complete the work of the Lords. As well as the examination of Private Bills—sharing about half the total with the Commons—much work is done on Provisional Order Bills and in the Special Orders Standing Committee. Powers are given under much delegated legislation for a Minister, after consultation with affected interests, to put directly before Parliament for approval certain Bills of a scope specified in the enabling Act, without their having to pass through the normal full Committee stages of the Commons and Lords. In fact these measures are rarely considered in detail by the

Commons and the examination falls to a sub-committee of the Lords. On Scottish Provisional Order Bills, when Parliamentary panels actually meet in Edinburgh or Glasgow, it is usually much easier for Peers than for MPs to attend.

Under many Acts a Minister is empowered to make orders and regulations that will become law by mere affirmative vote of Parliament or after having remained unchallenged before the House for a certain period of time. These regulations are similarly examined in detail and reported on by a Standing Committee called the Special Orders Committee. The congestion and pressure of work in the Commons would mean that few of these would be examined or revised but for the Lords.

Lastly, there is the function of the House as a Supreme Court of Appeal. By historical tradition or accident the House of Lords is a Court of Appeal (technically of 'Record') in Civil matters from the (English) Court of Appeal, by leave of that Court or of the House; in a Criminal matter from the (English) Court of Criminal Appeal if it is certified by the Attorney-General as of exceptional public importance; from the corresponding Northern Irish Courts in similar circumstances; and in Civil cases from the (Scottish) Court of Session.

Strictly the appeals go to the 'Supreme Court of Parliament' and the House of Lords in this judicial capacity is the same as for normal functions, although at least three Lords of Appeal must be present. But in fact, long ago, non-Laws Lord ceased to take part, and the Judicial business continues as a committee function, not merely during the recess, but even after a dissolution. The identity is purely theoretical, although when in 1938 it was suggested to move the Judicial business to another building, the theoretical or the traditional objections were thought too strong. This has little relevance to the general work of Parliament, except that it brings in the Law Lords who will contribute to the other work of the House. But it could, as we will argue, form the basis, in a reconstituted Second Chamber, of a much-needed Court of Administrative Appeals, or at least of some final advisory body to the Minister, to cover the whole field of administrative tribunals.

Four points emerge from this analysis of the routine work of the Lords: (i) They do much work essential to the smooth working of the House of Commons; (ii) They do very little, if anything, in fact, as distinct from form, which conflicts with the legal and political powers of the Commons; (iii) They could do much more useful work, except that—(iv) There is no clear and sensible division of work and functions between the two Houses; (v) That the real issues for reform lie in the type of work it does or could do, and that should determine composition and be the more relevant question than the (now largely settled) old question of powers. These last two propositions we will now explore further.

CHAPTER VI

NIBBLING AT THE ERMINE

The Parliament Act of 1949

The preamble to the Parliament Act of 1911 began: 'Whereas it is intended to substitute for the House of Lords as at present constituted a second chamber constituted on a popular instead of an hereditary basis, but such a substitution cannot immediately be brought into operation. . . .' None of the subsequent reforms has followed in this direction, nor are any likely to; but they have all exhibited the same quality of patchwork as the 1911 Act: immediate political improvisations to meet immediate circumstances with little attempt to relate the work of the two Houses to each other, or to consider sensibly the real work of the Second Chamber at all.

It is worth examining the circumstances which gave rise to the three subsequent reforms: the Parliament Act of 1949, the Life Peerages Act of 1958 and the Peerage Act of 1963. This will show the measure of agreement there is, although also the pleasure there has been in chasing false hares. But certainly the constitution of the House of Lords, all this will show, is far more likely than that of the Commons to be the subject of deliberate and fundamental reform in the near future. Our concluding chapter will want to show that of the many things Parliament does not do properly, or does not do at all, there are at least some which could be done by a reconstituted Second Chamber alone.

Our fathers were better practised at the debate about Reform of the Lords than we. From 1904–14 and in the first few years after the First World War, there did seem an urgency about the debate since lacking: proposals and schemes were freely canvassed. The Parliament Act of 1911 was intended by the Liberals to be but a prelude to more far-reaching reforms. Many on the Conservative side felt that it should be repealed and the Lords strengthened against further tampering with their powers. But, on the return of a Conservative Government, no serious intention to repeal the Act or 're-form' the Lords was apparent. In part, it was the extreme political difficulty of such a problem while the question of powers was felt to be the main issue; and, in part, the ending of the power utterly to reject Bills had in fact increased their prestige by spiking the guns of much of the opposition.

After 1918 there was no serious talk of abolition except from the rising Labour movement which, by the time it came firmly to power in 1945, was faced with a situation in which the volume of government work was so great that a Second Chamber could hardly be dispensed with. It seemed that the Government, in spite of the admittedly indefensible hereditary composition of the Lords, preferred their certain assistance, in the kind of work examined in the previous chapter, to the uncertainty of reform. The risks of reform were that almost any scheme would strengthen, not weaken, the popular prestige of the Chamber and thus embolden it to use its powers of delay more frequently than it dared with such a doubtful basis of composition. Also the peculiar difficulties of framing and drafting reforms were such that, with the pressure of more urgent business, time could scarcely be spared. In addition it must be recognized that a precise scheme of reform has never come from the Left: only general arguments mostly tending to abolition, ignoring the necessities of government, and confusing the House of Lords with other possible types of Second Chamber. There were several Conservative schemes of reform but they all, in effect, guaranteed a more powerful House, a permanent Conservative majority. 'Let sleeping dogs lie' was a sensible and practical policy for Labour during the great legislative drive of 1945–48. The dogs behaved and did good work; but they were plainly very much on sufferance; and the Tory Lords, passing and assisting measure after measure that they deplored, did so only to keep their power of three sessions' delay intact in case the time came when they should feel the need to use it. There was a feeling that sooner or later a trial of strength would come. Once again a Government chose to deal with the immediate problem of power rather than, as well, with the perennial problem of composition.

The Government chose that the trial of strength should come on the abstract power of the Lords rather than wait for an actual rejection of an important Government measure. The Parliament Bill of 1947 was introduced primarily to protect any legislation they might initiate during the last two years of the Parliament from being thrown out by the Lords under the 1911 Act's power of delay (thus giving the Conservative Party, through the Lords, the power either to cripple the last two sessions' work of a Labour Government's term of office or to force a General Election during those sessions). It limited the powers of delay to two sessions and one year. Actually, since 1911, the Lords had only twice used their power of delay; Conservative Governments were apparently deemed seldom, if ever, to get out of touch with the will of the people in ways that, according to the argument of the Conservative Lords, made a substantial delaying power necessary. The two Acts they did oppose, the Home Rule Act 1914 and the Welsh Church Disestablishment Act, were hardly fortunate choices to strengthen their case; the quicker passage of the one might have saved Civil War in Ireland, and the Anglican Church in Wales has been strengthened rather than destroyed by the other.

The Lords rejected the Bill of 1947 in three sessions and it was finally made law in 1949 under the Act of 1911 in the teeth of their opposition. When the Bill appeared for the first time before the Lords, Lord Salisbury moved the following Opposition amendment to reject the Bill:

'This House, while re-emphasizing its oft expressed readiness to consider proposals for modifying the basis of its membership which may conduce to the more effective performance of its Constitutional duties, declines to give a Second Reading to a Bill which would affect no change in this respect, for which the nation has expressed no desire; which would go far to expose the country to the dangers of a system of single chamber Government, and which can only serve to distract the attention of the country from the economic crisis and from the united effort towards recovery which is so vital at this time.'

Ignoring the last hardy annual there were three points of substance:

(i) That the reform of powers and composition cannot or should not be dealt with separately.
(ii) The Doctrine of the Mandate.
(iii) That single Chamber Government is in fact dangerous.

The first point is obviously the strongest; according to the sort of powers and functions a Second Chamber is supposed to exercise, so will the best composition vary. The Government, it was argued should have reformed thoroughly or not at all; they only introduced a disproportion between the balance of powers, composition and functions. Yet what are the implications of this argument?

That the Second Chamber should be constituted more sensibly than on a hereditary basis? Yes. If there was to be reform, there was no disagreement between the Parties on this point. But why could not one come before the other? Clearly the existing composition of the Lords had not hindered it from doing good work, and the Bill of 1947 was more a precaution than a remedy for any crisis already arisen. The fact is that not merely did the Lords dislike losing their substantial power of delay which they believed could be used in extremity, but they had always hoped for reform as a vehicle of actually strengthening the prestige and thus the effective political powers of the Chamber. Many had said that they saw no point in voting for reform of composition and destroying a traditional part of the Constitution if 'worth-while' powers were not to be given in return. Quite what these powers would be was vague. Possibly merely the strengthening of their ability to use their then existing powers of delay by the prestige of a more representative yet still Conservative dominated Chamber, and probably some 'entrenching' of their powers against the Commons.[1]

[1] This sort of Conservative case was well put in Martin Lindsay, MP, *Shall We Reform the Lords?* (Falcon Press, 1948).

On the second point the Conservative Peers argued that it was the function of the Lords, by delaying legislation for which a Government had no mandate, to allow the will of the people to be expressed; this the Parliament Bill prevented. The claim that this process—whatever it is—takes two years rather than one is hard to maintain, and was not, we will see, pursued in the 1948 conference. The increased range of the press, and the coming of the BBC, with the rise in educational standards, would seem to make the introduction of a shorter period than the two years deemed necessary in 1911, certainly no blow at the idea of reference back to public opinion. For instance, there was certainly little doubt that, on the death penalty controversy, a majority of the people were believed to be for retention (although there was much doubt as to whether this was not the kind of decision that the representatives of the majority do not make better than that majority itself). The majority of the Conservative benches in that debate hardly furnished inspiring examples of the ideal picture they had of themselves. But that is a too *ad hominem* remark; the issue is more fundamental. The Lord Privy Seal, Lord Addison, put the point well when replying to Lord Salisbury's 'preserve the mandate' arguments, he said:

'To claim to decide whether a subject is or is not in accordance with the mandate of the people contains the implication that, if this House is of the opinion that it is not in the mandate, this House is at liberty to reject [a Bill]; that is the deliberate and obvious implication. We challenge that implication from the very start. We claim that it is for the elected representatives of the people to decide whether an issue is or is not to be the subject of Parliamentary activity.'

The stark unsuitability of the House of Lords, or of any Second Chamber, to set itself up as a superior judge of what is public opinion, or as to what notice the public took of a particular vagary in an election programme, should at least be clear. This is not the place to discuss the whole 'doctrine of the Mandate', but this use of it seems more to discredit than exemplify the doctrine. Lord Salisbury talked of 'measures for which the government have no mandate' and claimed that substantial powers of delay are necessary for these. He would have entered the ranks of the Saints and Sages if he could have justified the broken pledges of the 1951 Election or have stated in precise terms what by their Election manifestoes the Conservative Party were mandated and pledged to perform. The doctrine was apparently only understood properly by Conservative Peers. The obvious and irreducible sense in which this doctrine can be understood is that, if a Government introduces legislation which it believes to be flagrantly against the wishes of a majority of the electorate, then it can expect to risk defeat at the next election. A Government is clearly a better judge of its own interests in this respect than the Lords.

The claim of the Lords—which they actually made in so many words in these debates—to be superior interpreters of 'the will of the people' appeared to involve them in arguing for referenda (an ultra-democratic idea which they normally, sensibly and properly, loathed). This contradiction kept spontaneously recreating itself during the debates. For speech after speech, with singular lack of premeditation, found itself judiciously claiming that the reason for the long period of delay was simply to allow 'the will of the country' to be ascertained. But then how? So it was quickly added that referenda and Gallup Polls did not discover what had by then become the *real will,* the 'permanent, real and not the temporary, vacillating will of the people'. The incident was fascinating, if only to see how much of the worst nonsense in Rousseau and Hegel could suddenly be recreated by empirically-minded English gentlemen in the common mental difficulty of wanting incompatible things. For it boiled down to this: the real will of the people was not something measureable, not something even to be explained, but something to be *understood* only by the remote and dispassionate House of Lords. But these rare explicit flights of metaphysics among the would-be purely practical are, perhaps, ultimately less interesting than the plain politics of the matter. The Lords did not dare suggest that their opposition should result in the normal way of sounding public opinion on great issues: a General Election. Clement Attlee put the matter clear and dry in the debates in the Commons: 'the House of Lords operates as an interpreter of the people's mind only when a Liberal or a Labour Government is in office. I challenge honourable members opposite to find any instance to the contrary in this long dispute'.

Lord Salisbury's third point, the fear of Single Chamber Government, was again part misunderstanding and part genuine difference of principle. It was a misunderstanding in the sense that in all modern unitary States the Second Chamber is never intended to share primary political power with the directly elected body. Only in Federal States, where there are deliberately both member-State and national interests to be represented, does the Second Chamber share the primary power. The difference of principle is that the Conservative Party often appears explicitly to believe that the Conservative approach to politics should be entrenched in the permanent Constitution by means of the House of Lords: the moderating and restraining force, the symbol of continuity and tradition, the representative of the great permanent interest of Property. One should not deny the strength of this argument, but it is one that if widely understood would certainly be rejected. If by 'Single Chamber Government' is meant literally a move towards the abolition of the 'Second Chamber,' then certainly the Labour Government, in moving the Parliament Bill, was not in favour of this; but if it is meant that the popularly elected Chamber shall have complete control over the political power of Central Government—only using the services and advice of, but not obeying, a Second Chamber in any and all circumstances—then, in this sense, the Labour Government was obviously for Single Chamber Government.

The debates were initially of a fairly high standard, but became painfully repetitious, especially the third time round. There was, in fact, no great popular feeling on the matter, and it was markedly obvious that Conservative MPs made little attempt to use it as a platform issue: as practical politicians they were much cooler about 'this fundamental attack on our liberties' than were their Lordships.

In spite of the Government's conviction that the question of powers was not merely fundamental, but also the first thing to be settled, genuine attempts were made to reach agreement over a much wider field by the device of a Conference of Party leaders, for which the Lords, in February 1948, adjourned their debate on the Bill. The agreed motion, setting out the terms of this informal Conference, stated that the discussion should cover both composition and the powers to be vested in any Chamber reformed in composition:

> 'These two subjects though capable of separate consid-erations were to be regarded as interdependent, and it was recognized that failure to agree either on Composition or on Powers might result in general agreement on the future of the House of Lords not being reached.'

This prophecy at least was fulfilled; the Conference broke down. In the words of the Official Statement:

> 'The representatives of all three Parties were united in their desire to see the House of Lords continue to play its proper part in the Legislature; and in particular to exercise the valuable function of revising Bills sent up by the Com-mons, and initiating discussion on public affairs. It was regarded as essential moreover, that there should be avail-able to the country a legislative body composed of men and women of mature judgement and experience gained in many spheres of public life. But the Government Repre-sentatives and the Representatives of the Official Opposition considered that the difference between them on the subject of powers was fundamental and not related only to the length of the "period of delay".'[2]

The nominal breakdown was only over a three-month dif-ference between compromise suggestions on the period of de-lay. The real reason was over devices by which the Conser-vatives sought for a strong House of Lords. Yet in spite of this fundamental difference, the area of possible agreement was shown to be surprisingly large and radical. If the Parliament Act of 1949 is regarded as the final word on powers, then the chances of obtaining agreement on the other aspects of reform are quite high.

It is worth quoting in full the section of the 'Agreed State-

[2] *Parliament Bill, 1947: Agreed Statement on Conclusion of Con-ference of Party Leaders* (Cmnd 7380), 1948.

ment' that shows, in spite of the vague and cautious wording, that an advance was made:

'Proposals relating to the reform of the Composition of the House of Lords were discussed first. If it had been possible to achieve general agreement over the whole field of Powers and Composition, the Party representatives would have been prepared to give the following proposals further consideration, so as to see whether the necessary details could be worked out and, if so, to submit them, as part of such an agreement, to their respective Parties:

(1) The Second Chamber should be complementary to and not a rival to the Lower House and, with this end in view, the reform of the House of Lords should be based on a modification of its existing constitution as opposed to the construction of a Second Chamber of a completely new type based on some system of election.

(2) The revised constitution of the House of Lords should be such as to secure as far as practicable that a permanent majority is not assured for any one political Party.

(3) The present right to attend and vote based solely on heredity should not by itself constitute a qualification for admission to a reformed Second Chamber.

(4) Members of the Second Chamber should be styled 'Lords of Parliament' and would be appointed on grounds of personal distinction or public service. They might be drawn either from Hereditary Peers, or from commoners who would be created Life Peers.

(5) Women should be capable of being appointed Lords of Parliament in like manner as men.

(6) Provision should be made for inclusion in the Second Chamber of certain descendants of the Sovereign, certain Lords Spiritual and the Law Lords.

(7) In order that people without private means should not be excluded, some remuneration would be payable to members of the Second Chamber.

(8) Peers who were not Lords of Parliament should be entitled to stand for election to the House of Commons, and also to vote at elections in the same manner as other citizens.

(9) Some provision should be made for the disqualification of a member of the Second Chamber who neglects, or becomes no longer fitted to perform his duties as such.'

Granted that the agreement might seem more formal than real when the actual details had to be worked out, yet the proposals are worth bearing in mind for the rest of this discussion. They set, so to speak, the official bounds of possibility.

The Life Peerages Act of 1958

Paragraph four of the *Agreed Statement* was implemented by the Conservatives, without further consultations, when the Royal assent was given to the Life Peerages Bill on 30 April, 1958. The Act stated that 'Her Majesty should have power by letters patent to confer on any person a peerage for life, and that a person receiving a life peerage should be entitled to receive writs of summons to attend the House of Lords and sit and vote therein accordingly'. The floodgates, as some feared, were then opened, but in a special Honour's List that July only a fairly modest trickle of fourteen names was announced—including, however, three women. (The number has now risen to forty-five such creations.) Both Government and Opposition made clear that this was not to be an Honours List in the usual sense; those on it had been appointed to help regularly with the routine work of the Second Chamber, and they had all expressed their willingness to work.

Thus 102 years from that afternoon when Sir James Parke's gout prevented him from immediately taking his seat as Lord Wensleydale, and thus gave their Lordships time to have second and decisive thoughts about accepting his title as one for his own life only, the hereditary principle in the composition of the House of Lords has at last been diluted. If, as will be suggested, the situation is still very fluid and there is no real prospect that the Life Peerages Act will alone be a permanent solution to the problem of reform, yet the way was at least clear for many useful members to join the Upper House without disenfranchising and embarrassing their heirs for ever (just as now the way is clear for them to leave it). Yet the fourteen appointments certainly did not mean that the intentions of the Preamble to the Parliament Act of 1911 were on the close verge of realization.

Strictly speaking, Life Peers have sat in the House of Lords ever since the Appellate Jurisdiction Act of 1876 which allowed at first two, and now nine, judges to sit in the House as barons for life, with the title of Lords of Appeal in Ordinary and with, furthermore, substantial salaries. The Act of 1876 was made necessary by the reluctance of the House of Lords to surrender its peculiar heritage as the highest court of appeal. The leading judges could, of course, have been given ordinary peerages; but, it is interesting to remember, the prejudice of the Order of Peerage against a non-hereditary element was less, even then, than their prejudice, and that of the Queen too, against creating men who might not be wealthy enough to endow their heirs with sufficient means to maintain the 'estate' suitable to a peer. The House of Lords was thus aware of the dilemma, even before the rise of the Labour party, that to create many new peers would devalue the Order of Peerage, but that failure to create at least a fair number of new peers might demonstrate to the country the incompetence of the Upper House to conduct its own affairs. In other words, two quite distinct issues confront all discussions of the House of Lords: that of making Parliament as a whole more efficient, and that of maintaining some connection between the order of hereditary peerage and the composition of a Second Chamber. The Life Peerages Bill was clearly intended to effect the best of all possible unions between these two issues: it strengthens the efficiency of the House of Lords and, at the same time, checks the dilution of the Order of Peerage. But even though the Parliamentary Labour party advanced no alternative object of affection (despite the positive prodigality of the Fabian Society), yet it is doubtful that it will ever recognize the legitimacy of such a marriage of convenience as a permanent feature of the Constitution. And, as Conservative peerage sadly knows, a stable and fruitful settlement demands the positive agreement of both great parties.

If we turn back to consider the vital second and third articles of the *Agreed Statement,* we find, of course, a most politic ambiguity. The opportunities for genuine and invented difference in trying to apply these articles are—and were—obviously great. But two implicit points of fundamental importance do emerge: firstly, that almost all sections of the Labour party are convinced that the work done in the House of Lords of revision and even initiation is indispensable (and, being the party of big legislation, they are, in a sense, more pressingly aware of this than most Conservative defenders of the utility of the traditional House); and, secondly, that almost all sections of the Conservative party are convinced that the days of the traditional House of Lords are numbered, unless their Lordships can themselves find, or agree to, a way of limiting attendance among the hereditary peers to only the most politically trained and responsible members (and they are more active in canvassing ways of doing this than the Labour party who, if they cannot find some way of reforming the Lords safely and utterly, and without increasing thereby their public prestige, seem quite happy that the composition of that House should remain 'indefensible').

Thus the Labour party is in earnest in wishing to keep a Second Chamber at all, and the Conservative party have been in earnest in wishing for a more radical reform of the composition of the House than has yet come from the working of the Life Peerages Act, or perhaps than could possibly come from that Act alone.

The Earl of Home, it is pleasant to recall, introduced the Life Peerages Bill for the Government in the debate of 3 December, 1957. He made quite clear that the Bill was not regarded as a 'final reform'. He pointed out that 'the arguments for the introduction of the Bill' were 'strictly and severely practical'. More people of the calibre of the existing peers of first creation were needed (who in fact do most of the work), people who might be deterred by the thought of saddling their children with a title. And Lord Home made clear that much of the concern was to help the Opposition, and that the Prime Minister 'would when appropriate seek the advice of the leader of the Opposition' on appointments. Thus far was common ground, but he continued: 'We on this side of the House, believing as we do that the hereditary principle has a part to play . . . having willingly modified the hereditary principle by the introduction of Life Peers so as to enable the Socialist point of view to be put more effectively . . . and if the noble Lords opposite in the years to come . . . will show a similar spirit of compromise, and be willing to include in a reformed House an element of hereditary peers, then we can arrive without much difficulty at the kind of scheme . . . which will appeal to the commonsense of the country.' Viscount Alexander of Hillsborough, the Labour leader in the Lords, denounced this mingled gift, appeal to reason and plea for future mercy, as mere 'tinkering with the problem' and an attempt to 'enhance the prestige of the House while retaining the hereditary principle'. But he was careful to offer nothing in exchange except well-worn generalities. The debate, in fact, found it hard to focus on any broad issue. Much of the time was spent by discussion of two fascinating, but relatively minor, anomalies left untouched by the Bill: that Peeresses in their own right still could not sit in the House (except if they happened to be made Life Peers), and that no way was then given by which the electoral disqualifications of a Peerage, or the title itself, could be renounced. So Mr Quintin Hogg, MP, was turned, protesting all the while into Lord Hailsham (and now back again), just as Mr Wedgwood Benn was to have to become Lord Stansgate (and now back again). The Earl of Home showed little sympathy for these politically motivated attempts, as he saw it, to avoid the burden of honour. He said that the Government were not willing to act on either matter because they would 'excite opposition and controversy'.[3]

[3] HL *Debates* (206), 3 December, 1957, c. 613. A most peculiar exchange during this debate is now worth recalling (17 December, cols. 1270–71).

Viscount Astor: If, during the war, there had been a reunion of all the male relatives of the Duke of Marlborough at Blenheim Palace, and that Palace had been hit by a bomb and everybody had been killed, the then Prime Minister might conceivably have become the Duke of Marlborough and might have had to be forcibly transferred to your Lordships' House. And in the interests of the nation as a whole that would have been a catastrophe . . . because under our present system it is essential that the Prime Minister should be a Member of the House of Commons, and by our present arrangements this country—I am sorry if I am interrupting the conversation.

The Earl of Home: I was only suggesting that, Sir Winston Churchill being such a special person, he would probably have required a special Act.

Lord Salisbury, while he voted for the Bill, criticized it strongly as inadequate; but it became clear in the debate that his own scheme, to limit the size of the House and strengthen its efficiency by some kind of selection among the peers who normally attended, would be completely unacceptable to the Labour Party since it would tend to increase the prestige, and thus possibly the real power, of a still hereditary and still overwhelmingly Conservative House.

After several amendments were rejected, the Bill was passed without a division on the Third Reading, 164 votes being the most cast on any of the amendments, contrasting to some 288 and 256 votes in the main Divisions on the Parliament Act of 1959. It did not even attract as many as the divisions on capital punishment and commercial television. Thus their Lordships, while they turned up in larger numbers than usual, did not seem extraordinarily aroused at the dilution (or rather, the improper fortifying) of their own vintage.

The debate in the House of Commons of 12 and 13 February was an even duller and more unreflective affair. The Opposition, after visibly floundering for several weeks, and showing every sign of wishing to avoid the issue, finally provided a *pro forma* amendment that: 'This House declines to give a second reading to a Bill which leaves the House of Lords overwhelmingly hereditary in character and with unimpaired powers to frustrate and obstruct the will of the elected representatives of the people.' But they advanced no alternative scheme of composition and, indeed, found it hard to appear suitably frightened at the prospect of what damage the Lords could do to legislation in the last year of a Labour Ministry—when they themselves had left the year's delay in the Parliament Act of 1949 and when, in any case, such actions would probably be more like electoral godsends than legislative disasters. The coverage of the Bill's passage in the press was unusually poor, if the measure was supposed to be important, and public reaction was apparently nil.

But from a Conservative point of view, if one needs to reform in order to preserve, a mere change in the Standing Orders of the House of Lords, which was adopted at the same time, was at least of equal importance. Following a report of a committee headed by Lord Swinton, the House of Lords voted on 11 April, 1963 that peers must reply to the Royal Writ of Summons which is sent to them (or rather, was deposited in the House for them to collect if they cared to attend); and that if they do not reply and appear to take the Oath within one month, they will be deemed to have applied for leave of absence for the remainder of the Parliament, and thus will not be able to take part in the proceedings in any way. What the numerical effect this would have was unclear, but some of the proponents of this change put it about that they expected as many as 500 or more peers to be excluded. In fact, by 1962–63 only some 210 Peers were excluded under slightly revised rules. But even if only some 300 peers had taken the Oath, that would be far above the number of regular attenders on any calculation, of men who can be presumed to have a responsible knowledge of the current affairs of Parliament.[4] Indeed it appears that the new Standing Order has stimulated more peers to attend occasionally, just as the Life Peerages Act has had a marked effect on the numbers who turn up regularly. But this has meant that the proportion of regular attenders to occasional, even just once-a-session, attenders has not increased. Far too many people still turn up who make no real contribution to the work or life of Parliament. And, as the following Table shows, while Life Peers make a better showing than all other Peers taken together, yet they are not much better in turning up than other Peers of first creation. Even these Life Peers, appointed to work, show less than half their numbers attending at all regularly.

At about the same time as the 1958 Act, Peers were allowed

[4] See, above all, P. A. Bromhead's *The House of Lords and Contemporary Politics* (Routledge, 1958), pp. 31–38; he found that over three years, 1951–54, sixty-eight peers had spoken on twenty-five or more occasions, fifty-eight spoke ten to twenty-four times, and 192 spoke at least once but less than ten times. See also, and on the whole issue, Sydney D. Bailey, ed., *The Future of the House of Lords* (Hansard Society, 1954), Lord Chorley, Bernard Crick and Donald Chapman, MP, *Reform of the Lords* (Fabian Society, 1954) and Wedgwood Benn, MP, *The Privy Council as a Second Chamber* (Fabian Society, 1957).

FREQUENCY OF ATTENDANCE OF PEERS ATTENDING AT LEAST ONCE, SESSION 1961–62

Days attended	1 Life Peers		2 Other Peers of first creation		3 Cols. 1 and 2 together		4 Other Peers		5 All Peers attending at least once	
	No.	%	No.	%	No.	%	No.	%	No.	%
1 – 20	15	(37½)	68	(50)	83	(47)	241	(64½)	324	(59½)
21 – 40	4	(10)	16	(11½)	20	(11½)	43	(11½)	63	(11½)
41 – 60	8	(20)	13	(9½)	21	(12)	21	(5½)	42	(7½)
61 – 80	6	(15)	12	(9)	18	(10½)	27	(7½)	45	(8)
81 – 100	4	(10)	15	(11)	19	(11)	17	(4½)	36	(6½)
101 – 115	3	(7½)	12	(9)	15	(8)	24	(6½)	39	(7)
	40	(100)	136	(100)	176	(100)	373	(100)	549	(100)

Possible number of sitting days—115. Total number of Peers—932.

to claim an attendance allowance of three guineas a day for expenses. But this, again, is either a temporary half-way house or it is nothing. The maximum yearly emolument would not be much more than about £300, so those who could not afford to serve anyway are not likely to be able to do so now. It helps some of the Labour Peers and ends some cases of real hardship among a handful of devoted public servants. It is hardly likely, however, to attract new blood; but, on the other hand, to pay a more realistic stipend to any of 549 hereditary gentlemen who care to turn up of a Friday to collect it (or they might all start coming again, 932 of them), would be a *job* beyond the ambition or tolerance of even the first great Duke of Newcastle. And it is relatively unlikely that any Chancellor of the Exchequer would suggest a Means Test for their Lordships. Proper payment must clearly wait on a reformed and reduced composition.

Thus each immediate expedient has fallen upon exactly the same stumbling block as larger schemes: the reluctance of the Conservatives to surrender the hereditary principle as at least the dominant principle of composition, and the ambivalence of the Labour leadership about whether they want reform at all.

The first list of Life Peers of 24 July, 1958, while composed of very able men and women, scarcely introduced a new type of member as distinct from increasing the supply of the old type. They would all have been suitable candidates for full peerages anyway, though they might not all have accepted. They did not, and nor did subsequent creations, represent any new thinking about the kind of person needed to perform the real work of scrutiny of the Second Chamber, so much as a fortifying of the existing Peers of first creation. It was a saving of the House against itself rather than any breaking of new ground. By far the largest group in both the old and the new first creations is still that of ex-MPs. *The Times* commented that the event was 'not very exciting' and, plainly puzzled how to set its mark on such a constitutional occasion, descended into a grumble that some of the new creations had actually been labelled as nominees of the leader of the Opposition (but only six), before rising into an intense discussion of whether the children of Life Peers should be given the same courtesy titles as those of ordinary Peers—as indeed they were.

The Act was a temporary expedient and it has not been made use of—with its forty odd rather conventional appointments—to transform the character and quality of the House; it has made thorough going reform more likely rather than less by complicating, to the point of absurdity, the whole status of both the Order of Peerage and the Second Chamber. But the ultimate expedient and absurdity had not been reached.

The Politics of Renunciation

In 1963 once more the mountain laboured and brought forth a mouse. The Parliament Act of 1958 had brought Life Peers and Peeresses into the Constitution to strengthen the repute and efficiency of the House of Lords. And now the Peerage Act of 1963, following the report of the Joint Committee on House of Lords Reform,[5] has enabled hereditary peers to renounce their titles and status for life, thus removing an injustice for some reluctant elder sons and, in some cases, their loyal and unhappy constituents. Another piece of patchwork has been added to the already crazy quilt of modern government in Feudal dress. In the same year that a British Parliament could tear apart and rebuild with great swiftness the whole structure of government of our largest urban area (albeit with a typical reprieve for the pageantry and jobbery of the City of London itself[6]), yet it still allowed the mouse of reform only the smallest nibble at the ermine.

When the Government introduced the new Bill in the Commons on 19 June, 1963, they proposed that the right of renunciation should come into effect on the dissolution of Parliament. They resisted amendments in Committee for it to take effect, as is more usual for Acts, on the giving of the Royal Assent. But then, on 16 July, the House of Lords staged one of

[5] HL 23, HC 38 (1962–63).
[6] See Belle Harris, 'Why Should the City Escape?', *Political Quarterly*, April 1963, pp. 194–99; I cite this as an example, very relevant to the Lords controversy, of the Conservative attempt to be modern without ceasing to be feudal.

their rare revolts and carried an amendment of Lord Silkin's, by 105 votes to 25, that the Royal Assent would be, as it were, devesting day. Normally, as we have seen, the House of Commons rejects such important amendments and the Lords then, having made their demonstration, climb down. But Mr Macleod, as Leader of the House, advised the House of Commons to accept this amendment, perhaps—as he said—because any delay so late in the Session might endanger the whole Bill with a crowded Parliamentary time-table ahead, but possibly —may one surmise?—because the change could have been one of Mr Macmillan's most prescient political decisions, since it was to release Sir Alec Douglas-Home, as well as Messrs Hogg, Benn and Grigg from honorific encumbrances. The quality of sheer opportunism and improvisation in the whole way the question of the House of Lords has been handled is now beyond either joke or belief.

The immediate political outcome of the Wedgwood Benn affair has been, if not an anticlimax, yet unexpected. However, the case is worth recalling and is highly relevant here for two reasons: it showed that there *is* some kind of public opinion on the issue (and that a Government will back down when faced by such a clear opinion); and it has resulted in the likelihood that the shot in the arm given by the Peerages Act of 1958 will now be counter-balanced by the loss of good blood back to the Commons. Radical reconstitution of the Chamber is now only a matter of time. The Lords have had given and the Lords have had taken away. Someone will have to try all over again.

Let us recall the main facts of the Benn case. The First Viscount Stansgate was created in unusual circumstances. On 21 December, 1941 a statement was issued from No. 10 Downing Street: 'The King, on the advice of HM Government, has been graciously pleased to confer peerages upon four members of the Labour Party. These creations are not made as political honours or rewards, but as a special measure of state policy. They are designed to strengthen the Labour Party in the Upper House . . . at a time when a coalition Government of three parties is charged with the direction of affairs.' He would certainly have been a Life Peer had the recent Act been then in force. Since this was a 'special measure of state policy' there was an element of ungenerosity throughout in successive governments invoking heraldic precedent, rather than using the sovereign power of the Crown in Parliament to find some relief for the Member for Bristol, South-East, before the crisis came. A Private Bill and a Public Bill promoted by Benn were both rejected. Then, on 17 November, 1960, the first Viscount died. The House of Commons referred to the Committee of Privileges Anthony Wedgwood Benn's claim that he was not disqualified.[7]

The Committee reported against Benn: that his 'instrument of renunciation' had no legal effect; that his status disabled him, not the Writ of Summons to the Lords for which he had not applied;[8] and that the issue of such a Writ, while plainly forcing someone to leave the Commons, yet constituted no breach of the Commons privileges.[9] And they rather gratuitously added, after voting on straight party lines, that they neither recommended the introduction of a special Bill to help Benn, nor were they called upon to express any view about the desirability of general legislation. The Committee, while accepting the view that the House of Commons is the sole judge of the qualification of its members, yet hid behind the law. (And the story went around that one Conservative Member of the Committee persistently committed the politically Freudian slip of saying 'Hogg' for 'Benn'.)

When the Report was debated and accepted, the House refused permission, voting again on strict party lines and against several clear precedents, for Benn to address them from the bar of the House on his own behalf. But on this division twelve truly honourable Conservative Members voted against the Government. Certainly, as one of the editors of *Public Law* wrote: 'such a refusal must . . . have injured the reputation of the House for generosity, courtesy and fair play'.[10]

[7] HC *Debates* (631), cols. 171–74.
[8] The *Roll of the Lords Spiritual and Temporal,* (1) HL, 1962–63, shows 68 peers who had never bothered to collect their Writs of Summons without which they cannot sit.
[9] *Report from the Committee on Privileges,* HC 142 (1960–61).
[10] Gordon Borrie, 'The Wedgwood Benn Case', *Public Law,* Winter 1961, pp. 349–61; see also Peter Bromhead 'Mr Wedgwood

Public opinion now entered into it, and Conservative MPs were left in no doubt from press, radio and television that Parliament had acted foolishly in the eyes of the public. It is hard to think of a case in which Parliament was so much at odds with an aroused and informed public opinion. The new Writ was at last issued for a by-election and Benn determined to stand. The Returning Officers have statutory power to refuse a nomination paper only if the formal particulars of the candidates and other persons subscribing the paper are not as required by law. Many odd holes in the Constitution began to appear. On 4 May, 1961, Bristol returned Benn by 23,275 votes to 10,231, *double* his majority at the General Election, despite much publicity by his opponent that his election would be invalid. And so the Election Court found when his opponent, Mr Malcolm St Clair, petitioned it. Meanwhile the House, on 8 May, 1961, yet again refused admission to Benn, though with growing ill-temper and doubt as it realized how clearly it was challenging the rights of the constituency; here was, indeed, the clearest clash between Parliament and a constituency since the days of Wilkes and the Middlesex elections in the 1760s, and between the hereditary and the democratic elements in the Constitution since 1911. But the Commons sheltered behind the Court.

There is no reasonable doubt of the soundness of the first part of the Court's judgement: that Benn was not elected because under a legal disability. He had argued that the disability of a Peer only arose from the incompatibility of duties imposed by the Writ of Summons. In practice the Crown only issues a Writ when applied for, and he had neither applied for nor received one. There were precedents on his side—the whole status of Peerage was much more uncertain and flexible until the mid-seventeenth century than today. But it is hard not to follow Victorian judges who held that these precedents and practices had fallen into desuetude (there is now, as with modern royal ceremonial, a kind of bureaucratic freezing and codification of customs and pageants once far more fluid).

Benn, the Peerage and the Constitution', *Parliamentary Affairs*, Autumn 1961, pp. 493–506, both excellent accounts of the whole case.

The modern law was quite clear. But what were the sources of the law? Nothing was to be found in statute. The sources were, of course, the decisions of the courts; the opinions of writers of authority; and the reports of the Committees of both Houses. This reveals what was shabby in the whole affair. Clearly the Election Court would give most weight to modern decisions of Parliament itself. But the Committee on Privileges had itself refused to contemplate change or innovation. What was, in the eyes of the Court, the only unchallengeable source of new law in these matters, itself took political shelter behind a refusal to consider anything except the precedents and the opinions of writers of authority.[11] This was to the discredit of Parliament (an example of the general timidity of Back-benchers in using their collective power).

But the Court went further. It declared that votes for Benn did not count and that, therefore, Mr St Clair was the Member for Bristol South-East—an injustice and a political absurdity. The Court relied on *Beresford-Hope* v. *Lady Sandhurst*[12] which had found that when the fact of incapacity was well known, votes for that candidate were thrown away. But was it as 'clear and notorious' that a Peer was disqualified in 1961, when seemingly allowed to stand at all, as was a woman in 1889—particularly when it was well known that a case was pending? The public might well suspect, wrongly, that if electoral law were not in a thorough muddle, an action would take place at the time of nomination, not after a campaign and the declaration of the Poll. The Court could easily have avoided the absurdity and injustice of declaring Mr St Clair elected. On this matter of opinion it could have declared the election invalid and ordered a new Writ to be issued. It was the first time—and one hopes the last—in which a candidate with a minority has been seated by order of a Court (the House of Commons acted directly in the case of Wilkes).

Two days after Wedgwood Benn (Viscount Stansgate) had

[11] The tautologous character of the doctrine of parliamentary supremacy has never been made more clear: Parliament is even supreme to ignore its own supremacy—but surely not its political responsibility?
[12] 23 Queens Bench Division 79 (1889).

been nominated for the British by-election, Mr Butler announced in the House of Commons that the Government intended to set up a Joint Select Committee (that is, of both Houses) to consider: (i) the composition of the House of Lords; (ii) whether Peers should have the right to sit in either House, to vote at elections or to surrender their peerages; and (iii) remuneration.

The terms of reference were subsequently narrowed to the second point alone. For the Labour Party simply refused to join a committee on such terms. Perhaps the wonder is that they joined it at all, but for the fact that they had already fully committed themselves on the Benn case largely on grounds of personal sympathy for a very popular colleague. For the Labour Party had and has no policy whatever on the House of Lords. The impetus for reform in recent years has been, with the single exception of the Benn case, Conservative. Since the breakdown of the 1947 Conference of Party Leaders and Mr Attlee's refusal to enter into fresh talks in 1953, Labour had pursued a resolutely conservative policy of letting sleeping topdogs lie. They feared that any reform or rationalization of the Upper House would strengthen its prestige even if the powers were left as now, or even reduced. And this was probably sound sociological sense; but it is political cowardice and, in the long run, politically untenable. It will be remembered that the Labour Party opposed the Life Peerages Act of 1958, though immediately co-operated in its working. Clearly it was absurd, theoretically and politically for Mr Butler to expect Labour to discuss the question of composition without discussing the question of powers. It is normally thought that the nature of a job is relevant to the selection of personnel. But the real objection was to discussing the problem at all. One supposes that the Government refrained from calling Labour's bluff by including 'powers' in the terms of reference only because they actually did want some result and not another stalemate. They were under, as usual, far more Backbench pressure from their own members to provide some remedy for reluctant Peers—after all, they have more of them—than was apparent in the Parliamentary debates on the Benn affair.

If the subsequent Report of the Joint Committee on House

of Lords was a mouse, yet it was a very pretty one—well suited to pseudo-Gothic surroundings. The Select Committee on Public Estimates should reprimand Her Majesty's Stationery Office for not having advertised it in the hopes of wide commercial sales among all the many literate eccentrics and men of humour still in the realm. The printed evidence showed the Lord Lyon King of Arms taking the committee relentlessly through the history of 'hereditary tribal representation' in the second of the Scottish 'Thrie Estaits'; Lyon showed that the Scottish Peerage had had the undoubted right of resignation *in favorem* and even powers of Nomination and Tailzie. Our own Garter Principal King of Arms struck closer to the eventual recommendations of the Committee and terms of the Act; Garter did, however, find need solemnly to reject 'the genetic argument', but to weigh judiciously the 'social argument' as being 'too deeply embedded in human nature to be changed easily'. And much more of the same—including several disingenuous proposals, notably from Lord Salisbury, that Peers should be allowed to stand for the Commons *without* renouncing their titles.

The report recommended that:

(i) Peerages may be surrendered. Existing Peers would be given six months to make up their mind from the date when the new law comes into effect; newly succeeding Peers one year, except if they are already in the Commons, then one month. The resignation would be for life, complete and irrevocable in every respect of title, dignity, precedence and privileges, but would be resumed by the heir on the death of the 'holder' of the dormant title (the Labour minority on the committee had voted for the extinction—technically, 'the drowning'—of such peerages).

(ii) The Peerage of Scotland (that is those created before the Act of Union of 1706) should all be admitted to the House of Lords. At present they elect sixteen Representative Peers; the additional number will be only fifteen. So here is an actual increase in hereditary numbers!

(iii) The Peerage of Ireland (that is those created before the Act of Union of 1800) have had no Representative Peers since 1919; so they should now be able to stand for any constituency in the United Kingdom and to vote if they fulfil normal residence requirements (previously they were excluded from election in Northern Ireland). This removed an anomaly without increasing (by about seventy) numbers in the Lords; but it left a class of people *with* titles who may stand for election and sit in the Commons. This seems, for obvious reasons, inequitable.

(iv) Peeresses in their own right (at present some seventeen ladies) of England, the United Kingdom and of Scotland should be allowed to sit in the Lords, or to surrender their titles on the same terms as all other Peers.

The subsequent Peerages Act (1963) followed these recommendations with only some minor changes in the timing and the procedure of renunciation. Justice was done—to Peers. But it is doubtful whether the Committee would have been appointed at all and the Bill brought forward if the Election Court had contented itself with disqualifying Benn and had not made nonsense of the electoral process by seating his opponent—unless Mr Macmillan was so very prescient in preparing the grounds for the Battle of the Succession in October 1963.

Once again a reform was brought in which did not infringe the right of hereditary peers to sit in the Upper House. And no one seriously questioned the undemocratic habit of Irish Peers and of holders of courtesy titles (among the sons of the hereditary Peerage) being able to use their titles in Parliamentary elections. This is a pretty small point; but it was a pretty small-minded piece of legislation. Mr Wedgwood Benn may have succeeded in his personal case; but both parties saw to it that no thin end of the wedge would be made towards an agreed and genuine reform of the Lords. Yet his fight could have very great political significance. His remarkable majority in the Bristol by-election should convince any future Labour Government that public opinion is not so wedded to the Lords as the Lords make out. If public opinion remains in this mood, may prior agreement between the parties prove politically necessary at all? Would there be much risk in a unilateral House of Lords Reform Bill, following the example of the Conservatives in 1958?

It is not too difficult to see a clear way to reform in the

sense of improving the utility of the Second Chamber. It may perhaps well be, as Lord Chorley has asked in a tone of amused despair, 'quite unrealistic to think that any such agreement can be reached'.[13] Let us grant that the Preamble to the Parliament Act of 1911 was a quite unrealistic red-herring; no one now wants a 'popular . . . basis' for the Chamber; the Commons is and should remain the only elected, national body in the Constitution. But agreement about the function of a second chamber is, in principle, great.

Let us go back again to Lord Bryce's Report of 1918 on the 'Conference on the Reform of the Second Chamber' of 1917—which is still the classic study of the function of the Lords. He distinguished four functions:

(i) 'The examination and revision of Bills brought from the Commons.'
(ii) 'The initiation of Bills of a comparatively non-controversial character.'
(iii) 'The interposition of so much delay (and no more) in the passing of a Bill into law as may enable the opinion of the nation to be adequately expressed upon it.'
(iv) 'Full and free discussion of the large and important questions . . . at moments when the House of Commons . . . cannot find sufficient time for them.'

As we have shown, the value of work in the first two categories is now actually greater than in Bryce's time, in terms of the time saved to the Commons, indeed for clauses of Bills and statutory instruments that often would not have been examined at all but for the Lords. (There is simply *no* case whatever for abolishing a Second Chamber.) The third function has been modified drastically by the Parliament Act of 1949. And the fourth function of general debate seems to do no one any harm and may sometimes do some good. The essential thing is that Bryce's first two categories point to the use of the Lords as an efficient working body.

The 'Agreed Statement on Conclusion of Conference of Party Leaders' in 1948 stated that: 'the Second Chamber should be complementary to and not a rival to the Lower

[13] See his thoughtful 'The House of Lords Controversy', *Public Law*, Autumn 1958, pp. 216–35.

House and, with this end in view, the reform of the House of Lords should be based on a modification of its existing constitution as opposed to the construction of a Second Chamber of a completely new type based on some system of election'.[14] The full concept imminent in the word 'complementary' is yet to be explored.

Then came the Parliament Act of 1958. It must be remembered that this was a Conservative measure, introduced without inter-party agreement and without any Mandate (the Conservatives, like ancient Chartists, invoked 'the Mandate' in 1948). It was clearly intended to restore the efficiency of the House of Lords without diluting the hereditary vintage. The repute of the House of Lords depends upon its efficiency, and upon its repute depends the social esteem that the public give to the Peerage.

Conservatives are well aware of the truth of Tocqueville's great maxim that aristocracies without function wither into contempt. And the Act might have killed the two birds with one stone. But the use made of it has been both half-hearted and contradictory.

Forty-five Life Peers had been created by the end of 1963 (including seven Peeresses), of whom two had died. It was said by the Government in the debates on the Bill that they would all be people who would be willing to play a regular part in the work of the House. In many cases this has been true, but not in all. There has been a tendency for the list to degenerate into, if not a window-dressing, then a supplementary form of patronage; and appointments have been made of people already so impossibly distinguished and busy that they have had little time for their duties. They seem to play no more or less a role in the recent life of the House than the other Peers of First Creation who provide most of the hard core of regular attenders who do the honourable donkey work.

About the same time the Standing Orders of the House were amended so that a Peer *may* apply for leave of absence for either a session or a Parliament, and will be deemed to have applied if he doesn't turn up at all. Then he 'is expected

14 HC 7380 of 1948.

not to attend the sittings' and 'he is expected to give notice
. . . at least one month' before he might subsequently attend.
At the moment sixty-two Peers have leave of absence for the
Session and one hundred and fifty-six for the Parliament. But
this is a purely informal and legally quite unenforceable tidying up—'is expected' forsooth! The Crown's Writ of Attendance
is absolute. There is no legal power to stop any absentee turning up if the spirit moves him.

Clearly the Life Peers Act could be an effective instrument
to create a Chamber of men and women experienced in the
administration of matters likely to come before the House
for scrutiny and revision. And the stress should be on relevant
experience rather than on 'public distinction' in the conventional way of the New Year and Birthday Honours Lists. It
can be said that no one has been made a Life Peer who could
not, with propriety, have been made an ordinary hereditary
Peer, were they willing. Yet a few good Town Clerks would
do far better service than most of the already over-busy people of public distinction who have been appointed. If an element in a reformed House should continue to be retired
MPs and failed Ministers, yet at least an equal element of it
could be, if properly paid, almost a career service, certainly
something to fill an important stage in the career of a lawyer,
civil servant, public official, some businessmen and some people in education: not all appointments need be for life, nor
need 'nomination' preclude application.

A Second Chamber

The true function of the Upper House is to save time for the
Commons; to give more time than can the Commons for the
scrutiny and suggested revision of complex public Bills and of
statutory instruments; and to discuss and debate not so much
great issues of public policy but matters of administration
and of the working of social policies for which the Commons
seemingly has little time, or even, with the declining use of
Select Committees, inclination.[15] If this administrative, bureau-

[15] See my 'A House of Scrutiny?', Observer, 1 April, 1962.

cratic, scrutinizing conception of an Upper House as a
Chamber of Review (or House of Correction?) could be
grasped, and the composition made appropriate, then one
could envisage many useful *additional* functions being undertaken by such a thoroughly de-politicized 'Lords'. Committees
could undertake work of investigation as well as scrutiny, to
allay the continued public worry, and to fill the real gap in
Ministerial accountability, about the workings not merely of
systems of public tribunals and inquiries, *vide* the Franks
Report, but also the greater un-tribunalled areas of ordinary
administration, *vide* the Whyatt Report. It would be a proper
place for the Standing Council on Tribunals and even, with
Law Lords active, a final Court of Administrative Appeals.
Many forms of public inquiry, even many topics handled by
inter-departmental committees, at the moment completely outside the scope or control of Parliament, could be undertaken
or reviewed by such a Second Chamber. In this context the
composition and work of the *Conseil d'État* of the French
Fourth Republic deserves far more sympathetic study from
British parliamentarians.

But the main point is that the functions of a reformed and
efficient Second Chamber should be studied in relation to the
work of the Commons. It is for the Commons to use the
Upper House as a policy-making body uses committees of
consultants, advisers and scrutineers. The solution to the
House of Lords problem will not be found until the next Select
Committee on Procedure of the House of Commons has, in
its terms of reference, the function of the House of Lords.

As for composition, the Labour Party must nerve itself, as
Mr Benn has suggested,[16] to cut the Gordian knot and divorce membership of the Peerage of the Realm from membership of the Upper House of Parliament. Half-way houses, such
as Lord Salisbury has been fertile in planning, all have the
same object: to preserve the social and political esteem of the
Order of Peerage. This consideration is simply irrelevant to
the work of Parliament—though it is relevant to the social mechanics of Conservative electoral prospects. And if this is

[16] Anthony Wedgwood Benn, 'The Labour Party and Lords Reform', *Guardian*, 28 January, 1963.

so, as most politicians would agree it is (even though different conclusions can be drawn from the observation), the Labour Party should attack the inequity of the Order of Peerage having any special role in Parliament at all. Since they may now lay down their rank and run for the Commons, let them do so. They could be appointed to serve in a nominated Upper House the same as anyone else; and they are likely to furnish more than their share of people with the right kind of experience of service on public bodies and in local government.

The Labour Party has been wise not to be affronted by the hereditary principle as such in relation to the work of the Lords. But the Life Peers Act recognized that the Peerage could no longer perform this work. And the Peerage is, after all, part of an undemocratic system of social influence exploited by the Conservative Party. Social esteem may be, as the worthy Garter argued, 'part of human nature'; but there is no justice in continuing to give it constitutional sanction. It represents a biased element in the system when the whole function of Parliament is to give opposition equality of access to the electorate with the Government.

The House of Commons could well, as Benn argues, be given power to override the decisions of the Lords by simple affirmative resolution. But his suggestion to leave the Peers of First Creation, together with the Life Peers, the Bishops and the Law Lords would still leave a Chamber of about two hundred and fifty members. If Mr Benn would consider what the functions should be, rather than putting composition first (in his animus against the hereditary principle), he might think that something far smaller was appropriate—perhaps no more than a hundred if most were genuinely full-time, not Lords but Councillors of Parliament.

So the House of Lords should be radically reformed for two reasons, which perhaps up until now have only been implicit in this argument, but reasons which should make the Labour Party think the question part of the matter of Britain and not just a silly, quite useful anomaly which can be ignored on sufferance. First, that the House of Commons is overburdened with work and thus drowned in detail. Second, that the prestige of the Peerage helps to perpetuate the un-democratic character of British life.

If a Labour Government will not reform the Commons (out of a false fear of losing real political control) to give the kind of 'Parliamentary control' the public wants and the kind of advice the government itself needs, then reform of the Second Chamber could provide some of these things. If a Conservative Government will not reform the Lords (out of a real fear of losing the false influence of snobbery), then it may be driven to reform the Commons somewhat. But ideally the two should move together and the work of the Lords should be rationally integrated to that of the Commons to provide the kind of advice and control which British Government is, at the moment, badly lacking.

CHAPTER VII

REFORMING THEMSELVES

The Select Committee on Procedure, 1959

The point and presumption of this book is that most Members of Parliament have not yet realized how deep a morass of ineffectuality they have fallen into, and that only strong outside criticism, ultimately public opinion, will make them move. The man outside will miss many of the subtleties and will get some of his facts wrong. But he should not be too worried about this. For part of the trouble is that, odd though it is to state, Parliament has become a very isolated club in its traditions and procedures. So long as it gives leadership to the public in the formulation of great issues at election times, it thinks that it is nobody's business but its own how it proceeds and how far it attempts to preserve the more outdated of its traditions. But, firstly, not all politics is a matter of great issues; and, secondly, the kind of issues which are put forward will be determined in large part by the routine way in which Parliament goes about its 'domestic' business.

How has this somewhat arrogant, almost feckless, ultimately dangerous lack of concern for public opinion and public understanding of the proper function of Parliament come about? In part simply through a decline in constitutional thought in this century itself, due to an almost total absorption in substantive issues and to the gentle and fallacious belief in a necessary and natural alteration in office between the two main parties; but also through a mood of stubborn nostalgia about procedural 'traditions' which dominates the House of Commons itself. The amount of mutual back-scratching about the 'glories of Parliament' that went on in a recent debate on Parliamentary reform[1] makes the flesh creep. One is sur-

[1] HC *Debates* (673), 15 March, 1963.

prised that grown men say such things to each other. It hardly needs saying that this self-glorification of ineffectuality by erudite Backbenchers receives little discouragement from the Frontbenchers. Members of Parliament are nearly as bad as the leaders of the legal profession at the moment: public concern is reproved as ignorant intrusion into private mysteries. The spirit of Parliamentary procedure can be likened to that much loved old body our Common Law: she is of so complex and arbitrary a nature, so full of whims, contradictions but then sudden delights, that to take the pains to master her fully is to become absurdly jealous of her precise retention, not because one really enjoys her all that much, but because one bitterly remembers the difficulties of gaining her; indeed, in time she becomes lovable, not for any gifts of form or intellect, but simply for her sheer capricious intricacy.

If this figure is acceptable, it will not then be surprising to learn that the few people who can master the procedure with habitual ease, the Clerks of the House, have shown themselves at all times, from the days of Erskine May to the Select Committees on Procedure of both 1945–46 and 1958–59, far more ready to contemplate and suggest large reforms, particularly tending towards specialization in the committee system, than have their masters the MPs. The servants of the House, the real (one apologizes) *technicians* of procedure, are not so servile and thankful in their suffering of existing inefficiencies. They recognize it as a means to an end—not as an end in itself: the end of putting through business in an acceptable manner, that is to say a manner that ensures it gets through, but only after close, careful and informed scrutiny of details and open criticism of principles. Many Backbenchers, frustrated from real work, take to chewing frozen procedure as a genteel anodyne.

These remarks are amply justified by what happened recently when the House tackled the question of procedure. Just as there has been a widespread sense of frustration with Parliament among the public, so there has been from time to time—in the words of the *Report* of the Select Committee on Procedure, 1959—'a sense of frustration which has on occasion been voiced by Members on all sides of the House'.

The debate of 31 January, 1958 on 'The Procedure of Parliament' was an interesting outburst and one to which the Government felt it wise to give way—at least as far as creating another Select Committee on Procedure 'to consider the Procedure in the Public Business of the House; and to report what alterations, if any, are desirable for the more efficient dispatch of business'. The 'frustration' to which the *Report* itself referred and which MPs spoke of in the debate was to most Members quite simply a matter of not being able to speak enough on the floor of the House, and of lack of time for debates of major consequence. The issue of reforming and specializing the committee system of the House in relation to the power of the Executive was certainly raised, but only very cautiously, very obliquely.

The *Report* made by the Select Committee is, at first glance, somewhat free from matters of general public interest. In the nature of procedural matters, of course, much of such a Report must inevitably be confined to matters of detail important only to the convenience of the House itself. But not the smallest part of the *Report's* proposals comes to grips with the real problem of the rapidly diminishing effectiveness of Parliamentary control of the Executive. Indeed, in several sections it sets itself against any altering of the 'balance' between the Executive and the House—with that sublime assurance that the House, by the Laws of God and Nature, rides a nag which is always a fixed and dutiful distance behind the great state-coach of the Cabinet. Only among a minority of the committee, mostly on the Labour side, was there any recognition that the Ministry is drawing farther and farther away from the House. The idea of a Standing Committee on Colonial affairs was called 'a radical constitutional innovation'—a palpable exaggeration considering the recent creation of the Select Committee on Nationalized Industries, but enough to damn it.

The committee, in other words, while doing some quite useful pruning and clearing, completely lost the wood for the trees. As on such exercises before, it was actually the Clerk of the House who put forward the most radical and comprehensive proposals for reform. Was Sir Edward Fellowes teasing or trying to frighten the committee when he said, in the discussion of a long memoranda on reform which he submitted: 'ultimately the only solution for the amount of legislation and the complexity of legislation in modern times is a vastly extended power of delegation . . .'? But he went on to remark that so little would the House of Commons be prepared to accept such a scheme, that he had not bothered to put it forward. It is surprising that none on the committee then argued that it was, indeed, time to face this alternative, but that it need hold no fears so long as Parliamentary examination and scrutiny of delegated legislation was greatly improved. The Committee on Statutory Instruments, it could be argued, only needs a professional staff to make it as effective an instrument of control as is the Committee on Public Accounts.

However, the committee made 37 piecemeal recommendations, some of which may have some general interest.

Paragraph 8 of the report made proposals for alterations in the composition and procedure of Standing Committees: the distinction between the nucleus of a Standing Committee and the additional members for each Bill should be ended—membership should be composed in respect of each individual Bill; and there were proposals to ease the difficulties of keeping a quorum in committee. The main proposals here would, of course, tend to create a type of committee composed more of specialists, but would prevent Members grouping together in specialized committees over a whole session: specialism may be tolerable to the House provided that the specialists are constantly reshuffled.

Paragraph 9 suggested that as an *experiment* some parts of the committee stage of the Finance Bill should be considered upstairs, thus breaking the—to some—sacred tradition of the whole House granting supply.

Paragraph 20 suggested that drafting assistance should be made available to Members, both for Private Bills and for amendments to Public Bills (but this simple reform was the furthest the Report went towards asking for more expert staff for either members or committees).

Paragraph 25 expressed the hope that preference be given to general debates in the use of time saved by the proposed procedural reforms (although the discussion in the *Proceedings* of the committee showed almost unanimous agreement that the Government would bag any time thus saved for their own business—yet this still did not turn the committee, as will be seen, in favour of morning sessions or a radical increase in use of committees upstairs).

Paragraph 27 made the sensible suggestion that in major debates an hour be reserved for five-minute speeches.

Paragraph 31 proposed that incidental reference to the need for legislative action be permitted on motions for the adjournment—an odd procedural restriction of great historical but no other relevance.

Paragraph 34 proposed relaxing the conditions by which successive Speaker's rulings had narrowed the original intention of Standing Order No. 9 to allow Private Members to move the adjournment to discuss urgent matters of public importance; they proposed returning to Mr Speaker Peel's early test of 'the occurrence of some sudden emergency either in home or foreign affairs', to escape from the present state of affairs in which 'scarcely any matter . . . could qualify for debate under the Standing Order'.

Among other proposals were for the form of the Order Paper to be revised and made comprehensible; for Privy Councillors to lose their automatic priority over ordinary Members in Debate; for the Business of the House to be announced longer in advance; for Question Time to be tidied up in several small and sensible ways; and for Members to be allowed to discuss the policy underlying the main Estimate in a debate on the granting of Supplementary Estimates.[2]

[2] For detailed accounts of the proposals and their reception, see H. V. Wiseman, 'Procedure: The House of Commons and the Select Committee', *Parliamentary Affairs*, February 1960, pp. 236–47,

What the Committee Did Not Say

The most interesting section of the Report is that of which the summary began: 'We have also examined the following matters but recommend no alteration in the present procedure and practice.' Four of these matters are worth keeping alive.[3] Firstly, the *Report* rejected the proposal that pressure on the Floor of the House would be relieved if the Report Stage of less important or less controversial Bills was taken in Standing Committee. This was proposed by the present Clerk of the House, as it had been by his predecessor, Sir Gilbert Campion, before the Select Committee on Procedure of 1945–46.[4] The Committee agreed that the relief afforded would be 'self-evident', but argued that the effect would be 'improper, since it would involve a departure from the principle that the whole House assumes responsibility for the details of legislation'. This kind of invocation of 'principle' is a remarkably fine example of an allegedly empirical conservatism turned static

---

and R. D. Barlas, 'House of Commons: Report of the Select Committee on Procedure, Session 1958–59', *The Table*, 1959, pp. 27–43.

[3] The Report also rejected proposals for 'mechanical voting' rather than the present system of divisions. Since this proposal gained much publicity, and since it appeared almost as a symbol of tradition versus efficiency, it is only fair to say that the Select Committee found that only two or three minutes a division could possibly be saved by 'press button' voting. Divisions are time-consuming because Members have to go to the Lobby, not because the telling takes long. Mechanical voting is only practicable where Representatives each have a desk on the Floor.

[4] Sir Gilbert had suggested that the House should have two large Standing Committees of 75–100 Members each—plus the Scottish Standing Committee. Each of these would have three sub-committees of about 25 Members. These sub-committees would consider what is at present the Committee Stage of all legislation and then 'report' not to the Floor of the whole House, but to their parent committee. See the *Third Report of the Select Committee on Parliamentary Procedure*, 1945–46. The Committee rejected this as 'a drastic interference with the rights of Private Members'—a sadly automatic response: such a scheme might affect the abstract rights of Private Members, but it would certainly strengthen their collective power.

and doctrinaire. The Committee genuinely wanted to save time on the Floor for more general debates by rescuing the House from detail, and yet it invoked a 'principle' which has already become so shot-through with exceptions (the whole field of delegated legislation, for instance, not to mention Scottish Bills) that it is not even an adequate description of present practice, much less a rule to be blindly followed. It is hard to see how the House would lose its responsibility for the detail of legislation when the hurdle of the Third Reading still lies ahead; it would be perfectly possible, without detailed amendments necessarily being offered on the Third Reading, for a Bill to be sent back to Committee for further amendation without defeating it as a whole.

Secondly, the *Report* advised against *morning sittings*, although it noted with considerable emphasis a difference of opinion between those who thought that Membership of the House should demand 'full-time service' and those who thought that the House 'would be better served by retaining a number within her ranks who bring to her deliberations the benefit of their knowledge and experience derived from other fields during such hours of the day as their attendance can be spared from the precincts of Westminster'. But the last phrase is really a little too ingenuous: there is in fact no question of deciding whether Members can be spared; there is simply a desire of the great majority on the Conservative benches to treat the House as a strictly part-time form of activity, and of many on the Labour benches to do so out of financial need. One sympathizes with this strange 'can be spared' formulation of the Committee: a franker statement would bring regrettable public scorn upon the House. No one really believes that the 'knowledge and experience' of making money in the morning is of direct relevance to the work of the House in the afternoon or evening; but everyone knows that at present salary scales Parliament would lose valuable Members if attendance in the mornings ever became obligatory—and it would also lose some others.

Certainly it is of the utmost importance that Parliament should, in a rough way, be socially and professionally representative as well as electorally. But two things should be clearly borne in mind: firstly, that the avoidance of business in the mornings allows lawyers and company directors to be greatly over-represented; and secondly, these same people could equally well serve full-time in the House just for a Parliament. The present distinction between full-time and part-time Members could to great advantage give way to the more natural distinction between Members with Ministerial aspiration, who would seek to remain in Parliament after each General Election, and men from the professions, from business and from the unions who would enter Parliament for a limited time and then return to their colleagues. If this seems fanciful, it is at least an answer to the 'outside experience' objection, and it would also improve the quality and enthusiasm of Backbench participation. Better that some men should be clearly professionals and that others should be clearly temporary, though for a period *full-time* representatives, of their constituencies and local parties, than that the present huge twilight majority of half-time Members should continue to leave the present work of committees to an overworked band of about a mere seventy Members.[5]

There was a vigorous move in the Committee in favour of morning sessions. Mr Wedgwood Benn moved an amendment to the Report, which was rejected by 9 to 6, in favour of morning sessions so as to create time for debates which might otherwise never take place because of the pressure of business. He had in mind debates on matters of current interest while they were still topical; on matters of specialized interest which tend to get eliminated from the time-table of the House; on Colonial affairs—for many of the smaller colonies are scarcely ever discussed in Parliament, until there is trouble; and for debates on the Reports of Royal Commissions and Select Committees. None of these matters would be legislative; all are things that peculiarly interest the private Member. Such debates would not call for the presence of the Minister himself, only of a junior Minister. 'The strongest case for this innovation,' argued the amendment, 'lies in the fact that it stakes a claim for the private Member at a time of

[5] See p. 86 above.

day and under conditions which make it very unlikely that any Government would want to steal it for its own business.'

Undoubtedly such a proposal would provide criticism and scrutiny of many neglected aspects of Government policy and areas of public concern, without in any way imperilling the Government's control of Parliament. The only doubt about such a proposal is that it smacks a little too much of debate for the sake of debate: one is a little sceptical as to whether more words would lead to the multiplication of wisdom. What is needed, surely, is not simply more time on the Floor, but more preparation behind what is then said on the Floor. If there are to be morning sessions (even with no compulsion on the majority of Members to turn up at all), they would seem the ideal time for the work of a reformed committee system.

It might be asked why no one simply proposed that the House begin its present business at 10 or 11 o'clock instead of 3 o'clock, simply so that the inconvenient night sittings could be cut out. But here the Committee is to be supported: full morning sessions for legislative business would place an intolerable strain upon the Ministers. The British system, after all, of having Ministers in the House is vastly to be preferred to the American separation of the Executive from the Legislature; but it does mean that men cannot be in two places at once; the Ministers must have the mornings for their Departments.

The Report's third important 'non-proposal' was the despairing: 'We have reviewed alternative methods suggested for providing a closer and more detailed examination of the Estimates, but have concluded that none of these methods is likely to prove more satisfactory than the present arrangements.' The Committee recognized that the Committee of the Whole House 'is no longer capable of conducting a more detailed examination', and that the 'Select Committee on Estimates can admittedly do little more than select certain votes from time to time for close scrutiny'; but it rejected the proposal of the Clerk of the House that particular sections of the Estimates, certainly the Defence Estimates, should be sent to *ad hoc* small, and presumably somewhat specialized, committees for examination by a fixed date.

And the fourth important non-proposal was the rejection of the suggestion by the Labour minority for a Colonial Affairs Committee. It is worth quoting their words rather fully for they illustrate the wilful confusion and stubborn traditionalism around the whole subject:

> The main argument against the proposal, and one which convinces us, lies in the nature of the committee, which in our view would constitute a radical constitutional innovation. . . . Notwithstanding that the order of reference might be drawn in general terms without conferring any express powers of direct interference, there is little doubt that the activities of such a committee would ultimately be aimed at controlling rather than criticizing the policy and actions of the department concerned. In so doing, it would be usurping a function which the House itself has never attempted to exercise. Although the House has always maintained the right to criticize the executive and in the last resort to withdraw its confidence, it has always been careful not to arrogate to itself any of the executive power. The establishment of a colonial committee would not only invade this principle, but also would lead to the establishment of other similar committees. . . . It is even possible that the regulation of discussion to a committee might be misinterpreted in many colonial territories as meaning that the House did not consider their affairs of sufficient importance to be discussed on the floor.

It would be hard to pack more tendentious nonsense into one sober-sounding paragraph. Of course 'criticism' leads to control, but, as we have seen, not necessarily to direct control in Parliament, but to the indirect control that the expectation of meeting an informed electorate creates in a Government. The Select Committee had need to reassure us that 'the House has always maintained the right to criticize the executive'! And why should the terms of reference of any such committee be drawn in 'general terms'? They could be drawn as narrowly as anyone cared if needs be. This was just scare talk. If the matter had not been one of Government policy, one wonders if even a majority of the committee would have agreed to this recommendation.

The Select Committee for all their cautious modesty and loyal desire not to embarrass their leaders, might well have saved their breath to cool their porridge. The report was debated on 13 July, 1959 and 9 February, 1960. There was some brave show of resisting the view of the majority in the committee that any growth of any form of specialized committees meant 'control' in the restrictive sense. But mainly the time was hogged—and this was one of the committee's complaints—by Privy Councillors, notably on the Labour side, very notably by Mr Herbert Morrison, who protested their love and allegiance for what one must call—in modern terms—the unreformed House of Commons. Mr R. A. Butler spoke for the Government in the first debate with a speech of bewitching evasiveness. The furthest he would go on anything important was that part of the Finance Bill might go upstairs in committee: 'all that we have said is that there might be an experiment in that direction'. But there has not been. The idea was repudiated in the next Session. And he thought the proposal for an hour of five-minute speeches in major debates a 'good idea'—and nothing has come of that either. He did deliver himself strongly against the idea of a Colonial Affairs Committee—and had to be interrupted and reminded that the Select Committee had *not* made such a proposal. The fears he had were apparent of what any such committee on procedure was likely to get up to; he plainly found it hard to believe that they had muzzled themselves. He also poured cold water on 'men of genius' who contemplate changing the 'antiquated procedure'. 'The answer may well lie,' he said, 'in the mouth of the younger Pitt, who said that he could not have run the House of Commons at all had not his supporters, the country squires, been extremely stupid.' Mr Butler is, even in his moods of pseudo-Bagehot, a deep and unexpected man—but that is another question.

So the net result was some improvement in the composition of the Standing Committees (but this was mainly to adapt them to the small numbers available for the work); some improvements in the Order Paper and in the notice the

Government must give for the business of the coming week; a reduction in the number of oral questions from three to two, and general support promised to the Speaker in checking the number and length of Supplementary Questions (but no thought of extending Question Time); the establishment of a drafting committee for Standing Orders of the House; and a few very small bits and pieces. But the Government rejected, as well as the Finance Bill proposal, the modest suggestion that drafting assistance be made available to Private Members from the Parliamentary Counsel's office for Private Bills and amendments to Public Bills. In fact no substantial saving of time for more general debate on the Floor—the one important thing the Select Committee were agreed upon—was gained at all. One of the Clerks at the Table has dryly commented: '. . . the limit appears to have been more or less reached in what can be done to economize in time spent on public business without a more radical reform than the House itself is at present prepared to concede'.[6]

The door was finally closed on any radical reform in the debate of 9 February, 1960. In the very next Session the Government was unable to complete its legislative programme through shortage of Parliamentary time, and consequently a number of important measures fell by the wayside, among them the Weights and Measures Bill and the Road Traffic Bill. The absence of a number of promised measures from the 1961–62 programme was excused on the ground that the list was already overcrowded. The Minister of Labour announced the postponement for a year of a long-awaited Bill to deal with the safety, health and welfare of shop and office workers: 'the programme of essential legislation for the current session is already so full that it has been reluctantly decided that there will not be time for the parliamentary examination of this complex and far-reaching measure'.[7] When the Government itself cannot find time for measures it values, one would expect them to give some thought and priority to

[6] R. D. Barlas, 'House of Commons: Report of the Select Committee', p. 43.

[7] Quoted in a *Guardian* leader, 'Parliament and Legislation', 20 November, 1961.

reform of precedure. But what the *Guardian* had called 'the narcissistic tendency' of the House of Commons extends from bottom to top. Ministers like Mr Butler, and former Ministers like Lord Morrison, need reminding that the last real shake-up of Parliamentary procedure took place more than fifty years ago in the time of Campbell-Bannerman. It is certainly time enough, if not too late.

One important matter was beyond the terms of reference of the Select Committee on Procedure: accommodation and physical facilities. Two subsequent debates took up these themes, one largely and other exclusively.[8] Many Members hammered away at the inadequacy of facilities generally and in particular the disappointingly small provision of accommodation in the proposed new Bridge Street site (as we have already noted).[9] Notable speeches were made by Mr Charles Pannell, Mrs Barbara Castle and Mr Richard Marsh, on the Labour side, and by Sir Lionel Heald, Sir Hugh Linstead, and Mr Airey Neave on the Conservative. These extracts may show that not all Members were as unadventurous as the majority on the Select Committee:

Mr Pannell in the debate of 15 March, 1963:

'The first job is to deal with the control of the Palace of Westminster. When I was a shop steward I thought that relationship was everything, and I still think so. I think that control of the Palace of Westminster by the Lord Great Chamberlain is something which we cannot put up with in 1963. . . . The House of Commons is very much subject to the whim of the Ministry of Works, acting almost as a sub-committee of the Treasury, and when the House wants further amenities there is a tendency, after it has resolved to do something to find that a pay pause has intervened and that the project is cut down. So I hope that we shall take over unified control from the Lord Great Chamberlain and set up a body which will manage our own affairs.'

[8] HC *Debates* (673), 15 March, 1963, and HC *Debates* (682), 1 August, 1963.

[9] See pp. 59–60 above.

Mrs Castle in the debate of 1 August, 1963:

'I suggest until we have . . . continuing democratic control over our affairs we shall never get the facilities we need to make us efficient. We all know what they are—and I recognize the reference in the Library Committee's report to the fact that we have for many years been asking for better services. New and young hon. Members often have a scientific background nowadays. . . . They are interested in various technical matters and they need facilities commensurate with the broad and challenging new age in which we live.'

Mr Marsh in the debate of 1 August, 1963:

'Any Member of Parliament who finds the Library adequate cannot be doing a proper job. It is a very brilliant Member of Parliament, who without any previous experience or training, can take on any Minister, with all the help and advice of the civil servants behind him, by popping into his local Library or the Library of the House and looking up a few books. Research is an important and skilled job, and a large section of the membership of this House is incapable of doing it. This is as much a specialized job as being a lawyer or an engine fitter. . . . There is no one in this House to whom one can go to obtain information or a brief on particular subjects. This facility is not a trimming. It is part of the tools of trade of Members of Parliament. This House can do as good a job as any other elected body if it has the facilities.'

Sir L. Heald in the debate of 15 March, 1963:

'I do not think we should regard with horror, as some of my right hon. and hon. Friends do, the possibility of a Committee of this House having technical advisers from outside to help it. It might even be possible—though this is a dreadful thought, some people would say—actually to co-opt such advisers to the Committees. . . . The Government do not like it and our friends the traditionalists tell us that we ought to remain a House of amateurs. I have heard that view expressed very eloquently. It is said, "We have always got on; we do not want to know too much about these scientific and technical matters, and it is much better to have people with a commonsense approach." But even in cricket we have had to give up amateurs. Do not let us have to retain them in the House of Commons.'

Sir H. Linstead in the debate of 1 August, 1963:

'Is the function of the House still to scrutinize and criticize the Executive and to ventilate grievances? If so, is its equipment adequate to discharge that task? If not, how is the equipment to be made available? Is it to be through the Library? Is it to be by creating a new form of secretariat? How is it to be done? Any development of this kind is an uphill task because neither the Executive for the time being nor the potential Executive . . . is particularly anxious to see a large reinforcement of the facilities available to Backbenchers, and we have to face that fact. The most we can hope for is a benevolent inertia. One hon. Gentleman said that the Government must give a lead. I think that in a matter of this kind it is the House which must give a lead, and the House must indicate what it wants and what it does not want, and then it will have to push extremely hard against both Front benches, to achieve what it wants.'

And *Mr A. Neave* in the debate of 15 March, 1963:

'I agree with the hon. Member [Mr C. Pannell] that accommodation is a very important aspect, but however much we improve the conditions in which hon. Members work here, we shall not improve Parliament and make it, as he described it, the great forum of the nation unless we courageously tackle the question of procedure. . . . The public as a whole sees us involved in what have been described elsewhere as "mysterious and esoteric process". Most hon. Members themselves think that our procedures are mysterious and could be much simplified. This means adding to the advisory functions of the House, as distinct from the legislative ones of the moment, a new system of advisory Committees covering the whole field of administration.'

The issue of accommodation can be overrated but, as these extracts show, all these needs and all these possible avenues of reform are related to each other. They form a fairly clear putative system. If one thing is gained, the rest will follow— which is probably why none of them are granted. Mr Macleod, as Leader of the House, spoke for the Government in the debate of 15 March; he said that there were 'constitutional problems' involved in any scheme for specialist committees, but promised as usual, to 'give the most earnest consideration' to everything. Mr Sharples, as Parliamentary Secretary to the Ministry of Works, wound up for the Government in the debate of 1 August; he gave no ground, expressed gratitude for the advice received and said, quite correctly, that he did not think 'the House would expect me to go into the very wide constitutional issues which have been raised'.

The Fear of Specialism

If Parliament is to make itself more effective at all, it must reform its committee system. This means at the very least that far more of its business must be conducted in committee— *both* in order to give adequate scrutiny of matters of detail of Government policy and to give more time for debate on the floor of the House of great matters of public concern. The distinction between detail and general policy does not lead in contrary directions so long as there is a sensible distinction between committee-work and general debate: at the moment there is not. Clearly 'Committee of the Whole' is now a quite indefensible procedure (though there is a traditional pleasure in such a puzzling phrase), and the taking of the detailed Report stage on the floor of the House is, in the case of most Bills, at least very hard to defend. Clearly any extension of the committee system will involve a greater specialization of that system.

Both sides in the procedural debate agreed that doing business by committee and the developing of specialisms become quite inseparable principles once an organization gets past the point where even its active Members cannot grasp the intricacies of much of the business before it. This is why many Ministers and other MPs prefer to jog along uncomfortably with the present procedural arrangements rather than strengthen, by any reform of committees whatever, tendencies towards

specialization among Private Members: they quite rightly see
the one as the thin edge of the wedge towards the other. But
the question is really—as the metaphoricians of Conservatism
usually forget—how far should the wedge be driven, not
whether it should not (when it palpably does) exist at all.
Even those who do not wish to drive this wedge too far have
felt that there are two areas of Government policy in which,
because of their extent and diversity, Parliamentary discussion
has been singularly inadequate and confused and in which
Governmental explanation has been singularly ineffable:
firstly, defence estimates and policy; secondly, colonial affairs.
They are both obvious cases—like the administration of the
Nationalized Industries—where discussions by a standing committee, either in the form of debates or hearings, would be
greatly to the public interest. It is hard to imagine that the
fantastic optimism of defence estimates in recent years could
have survived informed criticism.

The case for a colonial committee was put before the Select
Committee on Procedure, 1959 by Sir Edward Fellowes in
discussion of his evidence and more fully in the wording of a
proposed paragraph for the *Report* moved by Mr Hale, Labour Member for Oldham West. Briefly, Mr Hale suggested
that there should be a Colonial Standing Committee of between 32 and 40 Members established in proportion to party
strength in the House. It should meet for a morning session at
least once a fortnight; subjects for discussion should be chosen
by mutual agreement between members of the committee, and
there should be no motions or voting on any other but procedural matters. One Minister of the Crown responsible for
Colonial matters should be a member of the committee and
any Minister should be entitled to attend. 'We believe,' said
Mr Hale's motion, 'that this proposal would provide an effective means of calling attention to the necessity for redress of
grievances in the colonies in advance of an emergency'—a
grim but true implication about the normal occasions for Parliamentary debate.[10] This was the sole claim for a specialized

[10] It is, after all, a curious tribute to the Mother of Parliaments
that the only sure way her un-Parliamented children can get her
to discuss their affairs is, broadly speaking, by riot or rebellion.

committee put before the Select Committee and it was a minimum claim even of its kind: it did not even propose to give
such a committee power to send for 'persons and papers'; it
did not suggest that the committee should make formal reports to the House, nor yet publish reports or proceedings. It
seemed, in some ways, a slightly regressive proposal, in that
it might create the impression that even reforming MPs are
—once again—obsessed with the virtues of mere debate, as distinct from the need for more premeditation, inquiry and preparation. But, nevertheless, the proposal was rejected—as threatening the powers of the Executive—on a vote of eight to six,
splitting the committee exactly on party lines (the Liberal
Member, Mr Clement Davies, was absent).

Thus even a weak specialized standing committee, on a
topic which it defies credulity to believe that Parliament discusses adequately, was rejected, albeit on party lines. However, there is more cross-bench sentiment in support than the
Conservative vote in the Select Committee's proceedings be-
trays—the time of the Hola camp incident and of the Devlin
Report was not a tactful moment for a Conservative to suggest
the need for a better scrutiny of colonial affairs. But the case
for such a committee—and for one to debate Defence estimates adequately—remains the minimum and urgent ground
for reform of the Parliamentary committee system. And if
two such committees were created forthwith, they would give
the House some evidence on whether to go further by way of
reform or not.

More long-run proposals for reform would, of course, have
to emerge in some manner out of tendencies in the existing
procedure. It is extremely unlikely that sudden new schemes
would be accepted. But the present argument is not that such
tendencies do not exist, they are arising almost inevitably, but
rather that MPs are being singularly slow to recognize them.[11]
Reforms should be seen as growing out of the specialized but

---

[11] See A. H. Hanson and H. V. Wiseman 'The Use of Committees in the House of Commons', *Public Law,* Autumn 1959, pp.
277–92 for an excellent review of the whole history both of the dispute and the actual practices; the article was originally submitted
as evidence to the Select Committee on Procedure, 1959.

unofficial inter-party committees and out of the recent check in the decline of Select Committees as seen in the reports of the Select Committee on Nationalized Industries.

It is for nobody but MPs themselves to work out or evolve a detailed scheme—even though it is overdue for the informed public outside Parliament to insist that MPs make themselves more effective. But a more specialized committee system is likely to emerge in one of two different ways. Firstly, the existing Standing Committees which consider the Committee Stage of legislation could become specialized and then be given powers at least *to debate and discuss,* if not to report upon, the whole subject area of the type of legislation which is sent to them. Or, secondly, Standing Committees could remain unspecialized, or even if specialized, yet remain limited strictly to the scrutiny and amendment of legislation put before them; but alongside them there could grow up a comprehensive pattern of 'standing' Select Committees covering all areas of Government policy, debating and making occasional reports. Either system would be better than the present. And neither need scare any government in particular or the friends of good strong government—by our chaps—in general. Suppose there was a Standing Committee on the Colonies; suppose it was free to debate what it chose; it would still need to approach the whole House before embarking on collecting evidence for a Report—unless it were given an annual appropriation, which is very unlikely. (At the beginning of every Report from a Select Committee the cost is stated of printing and publishing and preparing the shorthand Minutes of Evidence—some £1,052 5s. 6d. for the one under discussion.) And the great power to 'send for persons and papers' is not one that the House is ever likely to delegate wholesale, though there would be no harm in an official specialized committee being allowed to table a motion asking for such powers for such and such a specific purpose.

Any debate or discussion in specialized standing committees would almost inevitably seek to follow as far as possible the experience of the Conservative '1922 Committee' rather than that of the Parliamentary Labour Party, and avoid motions and votes. The sense of the meeting and the published debate in the 'Committee' *Hansard* would speak for themselves. And if the new specialized committees did the work of the present Standing Committees, the Government—through the Committee of Selection—would and should retain the power to add additional Members to a Committee to ensure that Government legislation is passed if their existing majority on any such committee grew—as some profess to fear would happen—threatened by cross-benching follies.

Would not the public interest in the effective criticism of the Executive be greatly served by such a system? Would not the role of the House as a training ground for Ministerial talent be strengthened also? And would not the floor of the House be greatly relieved if at least the Committee Stage of all Bills was sent to one or other of these committees (and possibly, in time, the Report Stage) which would meet in the mornings? And if these committees could also consider estimates for particular Departments or parts of Departments, there would be a solution to what is admitted on all sides to be the inadequate scrutiny of estimates by the quite overwhelmed and under-equipped Select Committee on Estimates. And if either the Library of the House or the office of the Clerk was greatly expanded in personnel and facilities, so that committees could have—on affirmative vote of the House—clerks or research assistants seconded to them, one could then say that the Mother of Parliaments would at last have an organization reasonably adjusted to the complexity of modern administrative life and which would have evolved from one of the most effective, yet neglected, institutions within her—the committees of the two Parties. Such reformed committees, less cumbersome than Royal Commissions, less 'interested' than inter-Departmental committees, could throw light on many dark or obscure corners of modern administration—as did the best of the old Select Committees.

But before suggesting the basis for the precise specialisms and offering a specific outline for functions and powers, it would be best to consider certain objections to the whole principle.

The case for suppressing these tendencies towards more committee work and more specialization is based either on an outright desire to allow the Executive to continue to find it progressively easier to put through its business in the House— suffering random David sling-shots in Question Time, but rarely facing sustained and well-informed scrutiny—or else is based on a vast misunderstanding.

The majority in the recent Select Committee on Procedure rejected, as we have seen, even the modest proposal simply for a Colonial Committee as being 'a radical constitutional innovation'—like, presumably, the Select Committee on Nationalized Industries, and as likely to be aimed at 'controlling rather than criticizing' departmental policy and actions. The essence of this objection is simply a misunderstanding of the distinction between 'criticism' and 'control'. Obviously there is a sense in which all criticism is and should be a form of control. Presumably there are not real grounds on which a Government of a free people should be worried about any potentiality of criticism among its Parliamentary opponents—even among its followers; what worries it is not criticism as such but criticism so protracted through time as to be obstruction. But this is a matter of procedure on which no one is suggesting that the clock be turned back to Parliament before Parnell. By guillotine and closure a Government, governing as a Government has to govern, pushes its business through. In such a circumstance, when actual delay can be used but little by an opposition, it in fact becomes more and more important that the criticism there is should be more concentrated and more informed. Such criticism is, of course, control—in the ultimate sense that it may reach and affect public opinion and affect the government electorally. But the only valid sense of 'control' which would go beyond 'mere' criticism is one in which Parliamentary votes would go against the Government, either on the Floor or in Committee. In the only sense of control that can be a decisive objection to specialized committees, 'control' must mean an increased likelihood of the Government's being overthrown on the Floor of the House, or continuously obstructed by defeats in Committee.

But what is there in a specialized committee system as such that would threaten the basis of control possessed by any government with a working majority? For that control depends not upon the committee system of the House, but upon the historical fact that the powers of patronage, appointment and dissolution have made the Prime Minister also the unquestioned leader of his party, the majority party. He and his Cabinet control Parliament ultimately because no one stands much chance of being elected to the House without the help of a party. And disciplined parties exist not because the House is split down the middle by an aisle (as if they would cease to exist if it sat in a semi-circle), but because England is split down the middle. If one half of England ever comes to feel that it does not need protecting against the other half, then it may begin electing men for the smile on their face or the intelligence in their test and not for their certified likeliness to vote the same way as large numbers of other men. But until that time a Government with a reasonable majority will control the House in the only sense of the word that is a real objection to any committee system whatever.

It will naturally give itself a working majority on every committee and the wrath of the party will be as great and as effective as at present against any Member who treats his party as Burke, the great apostle of party, claimed to treat his constituents. A specialized committee system may complicate the life of the Whips and force them to extend their sphere of operations in, after all, what is their most frequent and important task—not coercing stubborn rebels, but informing willing colleagues what is in fact the issue and the party line on a particular vote;[12] yet such a system cannot destroy the basis of their power: the very fact of party itself.

It is really very odd that those who accuse the proponents of a specialized committee system of 'not understanding our system' themselves seem to have only the groggiest notions of foreign systems. When Mr R. A. Butler replied to the Debate of 31 January, 1958, which led to the establishment of the Select Committee, he warned—not once but several times— against the dangers to our fine old constitution of a committee system 'à l'américaine', as if to put it in French would remove

[12] An MP walks into a room or refocuses his attention and hears a chairman saying: 'The question I have to put is that the words proposed to be left out stand part of the question,' etc.

any lingering doubt among his followers that America is foreign. But no one had used such an argument in relation to executive powers, though several members had cast envious words at the secretarial facilities of American Congressmen, and Mr R. H. S. Crossman and—then—Mr Robert Boothby had bravely and rightly said that all was not rotten in the purely investigatory work of some great Congressional Committees. Mr Butler reverted to this theme again in his appearance before the Select Committee: 'it might well be that such a specialist committee would confound the French and American systems and imagine it had a direct say in the administration of colonial affairs'. And Mr Herbert Morrison had earlier warned the committee against 'importing into our Parliamentary system something like that which the United States and the French have'. But these warnings are strange, somewhat ignorant and certainly unnecessary. For it is not the case that the American committee system led to the separation of the Executive from the Legislature and therefore to periods of Congressional rule, but rather that the original and Constitutional separation of powers led the American Congress to develop specialized and legislating committees. The systems are so radically different that there can be no question of 'importing' anything, except a dubious analogy against the internal reform of our own for reasons of our own.

A more cogent argument was Mr Herbert Morrison's fear that a colonial committee, for example, would throw an almost impossible burden on the Minister. This is indeed something to be guarded against. The Labour Party, in particular, is not likely to forget the sheer physical exhaustion of many of its leaders towards the end of Mr Attlee's second Ministry. But three things should be said. Firstly, it would only be necessary in a non-voting committee for a junior Minister to attend—again by analogy to the 1922 Committee, and then not every time. Secondly, if the Minister himself did on occasion think it necessary to attend, it might stimulate thought about how to rescue himself from too much time-consuming detail within his own Ministry—something in which there is great variation of practice and room for experiment. And thirdly, the Ministerial attitude of automatic resistance to such committees might in any case be unnecessary. L. S. Amery, speaking from his own experience of office, actually thought that such committees would have been helpful to him as a Minister.[13] A committee, controlled by party sentiment, can be a sounding-board and a testing-ground for Ministerial projects; and it could be a valuable help to the Minister in his own problem—in itself almost as great as those we have been discussing—of keeping control of his own Department. Many of the present Party committees have amicable and mutually helpful relationships with Ministers.

Thus the general fear that any strengthening of the critical capacity of the House against the Executive would necessarily weaken our system of Cabinet Government is quite absurd. None of the fundamental controls by which the leader of an elected majority maintains his party's power are in question. It was, is and for ever shall be true that the British Cabinet system is, as A. L. Lowell said, simply an autocracy operating under constant criticism and with the need for periodic re-election. But what has happened is that the complexity of modern legislation and administration has made the Civil Service, with its sources of specialist information, and its elaborate inter-departmental committee systems, far too much the exclusive source of information both for policy making and for the evaluation of policy. The Opposition Members, or even the Government Backbenchers, have retained formal rights and occasions of criticism, but they will continue to lack the ability to make really informed criticism unless they can specialize or employ specialists of their own. If the cry is raised that there would be a danger of creating a 'counter-bureaucracy', one might ask just what is thought to be dangerous in that. On the contrary, it is one of the pressing needs of our time that the MP should not have to depend entirely upon the Government bureaucracy for the knowledge on which he will wish to evaluate their policies. So much of what he needs to know could, indeed, be readily found out for him, either as an individual or as the member of a committee, if he had

[13] See Hansard Society, *Parliamentary Reform* (Cassell, 1961), p. 43, and L. S. Amery, *Thoughts on the Constitution* (Oxford University Press, 1947), pp. 53–54.

access to proper assistance, which in turn would give him the vision of some leisure, some time for thought beyond the pressing business of the day—leisure which would be entirely in the public interest.

Ministerial fear of having a specialist committee trying to run or ruin their Ministry for them is equally unreal, for the party whips would still have the same influence over Members as before. Indeed, these committees could be of the utmost use to many Ministers, if once it were grasped that the problem of Parliamentary control of the Executive is inseparably linked to the Minister's own problem of how to control his own Ministry; and if once it were grasped that of all the outside bodies and interests to which Ministers turn for advice, Parliament itself could be the most useful, for it is the most representative of the least likely to be 'politically unrealistic'.

CHAPTER VIII

WHAT IS LEFT UNDONE

Advice and Investigation

The function of Parliament does not (and normally should not) consist in the threat of overthrowing Governments, but in the need to put relevant facts and fancies before the electorate which does sit in judgement upon Governments. Parliament is the broker of ideas and information; the Government must carry the final risks and responsibilities and the public is the long-suffering client (who often wonders quite who is doing who a favour). If such a function is a more modest one than the stress on legislation and 'control of the Executive' still found in the text books and on the after-dinner lips of Parliamentarians, yet Parliament is less well equipped for this modern task than it was for the nineteenth century task of influencing legislation.

What has happened is fairly plain. Both the power of the modern Executive and its scope have increased. This has happened, basically, because electorates have wanted it. There is no challenging this. But the procedures of Parliament mainly point in one direction which is, in fact, the least likely direction to help the public or to help or restrain governments: that of scrutinizing Government legislation and of constantly voting for or against the whole party power of the Government in the Commons. But scrutiny of the vastly increased scope of modern administration is badly underdeveloped. The nineteenth century assumption was that the electorate was only interested in the matters of legislation for which the Government took political responsibility. But the mid-twentieth century reality is that there is hardly anything on which the electorate is not prepared to hold the Government responsible, and, irritating though this is to particular Governments, it is the politics of our times: governments must be responsible for all those things that concern their citizens collectively. Therefore Parliament must be judged not merely for its efficiency in scrutinizing the things for which Ministers are legally responsible, but also for its effectiveness in airing and clarifying matters on which the public are concerned and—the true test of political wisdom—in anticipating the matters on which the public are likely to become concerned.

Here great gaps in the critical and informative function of Parliament appear. We have already seen the decline of Select Committees of the House of Commons in this century and the rise of Departmental and Inter-departmental committees to advise the Government on the methods, means and ends of public policy. The expert skill of these new committees is often beyond question. But they suffer from an inherent defect in any system where the ultimate restraints on government depend on an informed public opinion: their proceedings are almost invariably private and their reports often confidential.

The view of how great the gap is, of course, will depend on the assessment of the effectiveness of present Parliamentary procedures. But all these procedures, whether the work of the Select Committee on Estimates or the whole institution of Question Time, offer only 'spot checks', never a complete survey of the policies and actions of the Executive. This would be so in any organization as large as the modern State; but it is, indeed, a question of degree. It is never possible for everything to be looked into or discussed; but the presumption should be that as much as possible ought to be scrutinized by Parliament. This is certainly not the presumption of the modern Executive. If there is doubt, it is always resolved in favour of the Executive.

There must be, we are told, no Court of Administrative Appeals over the whole range of public tribunals, for this would interfere with Ministerial responsibility. There also must not be any single, central advisory committee on the substance of judgements, but only a Council on Tribunals to keep an eye on procedural matters. There must not be anything as un-British as an Ombudsman (or Parliamentary Commissioner, as in New Zealand recently). But there also must not be any growth of Parliamentary committees to fill the gap of Parliamentary responsibility and public concern. If the Government actually feels the need to shuffle off some responsibility and to get some new ideas in matters that have plainly got beyond it, then it creates a National Economic Development Council quite outside Parliament. And if need should arise for some thorough inquiry into some politically important impropriety or illegal action by a Minister, then a special tribunal under a Judge is established (under the Tribunals of Inquiry Act, 1921), no longer a Select Committee of the House of Commons.

The case of the National Economic Development Council is instructive. Its mixed composition, vague terms of reference, lack of real powers, but intended mission of planning and conciliation was clearly influenced by the French *Commissariat Général du Plan*. Jean Monnet's conception was that of the *'économie concertée'* in which all forms of enterprise, private and public, would consult together to form plans for a forward-looking economy. 'Planning must be done by those planned. Hence the planning authority must not be part of the ordinary Government service, but a new representative body, the members representing important firms, employers' organizations, trade unions, consumers, and experts (mostly academic).'[1] Its composition is peculiar—three Government Ministers, six trade unionists, six industrialists, two chairmen of nationalized industries and two economists; and its direct powers are none. It issues reports on goals, trends and priorities, though it has not yet become a planning body in any detailed sense. The Ministers who attend its meetings plainly do not feel bound by its conclusions, and nor is the Council bound by Government policy. But its influence is likely to be considerable. It has no power, but it has authority. Governments may ignore it, but since it appears to be authoritative, and for so long as it sounds authoritative, they will at least think twice before doing so. They may find themselves involved not in legal, but in *political* difficulties if they ignore it completely.

[1] See Joan Mitchell's excellent 'The Functions of the National Economic Development Council', *Political Quarterly,* October 1963, pp. 355–56.

And by the same token, the Council, while it can say anything, will undoubtedly be restrained by what it considers politically possible.

The NEDC is, in one sense, a symptom of the decline of Parliament. For when the Government does go outside Whitehall for advice, it takes care to by-pass Westminster. This may, in fact, be politically unwise—if such *planification* is to succeed it must carry the Opposition at least some of the way with it; but, the point is, the Government does not think so. Yet, in another sense, the NEDC demonstrates that Governments can set up authoritative-sounding advisory committees without risking their political control over Parliament (and, presumably, without fearing any bad electoral consequences). The function of NEDC makes the objections that Defence and Colonial committees, for instance, would infringe Ministerial responsibility sound like some ritual and no longer comprehensible utterances from out of a far distant past.

Its existence also raises a new issue. There are grounds for thinking that it might be strengthened if it included among its members, say, the Backbench chairmen of the Private Members' finance committees of the two main Parties. This would both help Parliament inform itself—and thus the country—better, and help to anchor NEDC down to political possibilities, prevent it becoming—as it possibly, and dangerously, might —quite literally 'irresponsible'. But, in the nature of the case, it is unlikely that a committee composed only of MPs could fill the intended role and do the necessary work, even sitting with economic advisers and even if it were a committee as 'representative' of differing interest which could easily be arranged as is the composition of NEDC. Clearly, for such work of mingled investigation and advice, there is scope for an almost infinite range of different compositions according to the task at hand. Why should not 'hybrid committees', composed of MPs, members of the Second Chamber, outside experts and civil servants, become a normal part of Government and Parliament?

The need for Parliament to become a centre of information, something that broadcasts ideas and facts relevant to political decisions rather than obstructs Government business, may lead more and more towards hybrid committees—particularly since one of the problems of our times is that of mutual comprehension between technical expert and politician. There exists a very large number of advisory committees upon which MPs do not serve, but could do so and to mutual advantage. For instance, one thinks of the National Production Advisory Committee on Industry, the National Advisory Council for the Motor Manufacturing Industry, the Advisory Council on Child Care, the Advisory Council on Scientific Research and Technical Development, the Television Advisory Committee, and the Agricultural Improvement Council for England and Wales—to give a variety of quite important examples.[2] Some examples could perhaps be found in which attendance by MPs would be inappropriate. There are some on which it would be illegal for MPs to serve under the terms of the House of Commons Disqualification Act, 1957, since payment is made. And there are some in which MPs are already to be found, either out of deliberate policy by the Ministers who make the appointments (as in the Advisory Panel on the Highlands and Islands of Scotland), or by virtue of some other function (some industrial consultative committees find that business associations or trade unions nominate members who are also MPs to serve on them). We have already seen that the normal committee system of the two Parliamentary Parties is more sensibly organized for an informed conduct of business than the official system of the House itself; but we should add to these examples of *ad hoc* 'hybrid committees' of Members and outside specialists or experts. The Parliamentary Labour Party's working party on Pensions and their committee on Science have both produced an extremely important fusion of political and expert knowledge.

So NEDC may serve as a rough model for the future, not the great exception. For what is important about it is that it mixes Ministers with outside interests and experts without any of them quibbling too much about 'responsibility' or, what it more often amounts to, fearing political guilt by association. If it is surprising enough and, in some sense, heartening that the Government established it at all, it is equally surprising

[2] See *Advisory Committees in British Government* (PEP and Allen and Unwin, 1960), pp. 58–60. See also Appendix F, below.

and heartening that the TUC, after much anxious debate, decided to join. But it is a very rough and imperfect model. It needs to be broadened out to include MPs. For just as there need to be more Select Committees of Parliament able to make use of outside knowledge, so existing outside advisory committees need to make more use of MPs.[2]

For MPs do have a very valuable and specific kind of knowledge rarely possessed by outside experts, civil servants or even, one should dangerously add, by Ministers who may have been in office too long: *political knowledge*.[3] They know that politics is the art and skill of conciliating, in some creative manner, differing interests. Individually politicians represent differing interests (both ideal and material); collectively they function to measure the differing strengths of these interests. If there is to be anything like *planification* in Britain—the positive task, or even more effective control of the administration —the essential negative task, then it would seem absurd to pass over that very body which best represents all the many differing interests whose support must be gained if these things are to be achieved.

Here is a theoretical issue so profound that people who take their theories completely for granted can only gaze at each other with blank incomprehension when their decisive practical objections do not appear to register at all. For to the objection that MPs would introduce a disruptive political element, we can reply that they would, indeed, introduce a political element, but that *the political element is normally a constructive one*. This is really the root of the *malaise* in contemporary British government—the belief that is growing up in Downing Street and Whitehall that if anything useful is to be done, it must be taken out of politics. It is this kind of non-political conservativism, frequently even striving to be 'above politics', and based on a confused view not merely of Parliament and Government but of politics and government, which obstructs both proper planning and proper control. There has grown up a cult of 'Wise Men' who are to be consulted if

[2] See *Advisory Committees in British Government* (PEP and Allen and Unwin, 1960), pp. 58–60. See also Appendix F, below.
[3] As even Lord Morrison of Lambeth, argues in his *Government and Parliament* (Oxford, 1954), p. 275.

anything 'goes wrong', distinguished public figures, but never politicians, all with an aura of 'very responsible fellows indeed' about them, to hide how politically irresponsible they are. For *political* decisions must be made by politicians: firstly, because that is their job and they are more experienced at it than the distinguished outsiders; and secondly, because politicians can be hurt—can be held responsible. The electorate can catch up on a Party, but it is next to impossible, it appears, to catch up on the folly of a 'distinguished public figure' or a high civil servant. But political *advice* should come from different quarters—political *and* lay (whether experts or 'wise men').

The truth is that if anything useful and significant is to be done in a free society, it must be done publicly and in such a way as to consult, involve and carry with it those affected. This is the function of politics. Experts advising in private can only affect matters of small public concern, unless Governments are desperate or so lacking in political skill that they spring great new measures upon an unprepared public. Quite obviously, any Government that wants to do great new things needs public awareness, support and participation far more than one that chooses to do little. In this sense Conservative Parties are always more likely to practice private government, or what Professor Ely Devons has called 'government on the inner circle',[4] than are Socialist or Radical Parties. These latter have, indeed, often been accused of being unfit to govern simply because of their tradition of taking soundings and making decisions publicly—or at least of talking freely about what is nominally conducted in private. But Conservative journalists have probably misled Conservative politicians. The weakness may in fact be a political strength. The true fault of Socialist governments, here and elsewhere, is often to stick grimly to publicly decided policies even when circumstances change or prove untimely; but the real fault of the recent Conservative administrations has been to hold their cards so high and to keep the lights so low that they have blinded themselves to the play upon the table. There has been of late an excessive in-

[4] Professor Ely Devons, 'Government in the Inner Circle', *The Listener,* 27 March, 1958.

formality in the way of 'taking soundings' before legislation
and an excessive secrecy about the processes of administration, both of which have led to great mistakes being made
through sheer lack of preparation and information. This is the
point where Conservatism and conservatism touch in the matter of Parliament. But it is not to deny, indeed to reiterate
sadly, that procedural conservatism pervades the older Labour
leadership who have had Ministerial experience, and begins
to corrupt the young as the spell of office grows upon them.

Consider three areas, not of major policy, but all important,
in which recent Governments have blundered into highly unpopular decisions, or found themselves creating a constant
source of troubles and sores: the control of aliens, police powers in relation to public meetings, and various anomalies in
election laws (the Benn and Bristol case, the problem of candidates from the Armed Services, concern about election expenditure in relation to the short period of the official campaign, and the curious working or interpretation of the law
as it touches the televising of politics, particularly at General
Elections). Each of these topics raises the kind of tricky mixture of law, fact and politics which MPs and some members
of a Second Chamber would seem ideally equipped to clarify
and advise upon, if only to act as a sounding board, at greater
depth than proceedings on the Floor of the House allow but
still without in any way impairing Ministerial responsibility.
The Government will have to make up its mind how to legislate, but it defies credulity to believe that advice both clear
and politically viable, say, on election law and television, is
more likely to come out of Whitehall than Westminster. It
almost shocks one that the Public Order Act 1963 or the Commonwealth Immigration Act 1962 were not discussed, either
as general issues or in some putative form, by a Select Committee of Parliament before ever the Bills were introduced.

Consider the Profumo affair. It is instructive to do so because it shows the weakness of the present dominance of the
'executive mind' over Parliament. Firstly, it shows the excessive trust that a Prime Minister could put in political friendship
rather than in publicly known procedures; and, secondly, it
shows that even when only Parliament was able to expose the

matter, Parliament was not then allowed to investigate and report upon it. Despite Opposition outcry, the procedure of the Tribunal of Inquiries Act was invoked so as to appoint not a Select Committee of the House, but a Judge with large and vague powers. (One might naïvely think that since the whole object of the exercise was to satisfy the Opposition, that their wish should be met—particularly at a time when the administration of justice was itself in some question; but it was made clear that it was 'the general public' who were to be satisfied by a Judge and not Parliament—again the assumption of a non-political public and of de-politicized methods of making political judgements).

Lord Denning himself had this to say (Paragraph 5 of the *Report*):

It has been much debated what is the best way to deal with matters such as those referred to me. The appointment of a tribunal under the Tribunal of Inquiries Act, 1921, is an elaborate and costly machine, equipped with all the engines of the law—counsel, solicitors, witnesses on oath, absolute privilege, openness to the public (so far as possible) and committal for contempt—but it suffers from the invincible drawback, in doing justice, that there is no prosecution, no charge, and no defence. The appointment of a Select Committee of one or both Houses of Parliament is a very representative body, but it is said to suffer from the drawback (to some eyes) that the inquisitors are too many and may be influenced in their, often divergent, views by political considerations, so that there may be too much dissent to carry authority. Now there is this inquiry which I have been entrusted with *alone*. It has the advantage that there can be no dissent, but it has two great disadvantages: first, being in secret, it has not the appearance of justice; second, in carrying out the inquiry, I have had to be detective, inquisitor, advocate and judge, and it has been difficult to combine them. But I have come to see that it has three considerable advantages. First, inasmuch as it has been held in private and in strict confidence, the witnesses were, I am sure, much more frank than they would otherwise have been. Secondly, I was able to check the evidence of one witness against that of another more freely. Thirdly, and most important, aspersions cast by witnesses against others (who are not able to defend themselves) do not achieve the publicity which is inevitable in a Court of Law or Tribunal of Inquiry.

This is a remarkable passage. Lord Denning himself throws doubt on the justice of such a procedure and then proceeds to give three advantages all of which could be gained within the procedural flexibility of Select Committees. He does note that a Select Committee could be drawn from either or both Houses and that the 'drawback' of divergent political considerations is only a drawback 'to some eyes'. Again, to other eyes this might seem an advantage. If it is hoped that some absolute truth can be arrived at on a matter of fact (perhaps *more* the case in the Lynskey Tribunal of 1948, the Bank Rate Leak Tribunal of 1957 and the Waters Tribunal of 1959 than in the Radcliffe or Denning Tribunals), then the case is strong for an independent judicial tribunal (though it might be still stronger for a Select Committee of the Second Chamber composed of Law Lords). But when Denning was asked 'to consider any evidence there may be for believing that national security has been, or may be, endangered', then the matter appears so inherently one of politics and political judgement that the 'representative' and 'divergent . . . political considerations' which would be found in a Select Committee of the House of Commons seem not a drawback, but a great advantage. The public would surely be better served and the real issues clarified by having, since politics is inevitable, the divergent viewpoints put before them, rather than to have a Judge asked to assess matters of national security and, indeed, air his views, inevitably personal, on 'the honour and integrity of public life' (the famous supererogatory Part IV of the Report).

Where party warfare and divergent judgements are inevitable, better that they are clarified and fairly stated by the device, if necessary, of minority reports and individual reservations, than that a Judge should be drawn into political matters which are the responsibility and function of Parliament. Better to have politicians trying to act in a semi-judicial capacity than to have Judges being required to act in a semi-political capacity. There are grave risks that the reputation for impartiality of Judges is endangered (particularly in the circumstances of the Profumo case and the prosecution of the late Stephen Ward; and the very mixed reception that the Government gave Mr Justice Devlin's report on the disturbances in East Africa might well have been remembered, both by the Government in appointing Denning and by Denning in accepting). And there are even more obvious risks that Governments will shuffle off their political responsibility, trusting in the discretion of a Judge arrogated to be the arbiter of national security, rather than to state clearly their own case and account of the things alongside less inhibited rival accounts and interpretations from the Opposition leaders and Backbench MPs.

The only study there has been of the working of Tribunals of Inquiry has commented: 'it is noticeable that as the number of Tribunals increases, the function of this fact-finding organization is found increasingly to be to establish what the facts are, and to leave the final verdict on the propriety of what has been done to public opinion'.[5] This is how tribunals have reacted to the inherent difficulty of their task—wisely if the Judiciary is to maintain its independence. But the nature of the cases put before them leave the public in need for greater guidance than this—indeed Denning did not hesitate to comment on the propriety of everyone's actions. The guidance could best come from having had the *divergent* interpretations clearly stated after a procedure at least more deliberative than that of debates on the Floor of Parliament. This case is put in extreme terms. In fact, there may be danger of underestimating the degree of detachment with which MPs can together arrive at a fair statement of the evidence on such matters, even though they then go on to draw different conclusions. If a matter seems inherently political, then a Select Committee of the House of Commons should be established. If a matter seems *more* purely fact-finding, then a Select Committee of the Upper House (particularly of a reformed Second Chamber which would become virtually a 'House of Scrutiny').

[5] George W. Keeton, *Trial By Tribunal* (Museum Press, 1960), p. 223.

There is room for judgement here. But there is more room in which to insist both that the working of the Tribunal of Inquiries Act is unsatisfactory, and that its use is a very prominent symptom of the decline of Parliament and the distrust of politics.

There is another most curious, large and important, general field of concern which the existing devices of Parliamentary control leave quite as full of holes as fences: civil liberties. Here one normally thinks, and normally it is true, that Parliament is at its very best. The traditional rights of the subject are jealously guarded by Questions and motions on the adjournment. Backbenchers have become famous through their passionate ransacking of the uttermost recesses of Parliamentary procedure when the rights of the subject are at stake; and they are well aided in this by the press, radio and particularly television.

But there are great gaps. The very concept 'civil liberties' until quite recently seemed somewhat un-British, the kind of over formalized thing the Americans needed while we rested secure in our traditional 'rights of the subjects' as defined by the Courts and the proceedings of Parliament.[6] But recently the concept is on everyone's lips. The number of matters which are determined by Ministerial discretion and are not normally reviewable by the Courts causes concern, and Parliament, although aroused, does not always seem to have provided any remedy. A series of deportation or extradition orders, those against Dr Soblen and Chief Enahoro particularly, have shown how little the Executive may be affected by Parliamentary opinion, although in the case of Miss Carmen Bryan, the Jamaican girl who was to be deported after a charge of shoplifting, the Home Secretary did yield. The Bar Council's investigation in 1956 of charges of unprofessional conduct against the barrister Marrinan brought to light, and produced justifications, of the practice of telephone tapping and the interception of mails by the police and security

[6] It is strange to think that Professor Harry Street's most able *Freedom, the Individual and the Law* (Penguin, 1963) is the first comprehensive book, as he correctly claims, on this subject in Britain. Presumably the need was not felt before.

services—all hedged around with talk of 'crown prerogative'.
A recent series of scandals in relation to nepotism, corruption and brutality in Police Forces have shown that MPs may
not even be able to question the Home Secretary on many of
these matters since they are generally not his responsibility,
unless they concern the Metropolitan Police, but that of Local
Authorities. Some of the proceedings of Local Authorities
themselves, both in relation to the police and the press, have
caused similar difficulties and concern. The granting of political asylum seems to be exercised in a manner so much more
illiberal than a hundred years ago. The Lord Chamberlain's
exercise of prerogative powers in relation to the censoring of
plays cannot be challenged in law—and some sadly stupid
decisions continue to be made. The discretion of the Home
Secretary in allowing public meetings in the Metropolitan
police area and the conduct of the police at some of those
meetings have similarly aroused grave concern, but resulted
in little more than nibbling attacks and attempts at clarifica-
tion in Parliament. And the fact that the clearest result of
the Vassal Inquiry was to put two journalists in prison for not
revealing their sources of information was, if debatable on
both sides, unexpected. It has become clear that freedom to
travel is limited by the fact that the granting of a passport is
a matter of the exercise of the royal prerogative, not something to which any British citizen is entitled. And Britain has
no laws to protect people against discrimination on grounds
of race and colour, although the courts have shown com-
mendable severity on persons committing offences in racial
disturbances (Mr Justice Salmon was clearly moved by considerations of public policy in the sentences he gave during
the Notting Hill disturbances of 1958).

Here, again, are questions of public policy (not just of administrative or legal practice) which all involve a mixture of
the inadequacy of the present law and of the machinery of
Parliamentary surveillance. 'Civil Liberties' is an area in which
one might expect permanent machinery for consultation between the Government and Parliament in relation to the
formulation of policy, both on the use of discretionary powers and the possible need for new legislation. It seems hard to

deny the need, as Professor Street concludes after surveying the whole field, of some form of permanent Civil Rights Commission.[7]

Administration and the Citizen

It was once the custom to petition Parliament for the redress of grievances arising from the actions of the Executive. Nowadays this is seldom done, except by way of political demonstration, and the few petitions received will not be debated. The Parliamentary Question is now the effective device that may follow from a citizen's writing to an MP, perhaps after an unsuccessful correspondence with a Government Department if he thinks that he has been unfairly or improperly treated by some branch of the administration.

The volume of complaints, however, is such that Parliament can only deal with those of real political importance, or of sufficient importance to individual rights to be potentially politically important. The matter will be investigated by the Department responsible who will alone have access to the files. The Minister may stonewall and then the most that an MP can do is then to keep on nagging at him, in and out of Parliament; only in extreme cases will there be any chance of forcing an independent inquiry—such as the Crichel Down case, the Chalk Pit affair or the 'Thurso boy' incident. As Professor John Griffith said in evidence to the Franks Committee:

I do not think that the theory of the constitution would say that there has ever been at any point in history a really completely effective control by Parliament of the whole of the administrative process. I think that the function of Parliament in these matters is to pick up things which do occur, and which members either get to know of or are informed about. The whole system of Parliamentary control

[7] Street, *Freedom, the Individual and the Law,* p. 288. One hopes that this book will get debated in the House of Lords as did Professor H. H. Wilson's book on the commercial television lobby.

is fundamentally a spot-check system, and it cannot be an entirely comprehensive one.[8]

The problem, as we have seen, has grown more intense both with the size and scope of modern government administration and with new methods: the growing use of delegated legislation and the gradual growth of administrative tribunals in all sorts of fields of administration to consider grievances and cases and to advise the Minister, or for various forms of public inquiries to be held before a Minister, a Local Authority, or some other public body may make a decision. Lawyers disliked both delegated legislation and the new quasi-judicial tribunals. A vigorous campaign against these specific things reached its climax between 1945 and 1951, and distrust of bureaucracy in general received a new lease of life from the Crichel Down case: the campaign which began with what Professor Brian Chapman has called Lord Hewart's 'insane masterpiece', *The New Despotism* of 1929. Hewart's colleagues and disciples argued that the Civil Service had replaced Parliament as the effective centre of government in Great Britain, and '. . . in some of the wilder writers we find dark hints of a conspiracy to dispossess the legislature and to govern by orders and regulations'.[9]

By the 1950s, however, most lawyers, having had some actual and less sensational experience of the working of tribunals, had come round to join the heresy of a few academics that the need was not for rejection, but for system. Professor W. A. Robson's *Justice and Administrative Law* of 1928 was the trenchant and learned gospel of this movement, ever in revised editions but always pointing to the need for a system of administrative law and for something like the French *Conseil d'État* to watch over the whole administration and to be a final court or tribunal of appeal for all those Ministerial powers which, while exercised by the Civil Service, yet escaped both the control of the Courts and Parliamentary control in any regular manner.

[8] *Report of the Committee on Administrative Tribunals and Enquiries,* Cmnd 218 of 1957, p. 984.

[9] Brian Chapman, 'The Ombudsman', *Public Administration,* Winter 1960, p. 306.

Thus following the Crichel Down case, and the general wave of concern for civil liberties, the Franks Committee was set up to inquire into (*a*) 'the constitution and working of tribunals, other than the ordinary courts of law, constituted under any Act of Parliament'; and (*b*) 'the working of such administrative procedures as include the holding of an inquiry or hearing by or on behalf of a Minister on an appeal or as a result of objections or representations, and in particular the procedure for the compulsory purchase of land'.[10]

The Tribunals and Inquiries Act of 1958 put into law many of the recommendations of the Franks Committee. These did *not* involve the creation of any true system of administrative law, but the Act did create a Council on Tribunals. It has three principal functions: to keep under review the constitution and working of specified tribunals (about 2,000); to consider and report on particular matters that anyone may refer to them; and to consider and report on administrative procedures which involve inquiries on behalf of or for a Minister when required by statute. They must also be consulted before tribunals change their procedures, or before a Minister, in the case of a statutory inquiry, may be exempted from the requirement to give reasons for his decisions. The Council appears from its Reports to be very active and to have done much good work in obtaining more procedural uniformity between Tribunals and more respect for their decisions, the aftermath of the Chalk Pit case, from Ministers.

But the limitations of the Franks Report soon became apparent. As Professor K. C. Wheare wrote: 'Many people were surprised to find that the redress of grievances arising out of the greater part of public administration in Great Britain were not covered by the terms of reference of the Franks Committee.'[11] They had been limited to the field of administration in which there were already tribunals or procedures of inquiry authorized by statute. The greater part of

[10] See W. A. Robson 'Administrative Justice and Injustice: a Commentary on the Franks Report', *Public Law*, Spring 1958, pp. 12–31, for an excellent summary and critique.

[11] 'The Redress of Grievances', *Public Administration*, Summer 1962, p. 125.

public administration was beyond their terms of reference (including the Crichel Down case itself), as was the task of laying down any sensible criterion to determine whether there should be tribunals in other fields of government activity. Professor John Griffith kept up the attack:

> The real issue . . . is whether we in this country are prepared to accept, perhaps as an experiment, the idea of an independent inquisitorial body with the power to ask Ministers to justify their actions. This must be a limited idea. It must not take the place of Parliament, the press, and other public institutions where the policy of Ministers is criticized. But there are two sorts of complaint, often closely connected, which do not appear to be adequately catered for in our present system. The first is the complaint that a particular procedure has worked unfairly. The second is that an individual has suffered, as the result of administrative action, to an extent which others in a similar position have not suffered. The Council [on Tribunals] could not directly force the department to alter its decisions. But its independent criticism, after investigation, would have considerable influence.[12]

Articles in the *Observer*[13] and elsewhere[14] began to interest people in a Scandanavian institution, the Ombudsman. The Danish form was the most cited and the general idea was that there should simply be, as New Zealand established in October 1962, a 'Parliamentary Commissioner' with power to investigate complaints and report on them, who would certainly require access, subject to various safeguards, to Departmental papers.

An independent legal organization called 'Justice' established a committee to carry on from where the Franks Report was forced to leave off. Its report was published in

[12] John Griffith, 'The Council and the Chalk Pit', *Public Administration,* Winter 1961, p. 374.

[13] See articles in the *Observer* for 31 May and 7 June, 1959; 10 and 31 January, and 11 December, 1960; and 12 June, 1961.

[14] See especially the three articles and the editorial comment in *Public Law,* Spring 1962 (with references to earlier articles in the same persistent journal), and Geoffrey Marshall, 'Should Britain Have an Ombudsman?', *The Times,* 23 April, 1963.

1961 as *The Citizen and the Administration*—gathering all
the kind of evidence, being composed of much the same sort
of eminent people and being printed much in the form of a
Royal Commission. The Prime Minister had already promised
in the House that the Government would give its conclusions
the most earnest consideration.

Sir John Whyatt and his colleagues came out in favour of
the creation of a Parliamentary Commissioner having a status
similar to that of the Comptroller and Auditor General. Sir
Oliver Franks wrote a Foreword underlining the narrow terms
of reference his committee had laboured under and indicat-
ing his sympathy for Whyatt's unofficial venture. And Lord
Shawcross set the stage in a Preface:

> With the existence of a great bureaucracy there are in-
> evitably occasions, not insignificant in number, when
> through error or indifference, injustice is done—or appears
> to be done. The man of substance can deal with these situa-
> tions. He is near to the establishment; he enjoys the status
> or possesses the influence which will ensure him the ear
> of authority. He can afford to pursue such legal remedies
> as may be available. He knows his way around. But too
> often the little man, the ordinary humble citizen, is in-
> capable of asserting himself. The little farmer with four
> acres and a cow could never have attempted to force the
> battlements of Crichel Down.

The Whyatt Report went on to consider two categories of
complaint: complaints against discretionary decisions, and
complaints against maladministration.

To deal with complaints against discretionary decisions it
suggested that there should be machinery embodying 'the
principle of impartial adjudication', the right of appeal to
some independent authority. The Council on Tribunals should
have its powers extended to survey those areas of Ministerial
discretion where decisions are made which are not at present
subject to appeal, and should be required to make proposals
for bringing such areas into the system of tribunals and inquiries where at all possible. We have already made clear
what we think of such chimeras of 'impartial adjudication' in
matters of *policy* (which is often itself a polite word for poor

old 'politics'). If the Minister is given discretion because flexibility in the application of public policy is thought to be needed, it is for him alone to carry the responsibility for its exercise; and it is Parliament's job to hold him to that responsibility.

But Chapter 9 of the Report did state cogent reasons why Questions in Parliament, even if increased in number, are not likely to be a remedy for complaints against maladministration. Parliament was already overloaded with work. Parliamentary Questions were usually framed not so much as a request for information as an accusation against a Government Department that it had failed to discharge its duties properly. Furthermore, the Department concerned carries out the investigation into the alleged offence; the investigation is based on documents which are not available to the person making the complaint; controversial matters of detail cannot be dealt with in the space of a single answer; and the complaints tend to become matters of party controversy making the Government unreasonably defensive on every point. They also pointed to the expense and delay involved in Departmental or other committees of inquiry, especially those under the Tribunals Act of 1921 (which has, indeed, only been invoked fifteen times).

Therefore, the Justice committee came out for this un-British thing, a Parliamentary Commissioner. Legal opinion has certainly turned a full circle since the days of Dicey's two fixed points of the Rule of Law and the Sovereignty of Parliament. They suggested, of course, certain safeguards. At first he should only receive complaints from MPs themselves, but later, as his jurisdiction became established and understood, he might receive complaints direct from the public. The Minister concerned should be able to veto the proposed investigation (but then, of course, to shoulder the political obloquy of having done so). The Parliamentary Commissioner should have access to files but not to minutes, so as to disrupt the informal workings of departments as little as possible. He should publish an annual report picking out cases of special importance, which would then be debated (not merely the cases but his conduct of his office, presumably).

The Government made its promised statement about eight months after the Report came out. It was a short and almost casual statement. Both Houses were simply offered 'the familiar dogmatic statement'[15] that the work of such an official would be incompatible with the responsibility of Ministers in a Cabinet system on the British model (quite ignoring the launching of such an office in New Zealand).

> The Government consider there are serious objections in principle. . . . They believe that any substantial extension of the system of reference to tribunals would lead to inflexibility and delay in administration, and that the appointment of such an officer would seriously interfere with the prompt and efficient dispatch of public business. In the Government's view there is already adequate provision under our constitutional and Parliamentary practice for the redress of any genuine complaint of maladministration, in particular by means of the citizen's right of access to Members of Parliament.[16]

The Editors of *Public Law* described this statement as 'disreputable' and commented that it was 'almost unbelievable' that such a document could be produced: 'for it reveals a state of mind which is exactly what all the fuss is about'.[17] It is, indeed, hard not to admire, in a perverse kind of way, the complacency of it and the easy way that the metaphysic of 'Ministerial responsibility' is used to eliminate any need for argument based on evidence or any examination of the facts. Plainly no such officer need effect the political responsibility of Ministers to the electorate, nor their political control over Parliament; but he could put back some real meaning into Parliamentary responsibility (for owning up and explaining why). Ministerial responsibility now means, in practice, irresponsibility: that the man legally responsible for doing something is the one who has to say that he is not constitutionally responsible for giving anyone any reasons why he did it.

There is a real and great problem. And an Ombudsman, in some form or another, might help the public in their

[15] G. Marshal, 'Should Britain Have an Ombudsman?', *op. cit.*
[16] HC *Debates* (666), 8 November, 1962, c.1125.
[17] *Public Law,* Winter 1962, p. 392.

difficulties and, more fundamentally, help them maintain confidence in the justice and efficiency of the whole system. Professor K. C. Wheare, no extremist, called the Whyatt proposals 'practical, sensible and worth trying . . . though . . . they are modest proposals and cannot be expected to do more than produce modest results'.[18] But one cannot help feeling that when so many noble, legal and academic minds turn to such a radical innovation there is an element in it of paper protest at the seeming incapacity or unwillingness of Parliament itself to provide the remedy. This may be pot calling kettles black. But which is the more realistic something-between-hope-and-fantasy: that a British Government will allow an Ombudsman or that a British Parliament will reform its committee system?

Sir Edward Fellowes, procedurally a moderate-extremist, has written:

> I do not think that an Ombudsman would work in this country. Such an institution creates a super-bureaucrat outside the responsibility of the Government but presumably answerable to the House of Commons, who would then have to set up a committee to control him. In my view it would be better to have the committee to whom the grievances could be brought and by whom they could be investigated. . . . Before departing from the traditional methods I would suggest for the individual Member a greater use of the non-oral Question . . . and for the House itself the revival of the Select Committee as an instrument of inquiry.[19]

It is conceivable, just, that if public concern continues to grow, the Executive might prefer the refined researches of an Ombudsman to the rough manners of Parliamentary Select Committees—particularly if exactly the right kind of person could be found to set the tone of the office (someone nearer, for example, an official of the Public Record Office in temperament than an Inspector of Police Establishments for the Midlands area). However, Sir Edward Fellowes's point is hard to evade: if an Ombudsman, then a committee

[18] K. C. Wheare, 'The Redress of Grievances', *op. cit.*
[19] Sir Edward Fellowes, 'Parliament and the Executive', *Journal of the Parliaments of the Commonwealth,* July 1962, p. 346.

to control him; if such a committee, why an Ombudsman at all? What the Ombudsman agitation has done is not so much to point to a viable solution, but to illuminate the character of the grievances which need some regular form of attention if British government is not to grow more and more irresponsible.

It is hard to better the words of an extremist (though on other matters of Governmental organization), Professor Brian Chapman:

> . . . it may be argued that it is better to have someone investigate the constable who slaps an errand boy than no one at all. But I would argue that this diverts attention from the basic point at issue in all this discussion. The control of public administration is above all a political matter which can ultimately be solved only by political means. It is perfectly proper for writers and publicists to be concerned at the extent of the arbitrary powers of the Executive in this country today; but it is quite unreasonable to turn on public servants for being responsible for this situation.
>
> The failure lies squarely on Parliament, and to some extent on the Parliamentary leaders. It is indeed an indication of decline in the status of Parliament and the standing of Members of Parliament that one should be hunting around in this way for some way of filling a lacuna which Parliament itself should fill. It is lamentable to find it seriously proposed that the right way to protect the citizen is by the appointment of an official, rather than by adapting parliamentary institutions to meet this new and urgent need. It would seem to me far more consonant with British history to appoint a permanent standing committee of inquiry of Members of Parliament, with its own staff, than to search around for a substitute. . . .[20]

Political activities must be conducted by politicians. But they are often ill-equipped and too ill-organized to do so. Advice and information should be sought for from every quarter: MPs should not be excluded. Experts need political advice as much as politicians need expert advice. And advice and information should be sought for both Government and Parliament.

[20] Brian Chapman 'The Ombudsman', *op. cit.*, p. 310.

CHAPTER IX

WHAT IS TO BE DONE

Here is Edward Bear, coming downstairs now, bump, bump, bump, on the back of his head, behind Christopher Robin. It is, as far as he knows, the only way of coming downstairs, but sometimes he feels that there really is another way, if only he could stop bumping for a moment and think of it. And then he feels that perhaps there isn't.   Alan Alexander Milne

No more exposition or argument, only one point of explanation before a summary. The purposes of this book should now be clear: to show the true function of Parliament in relation to British Government (basically that of informing the electorate); to sound yet another alarm that it is being badly fulfilled and that public confidence will decline if remedies are not found, and to suggest the broad areas of possible action. It is not intended to be so presumptuous as to offer a detailed scheme for Parliamentary reform. All it is proper, possible and needful to do is to set out the broad areas of need and the possibilities of action. If this seems evasive, I can only reply that I am not much taken by paper schemes by outsiders,[1] and that the method of this book may prove a welcome rebuttal to the usual view that people have of an academic's approach to politics. For I have sought to examine in detail and suggest only in general. Whatever happens, there will not be any sudden and great tearing up of Erskine May and beginning again on rational Benthamite principles. But there may be a concerted effort to stretch every existing procedure and institution of Parliament in the direction of reform, and to drop a few old bits of business by the wayside.[1] I am very serious in thinking that there had

---

[1] I find the tone and temper of *Change or Decay: Parliament and Government in our Industrial Society*, by a group of Conservative Members of Parliament (Conservative Political Centre, 1963), admirable on this point. They quote Bagehot as a legend: 'The very

better be some such effort, for there is ample evidence from the history of our times, and general grounds in political and social theory for believing that the strongest-seeming free systems of government can crumble from within if the masses cease to understand or care how they are governed, and begin to think that attempts to control or influence government are 'all a farce and a racket anyway'.

So I propose to set out certain general principles of constitutional interpretation and state the kind of consequences that should follow from recognizing them realistically:

1. Parliament serves to inform the electorate not to overthrow Governments

Therefore, too much time is spent on ritualistic forms of debates and divisions on legislation which is going to be passed anyway. Too little time is spent on scrutiny of the administration. Too much stress is laid by both Government and Opposition on voting and not enough on 'publicizing' (both by means of investigations and general debates—but more of the latter will only serve any purpose if there are more of the former). Too little use is made of committees of inquiry in Parliament and of MPs as members of outside advisory committees to the Government. Then if these things were remedial, Parliament could save time for both Floor and Committee by encouraging more, not less, delegated legislation.

2. Governments must govern, but strong government needs strong opposition

Therefore, the procedures of Parliament need rethinking to fit the concept of 'equal access to the electorate' by the Parties, and this for the whole life of a Parliament, not merely during the statutory campaign, since in a real sense *Parliament is a continuous election campaign* (but one which needs to be more fairly conducted). This concept is a more relevant key to Parliamentary procedure than concepts of Ministerial discretion and governmental secrecy, but it should complement, not threaten, the normal Government control of the

means which best helped you yesterday, may very likely be those which most impede you tomorrow.'

House to put its business through. The facilities available to the Opposition and Backbench Members in general should be greatly increased, particularly the expansion of the Library into a Parliamentary work-shop of research and investigation employing many trained research workers who could serve committees. There should thus be the deliberate creation of a 'counter-bureaucracy' to Whitehall, part complementary and part to break new ground, to obtain information for Parliament.

Failing all this, the Opposition needs to shed the influence of the modern 'Executive mind' and see itself again as an *opposition* whose primary duty is to *oppose,* not to preen and muzzle itself by too much conceit of being 'an alternative government'.

3. Government must plan and must control finances both in broad terms and in detail
Therefore, Governments should continue to consult more (and more openly) with people representative of those whose willing co-operation is needed in planning (certainly including, though not exclusively, MPs themselves). But there is little hope or sense in Parliament reasserting 'the power of the purse', as if financial control could ever be divorced from political control. The Government must take political responsibility for financial policy above all else. There is room, however, for great improvement in Financial procedure, by putting the Finance Bill 'upstairs', both to save Parliamentary time and to obtain closer and more informed scrutiny. Possibly the work of the Select Committee on Estimates could better be divided up among new specialized Standing Committees of Advice, Scrutiny and Inquiry.

4. Members of Parliament are elected to serve their country, their party and their constituency, not themselves
Therefore, the part-time MP should be discouraged. The job is too big for part-time service. Part of the present weakness of Parliament arises from the small numbers available for morning committee work. The small hard core of dedicated and hard-working MPs are exploited by the larger number of

gentleman amateurs. The Leaders and Whips should at least ensure better attendance in the mornings. If people are worried about *professional* politicians (though this is usually a silly animus against politics itself) or are worried, more realistically, about the 'representativeness' of the House, then it should be pointed out that representativeness may well be a function of a Member's previous full-time occupation rather than of his present part-time job (plainly there are some MPs who rely on their position to get *new* and part-time jobs when they come to Westminster). In any case, there might be a remedy if the Parties and Constituencies tried to encourage some people to serve in Parliament and then return to their business or profession. But MPs need greater facilities and larger salaries before they can all be expected to work full-time. One man, one vote; one MP, one secretary; and one MP and secretary, a private double-office.[2] Salaries should be increased together with a pension scheme, both tied to some quite high grade in the Civil Service to avoid recurrent disputes. But the more important principle in relation to salaries should be that all facilities, from postage to travel, which are a normal part of any professional man's office, should be provided free out of public funds.

5. Controls on any government are all ultimately political
Therefore, it is ultimately vain to seek impartial adjudication of the exercise of Ministerial discretion. So is the quest for an Ombudsman to make an impartial investigation of maladministration. At best such devices should be regarded as complementary to an increase in Parliamentary scrutiny. But Governments, by the same token, need not fear the direct power of specialized committees, since Party lines will hold, and ultimate political power is found only in the electorate (or, more subtly, in the self-control exercised by both Government and Opposition when they remind themselves, and are reminded, of how the electorate is likely to react: expectations

[2] And an individual telephone and proper modern office equipment, and a typing pool for all those November days when Miss Fortune is indisposed and for those spring budget days when her boss is churning it out faster than Miss Chance can manage it—it is ludicrous that these elementary things need to be mentioned.

are as important as experience). So, once again, all forms of
'control' as influence which can reach the ears of the electorate
need strengthening.

*6. No government can in fact be responsible or be held
responsible for every error or act of maladministration*
Therefore, we should recognize the obvious that Ministers
will not resign, nor ought they to, except occasionally when
they are personally culpable. Then there would be no threat
to 'Ministerial responsibility' from almost any degree of Parliamentary scrutiny and inquiry which stops short of sheer
obstruction or endangering national security. Control of the
administration should be seen as a joint task between Ministers and committees of MPs. 'Ministerial responsibility' is,
in fact, now a purely legal concept which defines who it is can
use certain powers and to whom Questions on them must be
put; but the concept is misused as a kind of knock-down
argument against any examination of a Minister's use of his
powers. The real meaning of the concept is simply political,
indeed all Ministers are collectively responsible to the electorate more than to Parliament. So Ministerial or collective
responsibility should never be invoked to refuse any form of
Parliamentary scrutiny and inquiry which does not threaten
political control of Parliament. That proceedings in Parliament indirectly and ultimately threaten the Government's control of the electorate *should be* no argument against them, for
Parliament should be a device (and easily could be) to ensure
something like equality of access to the public between Government and Opposition.

*7. Technical and Expert Advice is more and more necessary
to modern government but is more and more open to opinion
and interpretation*
Therefore, such advice should be given (with as few exceptions as possible) openly, and the presumption should be for,
not against, its coming through committees of Parliament.
This would seem a protection for the Government as well
as for the public. There are very few fields of applied knowledge where experts will not differ, on matters of priority if

not on principle. Certainly, the Government must alone make the final decision and carry the responsibility; but decisions are likely to be more wise and rational if the issues have been openly canvassed. Everyone suspects, for instance, that the real area of Defence secrets—whose discussion would endanger the safety of the State—is far smaller than any recent Government has allowed, even on the bleakest view of international relations and the lowest estimate of the efficiency of foreign intelligence services; a large part of what Professor Edward Shils called *The Torment of Secrecy* is that so many of the secrets are not secret. At the very least Parliament, by developing the Library of the House of Commons into a great research library, should offer alternative expert advice even if unasked. Members of Parliament will specialize more than they have done, but they will rarely be experts: they need regular access both to outside experts and to trained research workers (who would be employed by the Library) and more experience in knowing how to use them.

8. *Life is short, party politics is party politics, and the House of Commons will always be too busy to look at everything that needs attention*

Therefore, the House of Lords should be transformed into a small Second Chamber of about a hundred—let us call them —Counsellors of Parliament. They would be salaried people appointed in virtue of political, legal and administrative experience, and appointed not necessarily for life but perhaps as part of a career in some profession or some branches of the public service. It should have no political power but considerable authority for its tasks of scrutinizing legislation and debating general issues as at present, especially those Bills and issues of a less politically contentious nature; it should be prepared for the additional tasks, especially if the Commons is slow to change its ways, of reviewing administrative cases, surveying the whole field of delegated legislation, generally scrutinizing the conduct of administration, investigating grievances and conducting such public inquiries as the House of Commons may require it to do. There is a sense in which a reformed Second Chamber could fill many of the gaps which lead one to advocate more work in and by committees in the House of Commons—so, if necessary, a 'Chamber of Committees' or a House of Scrutiny.

9. Time and tide wait for no man and much of politics is the art of being present at the right time

Therefore, the time-span of the Parliamentary session should be increased, though without necessarily increasing the number of days the whole House sits. From the end of July to the third week of October Britain is without a Parliament. There would be a great gain for the public interest and probably for the efficiency of Government if the House only rose for a month in the summer, but spread its sitting days far more thinly over the rest of the year, even (as others have suggested) adjourning on Wednesdays to give time for research, reading, political and public business and general digestion of Monday and Tuesday and preparation for Thursday and Friday. Both Ministers and Backbench MPs would be less frantically over-busy, as they often are, and the public would see more of them. There would seem no general objection to some committees seeking to continue their work during periods of recess.

10. British government and politics is British government and politics

Therefore, it is misleading (and usually deliberately so) to suggest that greater use of committees of advice, scrutiny and investigation would lead to their controlling the policy of the Executive, as happens in the United States and in the France of the Third and Fourth Republics. No procedural changes in Parliament whatever could rewrite British social history which has created the two party system in its highly disciplined form. The constitutional arrangements of these other systems of government are entirely different, indeed they have (or had) written, fundamental constitutions which encourage deliberate divisions of power and formal checks and balances, unlike the British 'sovereignty of Parliament' (or complete Executive power limited only by political considerations). Even further than this: such systems are as they are largely because they do not have parties as disciplined and political divisions so relatively clear-cut as in Britain.

All this points, in and out of every other consideration, to the need for a reformed committee system. Let us try to be more specific. There is a minimum position and a maximum position. The minimum position is simply that the nineteenth century use of Select Committees should be revived, both to discuss future policy and to investigate particular topics or grievances. The maximum position is that Standing Committees on legislation should become specialized to definite areas and should be given general powers to discuss matters in these areas, and to scrutinize and investigate the work of Departments concerned (even this maximum position rejects firmly, once again, any suggestion that they should share executive authority with the Minister).

Something between them is more likely to be reached and more likely to work well. The existing Standing Committees should be left with their existing work of considering Bills in the Committee Stage (though there is room to argue that more Bills should go to a Standing Committee, that is less to 'Committee of the Whole', and even, as Sir Edward Campion argued, that reconstituted Standing Committees could well consider the Report Stage of most Bills). They should not be confused with what I will now call cumbersomely, for the sake of clarity, Standing Committees of Advice, Scrutiny and Investigation. The House, we have suggested, spends too much time in any case considering the preordained passage of legislation; and any scheme of reform must avoid any threat or even suspicion of a threat to the passage of Government legislation.

I use the word 'Standing' Committees of Advice, Scrutiny and Investigation simply to differentiate them from the traditional idea that Select Committees are *ad hoc* committees. But in fact, as we have seen, there are certain Select Committees which are perennial—those of Estimates, Accounts and the Nationalized Industries, for instance.

The kind of new committee that is needed should be set up for the whole life of a Parliament to give its members time to specialize and see things through. The basic power these committees should have would be to discuss matters and have their deliberations published—as in the normal *Hansard* for Standing Committees. But then they could have general power to send for persons and papers and to instigate inquiries within their field of competence; they would thus do much or all of the work for which some would wish to invent —a fantasy of despair in Parliament—a British Ombudsman. If they work well on these grounds one would expect them to become used more and more by Ministers, both as sounding boards for future legislation, and as partners in investigating the efficiency of sections of the administration. And, finally, their specialized knowledge and growing familiarity with expert opinion could make them far more useful than the present committee to perform the work of scrutinizing the annual Estimates. This work could be shared round the specialized committees to ensure a far closer scrutiny of estimates than is at present possible. They would also take over the work of the present Scrutiny Committee on delegated legislation.

What should the areas of these committees be? There is a superficial attractiveness in schemes for one committee to each Department. But there are strong objections. There would be too many committees—if they are each to stand any chance of gaining, from time to time, the attention of the Floor of the House for their more important reports. Such a system would carry a greater risk of interference with the routine work of Departments. It would certainly carry a great risk of creating committees as narrow-minded as some Departments. One of the functions of Standing Committees of Advice, Scrutiny and Investigation would be to bring together considerations relevant to several Departments and to take broad views, even where not immediately politically or administratively applicable. Cases may vary. The range of concerns of the Home Office are already so wide that no useful committee could have terms of reference any wider; but a committee on the Ministry of Works, for instance, even with its recently expanded functions, might prove hard to man.

There is a very obvious and neglected model which might prove to be what many people have in mind but find hard to formulate precisely: the specialisms which the two Parties themselves have found the need to create in order to discuss policy and inform themselves effectively (see above pp. 100–3).

If one looks at the subject groups which the two Parties have in common, ignoring the question of sub-committees, amalgamating two or three Conservative groups which have no Labour equivalent, one can find a sensible, though highly flexible, model for the committee system of a reformed House of Commons:

> Agriculture, Fisheries and Food
> Arts and Amenities
> Colonies
> Commonwealth
> Defence and Services
> Economics and Finance
> Education
> Foreign Affairs
> Fuel and Power
> Health Services
> Home Office Affairs
> Housing and Local Government
> Pensions and Social Security
> Scientific Development
> Transport and Civil Aviation

And in addition there is need for committees on *Legal and Judicial Affairs* (to survey the whole field of the administration of justice and to discuss law reform); the *Machinery of Government* (it is quite fantastic that Governments are so free from informed Parliamentary criticism in respect of the making and remaking of Ministries and Departments and the allocation of responsibilities between them—a freedom which we have noted, contrasts vividly with the tactical traditionalism of Governments when Parliamentary reform is discussed); the *Select Committee on Nationalized Industries* would continue, and in addition to the 'domestic' committees of the House, such as Privileges, there should be a *House of Commons Commission* (the long overdue recommendation of the Stokes Committee on accommodation of 1954 should be implemented to make the Commons master in their own House, no longer the uneasy tenants of a Royal Palace with its grotesque divisions of responsibility between the Lord Great Chamberlain, the Minister of Works and the Speaker).

Government should govern and lead, not follow; in Britain we even think that governments that try to stand with their ears permanently to the ground are in an unbecoming and dangerous posture. Few Socialists would not agree with a random remark of Sir Winston Churchill the last time he held a press conference in Washington (during the time when President Eisenhower was trying not to make up his mind what to do about Senator MacCarthy): 'politicians who cannot stand unpopularity are not worth their salt'. But this does not mean that we have not something to learn and much to amend. The procedures of Parliament itself are more than a symbol of much that is wrong in Britain today, where tradition seems to have grown sour and dogmatic. They are a brake on reform and renewal. Too many Conservatives are cynical about public opinion and so have little interest in Parliament while in office; but equally too many Socialists are only interested in Parliamentary reform while in opposition, and think that they can create a more democratic Britain by taking over what have become radically undemocratic means. Governments at the moment get away with too much too easily; and this, to my mind at least, is as true for the proper Goose as it may be for the proper Gander. Strong government is demanded by the electorate but strong government needs strong criticism. Parliament has only itself to blame that its procedures have fallen so desperately behind the times and the still growing powers of the Ministries. The public, while government ultimately depends on their confidence, has a right to demand that the House of Commons wakes up and reforms itself—no one else can.

One is not optimistic. In December 1963 the straw in the wind was Mr Harold Wilson. He was reported in *The Times* for 23 February, 1963, as having resolved, little more than a week after his election as Party Leader, that a future Labour

Government would bring in immediate plans for Parliamentary reform. But by the autumn, Mr Wilson was 'yet to be convinced' of the need to change anything,[3] particularly of the need for a system of specialized advisory committees. One hopes that he will realize, in his evident anxiety to keep things as easy as possible for the passage of great new legislation, that it is not primarily a moral maxim, but a political truth that the means determine the ends.

If the Conservatives are returned, then there is great need for them too to try to take, not an altruistic view, but a long term political view: Parliament should adjust itself to the consequences of prolonged one-party government. The capacity for Opposition would need every strengthening it can be given if Britain is not to blunder into a kind of remote and secretive government which, even if it pleases the public, is likely to evade that public discussion of public issues upon which free politics depend.

Britain today suffers under the burden of three native curses: that of amateurism, that of 'inner circle' secrecy and that of snobbery. All three serve to debase both the quality of political life and the energy of economic activity. The unreformed Parliament is more than a symbol of these things; it helps to perpetuate them by the most effective of all forces in politics and society—example. If Parliament were reformed, the whole climate of expectations could change, much of the sweet fog we muddle through might lift. Continued decline may be our lot, decline not merely in external influence but in any internal belief, both individually and together, that there are things worth doing in Britain. But if renewal in industry, learning and the arts, if it comes at all, comes in such a way that it by-passes Parliament, then this could mean the rule of the expert and the bureaucrat alone—a condition far more frightening than that 'mere politics' of which at least ensures the existence of that which is the greatest of all things, freedom (or, more precisely, the ability to enjoy freedom). Politics is the great civilizer, the activity which mediates be-

[3] See the two woeful BBC interviews with Mr Wilson, by Norman Hunter, on the subject in *The Listener,* 14 and 21 November, 1963.

tween the expert and the public, between declining classes
and rising, indeed between all competing interests, whether
of mind or matter, which compose society—competing so long
as resources remain limited and demands (or imagination)
infinite. Parliament is the greatest forum of politics in Britain
and any neglect of it means danger for freedom and for all its
derivative qualities of spontaneity, adaptability and invention
upon which depend both the very survival of States and their
worthiness to survive at all.

CHAPTER X

POSTSCRIPT:
PROSPECTS OF THE MOMENT[1]

Since the above pages were written a change of government
has taken place, for the first time since 1951, but the system
has not changed and neither has the need to change some
secondary aspects of it. British voting behaviour since the
war has remained astonishingly fixed (as the Table shows):
even 1945 was by American standards no real landslide in
terms of the popular vote. And in 1964 the Labour Party increased its share of the total poll by only 0.3 per cent. As
Dr Richard Rose has clearly summarised it: 'The Labour
majority in the new Parliament was the result of a marked
reduction in Conservative support, rather than a sharp rise
in Labour support.'[2] But even a majority of only five over the
other two parties in the House of Commons, now reduced
to three by a by-election defeat, can be politically solid in
the actual working of the British constitution.

The unexpectedly wide limits of manoeuvre will be apparent if we answer three questions. How strong is the present government? How may it properly use its power? How
does this affect the prospects for Parliamentary reform?

The Strength of the Government

The election was, as Wellington remarked of Waterloo, 'a
damned near thing'. But in general elections as in that sort of
battle, 'enough', as our mothers taught us, 'is as good as a

[1] I have added this in February 1965 for the present American
edition, adapted from my 'The Limits of Manoeuvre', *Socialist
Commentary*, December 1964.
[2] *The Times Guide to the House of Commons, 1964*, London,
1964, p. 240.

RESULTS OF GENERAL ELECTIONS BY VOTES AND SEATS, 1945–64*

	Electorate	Votes Cast & Total Seats	Conservative	Labour	Liberal	Communist	Other
1945†	32,836,419	100% 24,082,612 *640*	39.8% 9,577,667 *212*	48.3% 11,632,891 *394*	9.1% 2,197,191 *12*	0.4% 102,760 *2*	2.4% 572,103 *20*
1950	34,269,770	100% 28,772,671 *625*	43.5% 12,505,567 *298*	46.1% 13,266,592 *315*	9.1% 2,621,548 *9*	0.3% 91,746 *0*	1.0% 290,218 *3*
1951	34,645,573	100% 28,595,668 *625*	48.0% 13,717,533 *321*	48.8% 13,948,605 *295*	2.5% 730,556 *6*	0.1% 21,640 *0*	0.6% 177,329 *3*
1955	34,858,263	100% 26,769,493 *630*	49.7% 13,286,564 *344*	46.4% 12,404,970 *277*	2.7% 722,405 *6*	0.1% 33,144 *0*	1.1% 313,410 *3*
1959	35,397,080	100% 27,859,241 *630*	49.4% 13,749,830 *365*	43.8% 12,215,538 *258*	5.9% 1,638,571 *6*	0.1% 30,897 *0*	0.8% 224,405 *1*
1964	35,952,993	100% 27,656,149 *630*	43.4% 11,980,783 *303*	44.1% 12,205,581 *317*	11.2% 3,101,103 *9*	0.1% 44,576 *0*	0.9% 302,518 *1‡*

* Adapted from D. A. Butler and Richard Rose, *The British General Election of 1959*, London, 1960, p. 204, and supplemented from *The Times Guide to the House of Commons*, London, 1964, pp. 244–47.

† Excluding University seats and weighted to eliminate the element of double voting in the fifteen two-member seats then existing (both these categories were abolished by 1950).

‡ Mr Speaker.

feast'. And it will be more of a feast than many at first thought. Even the Conservative press agrees correctly, if rather surprisingly, that Mr Wilson, even with such a slender majority, is in a position to do too much, rather than too little, as the election results at first suggested. This is so for eight good reasons. Some of them are endemic to the system, some to the peculiar situation of the moment. But this distinction does not effect the argument: it is enough that the peculiar factors can occur at all within the system.

First, the Conservatives, like any Opposition, do not even wish to overthrow the Government by a vote in Parliament until some great and clear change in public opinion takes place. One of the main facts of British political life is that the country is normally governed by the Conservatives. The incumbent administration has great advantages in picking the time for, in planning, and in conducting a general election. They fight it with all the practical advantages and all the symbolic majesty of being *the Ministry*. And yet the Tories lost. One prophecy is fairly safe: that the next general election will be fought by a Labour Government able to pick the time and the issues for the engagement.

Secondly, the Liberals are not anxious to overthrow what is, at least, a radical Government and the first to be tried for over a decade. The reputation of being able to hurt but not to help could prove fatal to the Liberals, as to any small, third party in what is behaviouristically a two-party system. They will seek, at almost any price, to avoid responsibility for the death of the new Labour Government. They could have their moment of power, but only at the price of reviving every doubt about the consequences of voting Liberal.

Thirdly, no Prime Minister will take a snap or contrived defeat in the division lobbies as sufficient grounds for resigning and dissolving Parliament (unless he is ready and seeks an excuse). The Tory whips may have a greater job restraining their eager cohorts, come the prophesied 'Great Westminster 'Flu Epidemic of 1965', than the Labour whips in resuscitating their noticeably more elderly ranks. A modern Prime Minister is only under an obligation to resign on a vote in the Commons either if both party leaders have beforehand made solemn, public noises that it is a 'vote of confidence', or, if following any vote, or series of votes, the Government simply cannot carry on. A vote of confidence is what a Prime Minister takes to be a vote of confidence or discovers afterwards to have been a vote which lost him the confidence of the House (meaning in fact the loss of enough members of his own Party to overthrow him). It is a thoroughly political matter. After all, a vote of confidence need not even be a defeat in the actual tally of votes, as Neville Chamberlain discovered in 1940. He had a handsome majority, but with so many regular Conservatives abstaining, *a few even voting against him,* he knew that he had not sufficient confidence behind him to govern decisively in times of emergency. A British Government whose party was elected with a majority of seats in the House has not been defeated on a vote of confidence since the fall of Gladstone's third ministry in 1886 on the defeat of his Irish Home Rule Bill. If 'the Constitution' is based on precedent and practice, then we can almost say that it would be unconstitutional for a Parliament to defeat a Government whose party was returned by the electorate with a majority of seats in the Commons. What this means is simply that electorates are likely to punish parties which overthrow properly elected Governments before they have had, in some sense, utterly vague legally, but concrete enough politically, 'a fair chance'.

Fourthly, the fact that Labour has won at all, perhaps for the first time in normal peacetime conditions, may affect the fundamental factor of British electoral politics: that is, the fact that about one-third of those who regard themselves as working-class normally vote Conservative. The Tory working-man dominates British politics. For all the debates about policy and image, the Labour Party could have fought any election since the First World War on *any* platform whatever, from Bolshevism to Free Trade, and would have won every time, if it could only have cut into the working-class Tory vote by a third or even a quarter. Now in part that vote is agreed to be *aspirant*—voting Tory to feel or be like a Tory; but in part it is agreed to be *deferential.* Labour will gain some of this vote simply by being neither more nor less socialist, but simply *the Government*. Hitherto this has been a factor largely beyond its control, except in the atmosphere of postwar shortages. But nothing, in politics at least, succeeds like success.

The deferential voter is impressed by being, not becoming. The Tory workingman has a year or two ahead of him of seeing Labour men as Ministers of the Crown. And this time, unlike in MacDonald's two Governments, they look like it and have, to put it mildly, no diffidence. Nor should they. The Labour Party is much helped by a Prime Minister who is not frightened by power, novelty or risk—a quality likely to attract those poor souls who prefer hierarchy to fraternity. They have now seen on telly the Queen in her Crown amid all her Peers at the State Opening of Parliament reading a socialist program of government—and more such wonders are to come. The working-class Tory could not be gained to Labour by any obvious rational appeal; but he may be gained by what is, in a sociological sense, almost an accident: the *sheer fact* of a Labour Government that means to govern and to be treated as a Government—if it survives.

Fifthly, there is the personal factor of Wilson himself. The Labour Party is at last superbly led by a man who knows both its heart and its head—a man with left-wing prejudices and right-wing realism. If the Party runs into Parliamentary trouble, it is unlikely to be through any failure of leadership. Wilson has had the sense to see that the Labour Party is a great coalition, but that properly managed this is its strength, not its weakness. It stands for all of nonconformist Britain— from no-nonsense, middle-class radicalism, through the massive inertia and strength of organized trade unionism, all the way to the many small and brittle, but always energizing, traditions of intellectual socialism. Properly led, this breadth and representativeness is a great strength: it has direct contact with every important section of the community. And the existing flexibility of the office of Prime Minister is all in its favour, though Wilson has gone further than ever before in expanding the staff of the Cabinet office.

Sixthly, the Government is stronger than it seems because the public appears to like a Government to look like a Government, does not judge election statistics too precisely, and dislikes frequent general elections. The signs are that the electorate does have a great sense of 'give them a chance' and 'fair play' (which underlies all the lack of formal constitutional restraints). They would punish the Conservatives if they turned out Labour before Labour had had 'a chance to do something'.

Seventhly, it is unlikely that the Conservatives will want a general election until they have had time gracefully to get rid of their present leader, and time powerfully to establish the reputation of a new one—so important have the offices of Prime Minister and Leader of the Opposition become. Perhaps, to be fair, nobody could have saved them from defeat; but 'nobody' won't help them win the next general election.

And, eighthly, party discipline, always so strong (this key peculiarity of the British political system), becomes even stronger, not weaker, when the majority is small. Any MP who threatened his own party in Parliament would quickly find himself without a party in his own constituency.

How May It Use Its Power?

Where there is power, there is responsibility. Basically the British system of government is quite simple. A general election returns a party which forms a Government which continues to govern, subject to only Parliamentary criticism (but only very rarely to the threat of Parliamentary defeat), until it is re-elected or defeated in the next general election. Acceptance of general elections is the only ultimate restraint upon British government. There are no more and no less constitutional restraints on a Government with a very small majority than with a large one (particularly because there is such a flagrant disproportion between seats and votes—the Conservatives were not inhibited in 1951 by getting more seats but less votes than Labour). The only restraints are political: factors which affect a Government's *expectation* of what will happen in the next general election.

The first business of government is to govern. And the public knows this, for it supports party candidates and punishes independents. It will expect a Government to be able to take what steps are necessary to put its business through the House of Commons. The public would surely punish a party which did not allow adequate criticism of legislation, but it does not hold strong procedural prejudices about the length or number of stages needed to create 'adequate'. The Government will have to run the risk with the electorate; no Government can be expected to accept the judgement of the Opposition on what is adequate. There is nothing sacred even in the number of stages of a bill, still less in whether they are taken upstairs, downstairs, or in my lady's chamber, so long as they are known to be taken and can be publically criticised.

The needs of government in different circumstances will create different conventions. So it is nonsense for the cry to be raised that Labour may have to 'violate the constitution' —easy enough to do if one can first catch it. One thinks again of a famous cry of Mr G. Marx's: 'I was fighting to save the honour of this woman—a thing she has seldom done for herself.' One's reputation for fairness will be judged not by tamely and lamely accepting other people's conventions about constitutional behaviour in every detail, but by making clear how one's own differ by abiding by one's own. New conventions may be created and new informal restraints discovered, many of the old may perish or, more often, diminish, but there will always be some restraining notions of constitutional propriety.

So in a constitutional sense this Government, like any other British Government, can attempt what it likes, subject only to political restraints. So long as the public does not feel that the basic political system of public criticism, the free press and the acceptance of general elections is threatened, then the Government can try on what it likes—at its own political peril. However, two factors do raise special and immediate problems: the machinery of government and the power of Parliament.

Plainly in politics, as in war, lines of retreat can be as important as those of advance. However flexible the constitution, there is practical sense in keeping it as settled as possible. Recently there have been huge changes in the machinery of central government. The size and extent of Mr Wilson's changes in the structure and function of the Ministries have been without precedent in peacetime. There are now 120 MPs in the Government (eighty-nine Ministers and thirty-one Parliamentary Private Secretaries) compared to 101 in the last Parliament.[3] What is done is done. There is little point in wondering if they were all equally wise or necessary. Some of us may delight at the carving up of the Treasury but shudder at the multiplication of symbolic Ministries. Opinions will differ; only experience will tell.

But there might be some advantage in trying to avoid such huge changes every time there is a change of Government. It might be prudent of Mr Wilson to offer some kind of commission or recurrent Select Committee of Parliament on the machinery of government.[4] It is a neglected subject for public examination and might be a fair price to pay for the bold and untrammelled initiative of a new Government. Otherwise, though this is a fairly sophisticated idea, not likely to affect public opinion, some people may rightly fear that there has been some real breach of constitutional propriety.

But a more real and public suspicion attaches to the position of Parliament itself. Strong government needs strong opposition; it can benefit from strong opposition and it can stand up to it. The interest of the newly elected Leader in Parliamentary reform appears to have evaporated. Even the pledge to create an 'Ombudsman' is ambivalent; the office could take a form that would by-pass Parliament. The Tories will be quick, and properly so, to raise a cry on this.

The public is worried about the apparent decay of Parliament, not just about 'administrative justice'—which is an issue whose importance is understood by very few. Granted that part of this worry is misunderstanding of the nature of Parliamentary control anyway: that control does not mean direct power, but simply influence; not command, but advice; not

[4] As suggested by the Rt. Hon. Jo Grimmond, the Liberal leader, in a debate on these recent changes, HC *Debates* (702), 19 November 1964, cc.677–84.

obstruction, but criticism; not initiative, but scrutiny; and not the prohibition of actions, but the publicizing of them. But then Governments should be wiser than electorates and see that this type of political control does not directly hinder them (sometimes it can even help them, to anticipate trouble, for instance). The facilities for this type of Parliamentary control, it is generally admitted, have fallen into decline and are ludicrously unadapted to modern changes in the machinery of government itself. Labour might have gained a reputation for democratic innovation (in the sense of making more things public); it must now beware that it does not gain a reputation for being autocratic.

Any Government can properly use its Parliamentary majority (however slender) to put through whatever legislation it thinks worth the risk; but if it uses its power to weaken Parliamentary control still further, either by sins of omission or of commission, then people may come to think that it has broken the rules.

British Governments have great and proper advantages in picking the time and occasion for a general election. The Conservatives can hardly expect Labour to behave, on their own view of things, even as well as themselves. And they used the opportunities of office in a way that almost calls for a new definition of corruption. For three successive elections the bank rate and the whole volume and incidence of public investments were adjusted for electoral advantage. We have seen a kind of political Keynesianism, that has been variously called 'quadrennial inspiration' or 'fourth-year democracy'.

Labour is unlikely to play politics with the economy in that kind of way; but it would be hard to blame Mr Wilson, if, 'consummate politician', as his opponents call him, he were to save up a little something for electiontide. This kind of thing seems politically venial. It is no damnable sin so long as it can be discovered and denounced in time. The remedy is more publicity, some deliberate attempt to end the excess of discretion and secrecy in the British official mind. But again this throws us back to the question of the effectiveness of Parliamentary control.

The Prospects for Reform

Parliament under modern conditions is to be seen as a permanent election campaign. It does not govern, nor does it directly control Governments. But it does help to control them indirectly, through its effect on the electorate. Nearly everything that is said in Parliament is aimed at the public who become the electorate. There is nothing regrettable in this by itself—except to silly liberals who dislike politics. But it is regrettable that Parliament is such an inefficient device for reaching the public ear, and has so little facility itself for discovering information to rival the sources of the Government. Parliament, in a word, should not threaten the life of a Government; it should only threaten its renewal at the next election. A Government may legitimately defend its Parliamentary life by almost any means; but it may not legitimately hinder Parliament's ability to conduct the next election campaign in a continuous and potentially effective manner.

Election law itself needs to be rethought in the light of this concept. It is beginning to be realized that the three weeks of official campaign known to electoral law are quite meaningless in real terms. This simple discovery lies behind the Labour Party's apparently purely partisan pledge to get business firms to disclose their political donations. The campaign is a continuous one: if it is sensible to control election expenditure at all, then it must be controlled all the time. Disclosure and publicity are forms of control and they are likely to be effective as financial controls on total expenditure—always hard to enforce.

But there is even more need for Parliamentary procedures to be rethought by analogy to the purpose of election laws. They are at the moment the residue of a period when the division lobby was held to be the true instrument of Parliamentary control, rather than the ability to catch the ear of the public. Thus far too much time is taken up with legislation—which will and should pass anyway; but far too little time in scrutiny, investigation, and general debate.

Mr Wilson does not yet appear to have grasped this aspect of political and social change. This could lead to political trouble. If the powers of Government continue to expand and those of Parliament to decline, the public will scent unfairness, will suspect a breach of the basic conditions of British politics. Labour has more to gain and more to lose. The imbalance between Government and Parliament was apparent during the 1950s, but the relative inactivity of the Tories made the matter seem scarcely urgent. Labour by trying to do more makes the matter more evident. Labour is not to blame for past neglect of Parliament, but will reap the cumulative consequences if it does not offer more realistic facilities for Parliament as a price for putting through Government business more quickly. A new Select Committee on Procedure has been appointed, but its terms of reference are narrow, keeping it well away from both facilities and research.

It all comes down to this. The present Government has almost as much hope of an effective spell in office as any. It will take every chance it can to affect favourably the result of the next general election, and it will fight that election when it wants to and not before. But the system is known by everyone in it to be, in some sense, a Parliamentary system. If that is ignored, if it is treated as if it were a Presidential system, then there will be trouble: the electorate will suspect it of and punish it for great unfairness. The Opposition would be given something like a crusade on a platter, to fight the election to defend 'British institutions'. So it is likely that the Government will make some move—even for purely political considerations (as ever and why not?).

Great changes in the machinery of central government must find their functional equivalent in modernizing Parliament. Nothing could make the Labour Party look more power-hungry and dogmatic and less humane and intelligently flexible than if it allows itself to get a reputation for caring only for the ends and not for the means. If Labour is 'just as bad as the Tories', it will be defeated—for Britain is normally Tory and is normally deferentially indulgent to the Tories; Labour is judged by higher standards, alas, but it has now a real chance to live up to them and to prove that good government is worth votes. Good government means (perhaps a rather British view of things) choice more than mere consent, publicity of government actions more than—which is unrealistic —widespread participation in them. The British political system is, indeed, properly called 'responsible government' and not 'representative democracy'.

APPENDIX A

THE DECLINE OF SELECT COMMITTEES
OF THE HOUSE OF COMMONS

The following table shows Select Committees divided into categories for selected sessions:

	1	2	3	4	5	6
Session	Domestic	Procedural and Privilege	Financial and Scrutiny	Public Policy	Legislation	Total
1868–69	2	9	1	9	16	37
1875	1	5	1	7	11	25
1881	2	6	2	5	17	32
1887	1	9	2	8	18	38
1896	1	7	1	10	4	23
1909	1	6	1	6	3	17
1924–25	1	7	2	3	3	16
1930–31	1	10	2	3	2	18
1937–38	1	5	2	1	5	14
1946–47	2	5	3	—	5	15
1952–53	3	7	4	2	1	17
1956–57	1	7	4	—	2	14
1960–61	1	6	4	—	3	14

Sources: *Returns of Select Committee* and *Journal of the House of Commons*

Note that in 1888 two large Standing Committees (60–80 Members) were established to deal with legislation, thus replacing either the Floor of the whole House, or else Select Committees for each Bill (which inflates Column 6, the Totals, prior to 1888). Until 1906 these two committees were specialized, between trade, agriculture, fishing, shipping and manufactures, and law, courts of justice and legal procedure respectively (see p. 85 above). From this developed the present system of Standing Committees (not included in Column 5 of the Table). It is arguable whether more legislation should be put to Select Committees rather than Standing Committees; but the unquestionable index of decline is Column 4: how very rare it now is for Select Committees to be allowed to consider matter of public policy.

Note that Column 3 includes the Select Committee on Nationalized Industries.

Note that the above figures include Joint Committees (i.e. of both Houses), but do not include Private Bill Select Committees.

Here are some *examples* of the kind of subjects considered:

Examples of Subjects Considered

1868–69 Abyssinian War, Endowed Schools Bill, Mail Contracts, New Law Courts, Salmon Fisheries, Seeds Adulteration Bill, Telegraph Bill, Wizley Common

1875 Banks of Issue, Epping Forest Bill, Hampstead Fever and Small Pox Hospital, Loans to Foreign States, Public Worship Facilities Bill

1881 Contagious Diseases Acts, Artisans, and Labourers' Dwellings, Married Women's Property Bill, Tithe Rent Charges, Railways, Bills of Sale Act (1878) Amendment Bill

1887 Butter Substitutes Bill, London Corporation (Charges of Malversion), Police and Sanitary Regulations, Temporary Dwellings Bill, Metropolitan Police Bill, Sunday Postal Labour

1896 Divorce Bills, Distress from want of employment, British South Africa, Petroleum

1909 Daylight Saving Bill, Debtors (Imprisonment), General Committee on Railway and Canal Bills, Asylum Officers' Superannuation Bill

1924–25 Indian Affairs, General Nursing Council, Moneylenders Bill

1929–30 Capital Punishment, Ministers Remuneration, Musical Copyright Bill

1937–38 Food and Drugs Bill, Welsh Church (Amendment) Bill, Official Secrets Acts
1946–47 Trafalgar Estates Bill, Public Offices (Site) Bill
1952–53 Army Act and Air Force Act, Delegated Legislation, Members Expenses, House of Commons Accommodation
1956–57 Obscene Publications Bill, Nationalized Industries
1960–61 Army and Air Force Bill, Covent Garden Market Bill

Compare some of these subjects with those in Appendix F. It is hard to see any particular reason why some inquiries should be parliamentary and others not; it is hard to see any general reason, to put the matter purely negatively, why many of the topics in Appendix F could not be at least as well handled by Select Committees of Parliament (see pp. 96–99 above).

APPENDIX B

WHAT MPS THINK OF THEIR JOBS

by RUDOLF KLEIN

(reprinted by permission of the Observer *from their issue of 27 March, 1963)*

Criticism of the House of Commons by outsiders is largely echoed by its own members. A special survey of MPs, conducted by the *Observer,* shows that many of them are highly dissatisfied with the conditions of work and pay at Westminster.

Salary

Overwhelmingly, MPs want higher salaries: 77 per cent. But a majority are disturbed by the trend towards full-time politicians (56 per cent) and consider that the control exercised by the Commons over Government expenditure is too loose (61 per cent).

A high proportion of them also think that the individual Backbencher has too little influence (44 per cent) and believe that the prestige of the House as a whole is falling (36 per cent).

The findings will give new force to the demands made in last Friday's debate for procedure to be reformed and the organization of business to be improved. They show that a majority of MPs recognize the need for change—although few would go all the way with Lord Altrincham's article in the *Observer* last Sunday.

The *Observer* survey is based on the view of 163 MPs who replied to a questionnaire sent to all members of the House. This represents a quarter of the total membership—but a much

higher proportion of the rank-and-file. Most members of the
Government thought it tactful to abstain. So did most Labour
Frontbenchers.

Conservative and Labour MPs replied in direct proportion
to their total strength—28 per cent of each party. Three Liberals answered—43 per cent of the party. The 162 replies
therefore represent a fair cross-section of the House.

Do you think that the salary of MPs is

	Per cent of Total	Per cent of Conservative	Per cent of Labour
reasonable?	13	18	6
generous?	2	4	—
inadequate?	77	64	94
Mixed views or none	8	14	—

Opinion is most emphatic on the issue of salaries. A majority of both Conservative and Labour MPs are agreed that
their present pay is too low. Cynics might explain this near
unanimity on grounds of self-interest, but a breakdown of the
replies does not entirely support this interpretation.

Support for higher salaries comes in many cases from Conservative MPs with other forms of income. 'With an outside
source of income I can survive. Without it, I could not without a great reduction of expenses on parliamentary duties.'
(Sir John Langford-Holt.) 'I have no difficulty in managing
and do not need an increase. I would, however, vote and speak
in favour of this, since the Member of Parliament who has no
other source of income lives in conditions of humiliating and
unreasonable poverty' (Mr Humphry Berkeley).

Another Conservative explains: 'My constituency is 200
miles from London, nearly 700 square miles in extent. This
means two homes and a yearly mileage of 20,000. I get paid
£1,750 and pay out £2,500, which means I pay £750 out
of my own pocket for the privilege of working a forty-hour
week.' This is echoed by a Labour MP: 'My overdraft at the

bank, after three years as an MP, is now equal to my deposit balance when I was elected.'

Sir Gerald Nabarro (Conservative) is more explicit still. He gives a precise breakdown of his expenses as they will be returned to the Inland Revenue. The cost of a secretary (proportion of salary only) for handling about 15,000 letters a year: £1,000. Living in London for Parliamentary sittings ('My home is in Worcestershire'): £750. Telephones, telegrams and postage: £250. Constituency travel by car, excluding the cost of driving to the constituency: £200. Total £2,200—showing a deficit of £450 on the parliamentary salary and expense allowance.

Sir Gerald concludes: 'I am not grumbling. . . . What I *am* doing is explaining to Lord Altrincham why I am an amateur politician and a professional businessman. I think my constituents like me that way.'

But some Conservatives had reservations. There is a danger, they felt, that men or women might want to become MPs simply for the sake of the money if salaries go up. 'The important thing is to strike a balance,' one commented, 'between, at one end of the scale, allowing a full-time MP to do his job efficiently without excessive financial worry whilst, at the other end of the scale, avoiding making the job financially attractive.'

Asked to suggest what salaries ought to be paid, most MPs thought that about £3,000 a year would be fair—but that it might be best to relate it to Civil Service salaries. Some thought it should be £5,000 or more.

Full-time, Part-time

There is a much deeper split on the basic question of an MP's duties. Should he be a full-time politician—a professional? Or should he be part-time—an amateur? A majority of MPs thought that the trend towards professionalism was regrettable. But the parties divided on this.

Do you think that the trend towards MPs becoming full-time politicians is

	Per cent of Total	Per cent of Conservative	Per cent of Labour
inevitable?	17	4	35
desirable?	17	4	33
regrettable?	56	78	26
Mixed views or none	10	14	6

Labour MPs, on the whole, have no regrets about this trend and some welcome it: 'Amateur status in politics has always been overrated; it is today an anachronism.'

But from the left-wing of the Labour Party comes a note of dissent. The trend, Miss Jennie Lee categorically states, is undesirable. 'Contacts with trade, industry and the professions are all the better if up to date. Again, diversity is the best rule. Some MPs will choose to be full-time, others to bring to the House the refreshment of outside contacts.'

Conservatives are more outspoken still. 'If the House of Commons finally loses its amateur status it will be the end of parliamentary government. The fall in quality would be disastrous. What sort of professional is likely to be attracted by a job which may only last four years?'

But this snorting contempt for the professional is not shared by all Conservatives. 'There always have been full-time politicians—the place could not run without them. The change is that they are not now supplied exclusively by the leisured classes' (Mr William Shepherd).

Whether they consider themselves professional or not, MPs tend to spend long hours at Westminster. The question 'How much time do you spend, in an average week, at the House of Commons?' produced some evasive replies. Mr Woodrow Wyatt was unusually frank: 'Nobody is bound to reply to questions when the answers might be incriminating.'

The majority, however, gave figures. On an average, MPs seem to spend about thirty hours a week at the House. But the extremes tend to fluctuate from two to sixty hours. Some said they are at the House 'all the time' (Mr Harold Davies, Labour, and Wing-Commander Grant-Ferris, Conservative).

Most MPs stress that the time actually spent at Westminster represents only a part of their parliamentary duties. Indeed, in many replies there is a distinct note of resentment at their constituents. Too many of the public, one man complains, seem to think of MPs as glorified social workers.

A Conservative, Miss Joan Quennell, argues that the public will have to decide whether it wants welfare workers or senators. A Labour MP, Mr Richard Marsh, suggests a way of easing the burden of constituency work: 'I see no reason why groups of perhaps half a dozen MPs should not share a graduate welfare worker.'

Influence of Backbenchers

Complaints about too much work go hand in hand with grumbles about too little influence. Not surprisingly, Labour MPs voice this particular grievance most often: being in opposition is frustrating enough for party leaders, let alone Backbenchers.

Do you think that individual Backbench Members have

	Per cent of Total	Per cent of Conservative	Per cent of Labour
enough influence?	44	56	30
too little influence?	44	32	59
too much influence?	1	1	—
Mixed views or none	11	11	11

After less than a year in the House, Mr Dick Taverne (Labour) is already finding the opportunities for Backbenchers too limited. 'Question Time, supposedly the Backbencher's moment of glory, is very threadbare in its yield of important information, particularly if it might embarrass the Government.'

But a frequent opinion is that a Backbencher's influence is

what he makes it. 'In my experience Backbench Members have
as much influence as they care to exercise' (Mr John Stone-
house). More plaintively, a Conservative puts it: 'I am content that the Government should govern. But I should like
to be heeded sometimes' (Mr J. Talbot).

Many Conservatives think that Backbenchers make up in
influence as members of groups what they lack as individuals.
One Conservative ex-Minister tartly remarks. 'The assumption
that Backbenchers are lobby-fodder is a figment of the imagination.'

Party Discipline

Indeed one of the most surprising results to emerge from the
survey is that MPs do not, on the whole, share the view—
widely held outside Parliament—that they are so many voting
machines. Only a few in both parties think that party discipline
is too strict.

Do you think that party discipline is

	Per cent of Total	Per cent of Conservative	Per cent of Labour
too lax?	2	2	3
just about right?	76	81	70
too strict?	20	15	26
Mixed views or none	2	2	1

But the minority tend to be eloquent. 'The fact that there
are two main parties in the State makes it urgent to have reasonable diversity within each party or we are well on the way
to a *gauleiter* atmosphere' (Miss Jennie Lee). A Conservative
is almost equally sharp: 'The Whips' Office tend to behave
like a collection of prep school prefects.'

But mostly there is scorn for the advocates of less rigid
party discipline. 'There is a lot of nonsense talked about party
discipline, usually by so-called Liberals who haven't got a
party and have the quaint notion that if they had it would

work effectively as a sort of anarchists' federation' (Mr George Darling, Labour). Some Conservatives go further still, and write of the Whips as if they were father figures: 'The average Backbencher spontaneously puts an enormous reliance on the Whips, without whose advice parliamentary life can be extremely difficult.'

A few Conservatives complain of another source of pressure. The real trouble, they argue, springs not so much from intolerant Whips but from narrow-minded constituency parties.

Wistfully, some MPs ask why more cross-voting should not be allowed. Why, they want to know, has every division to be one of confidence where the Government must win to survive?

Use of Time by the House

The way the House operates is the root of most of the complaints made by MPs. There is a feeling that not only has the power shifted towards the Government but that even the average Member's ability to know what is going on is declining.

There is wide agreement among MPs that the House spends too much time discussing details of legislation which only experts on the subject can understand. Hence they explain, MPs are bored—and the Chamber is left to a handful of experts.

Do you think that the House of Commons spends too much time

	Per cent of Total	Per cent of Conservative	Per cent of Labour
debating details of legislation?	60	56	64
discussing broad principles of policy?	—	—	—
neither?	18	16	21
Mixed views or none	22	28	15

Equally, many MPs think it would be best for the House to spend its time discussing the broad principles of policy and

delegate some of its work to specialized committees: 54 per
cent thought that such a change would be helpful. Defence
and agriculture are the subjects which most MPs think would
be best dealt with by such committees.

Control of the Executive

One result of such a change, MPs think, would be to allow
them to exercise a closer check over Government expenditure.
There is surprising agreement between the two parties that
this is too loose.

Do you think that the House of Commons' control over the
Government's expenditure is

	Per cent of Total	Per cent of Conservative	Per cent of Labour
sufficiently strict?	32	29	38
too strict?	—	—	—
too loose?	61	60	59
Mixed views or none	7	11	3

Such a scrutiny by specialists might, MPs hope, redress the
balance of power within the House of Commons. The extreme
view here is that of Mr Humphry Berkeley: 'Since 1945 the
parliamentary Party machine has become too powerful. The
day of the Backbencher with influence has gone, even if he is
an ex-Minister. Not one former member of the Government
still in the House of Commons has any position comparable
to that of Sir Austen Chamberlain before the war.'

Less gloomy and less fatalistic is the view taken by Mr
George Darling. The balance has shifted—inevitably, he argues, because of the increasing complexity of modern government. 'The Executive has, however, become far more powerful
than it ought to be simply because we have not adjusted parliamentary procedures to meet the new conditions.'

Do you think that the balance of power within the House of Commons since 1945 has shifted towards the

	Per cent of Total	Per cent of Conservative	Per cent of Labour
executive?	63	56	71
remained the same?	23	20	26
shifted towards the Backbench members?	7	12	1½
Mixed views or none	7	12	1½

Efficiency of the House

Apart from delegating more work to specialist committees, so freeing the House for discussions of major issues of principle, MPs are most enthusiastic for improvements in their working conditions. 'Use the present building for State occasions and let's have a modern working building,' urges Mr Wilfred Proudfoot (Conservative).

'Physical conditions are bad. I calculate that I spend 15 per cent more time than necessary in doing my work, simply because of inadequate facilities in the Palace of Westminster. Only the Library facilities and staff are up to the needs of 1963' (Mr Robert Mathew, Conservative).

Do you think that, on balance, the House of Commons does its work

	Per cent of Total	Per cent of Conservative	Per cent of Labour
efficiently?	15	20	8
adequately?	44	42	45
inefficiently?	33	27	41
Mixed views or none	8	11	6

Another demand is for a fixed time-table which would put an end to night sittings. The present time-table, Mr A. E.

Oram (Labour) complains, is 'suited to the life of an eigh-
teenth-century gentleman but not to the needs of a modern
Parliament'.

The system of voting, with all the Members having to troop
through the division lobbies, is another frequent source of
grousing. 'If there are three divisions in a row, as not infre-
quently happens, MPs can spend half an hour merely walking
about. A mechanical voting system is a necessity'. (Mr William Warbey, Labour).

An even more fundamental inadequacy, in the view of many
MPs, is the shortage of private office and secretarial help.

But some Conservatives have reservations. For some of
them the House of Commons is still, essentially, the greatest
club in the world. If all MPs had private offices, they warn, the
clubbable atmosphere of the place would be destroyed.

Prestige of the House

Do you think the prestige of the House of Commons, in the
eyes of the public as a whole, is

	Per cent of Total	Per cent of Conservative	Per cent of Labour
rising?	6	4	9
static?	48	46	50
falling?	36	37	36
Mixed views or none	10	13	5

The readiness to change their ways reflects, perhaps, the
feeling among MPs that the prestige of the House of Commons is not as high as it might be. But on this issue MPs show
considerable bitterness. If the House of Commons was not as
highly regarded as it ought to be, many feel, it was largely
the fault of the Press. There was a strong streak of resentment
at what one MP calls 'newspaper tittle-tattle about personali-
ties'.

But others are less sure whether all the blame can be put on
newspapers. 'Too many politicians; too few statesmen' (Mr

Henry Price, Conservative). 'Hedonism comes before political interest nowadays, more's the pity' (The Rev Llewelyn Williams, Labour). 'Public ignorance of the proper functions of Parliament' (Mr Gordon Matthews, Conservative).

Some MPs are inclined to blame those of their colleagues whose excessive loquacity takes up too much parliamentary time and reduces the chance of other Backbenchers being called to speak. They are particularly resentful of the prescriptive right of Privy Councillors to speak.

One Conservative, whose experience spans the Backbenchers and office, writes: 'I believe that Ministers and Members must discipline themselves about long speeches. Given enough preparation and thought, a Minister can generally say all that he wants to say in thirty-five minutes. . . . I think Backbenchers' speeches should be limited to fifteen or twenty minutes when other persons are waiting to make a speech.'

Do you think that, in your period in the House of Commons, the quality of the Members has

	Per cent of Total	Per cent of Conservative	Per cent of Labour
gone down?	15	10	23
remained the same?	30	27	33
gone up?	37	40	35
Mixed views or none	18	23	9

On one point, at least, there was optimism. The quality of new MPs coming into the House is going up in the general view: only 15 per cent think that the quality of Members has been falling, 37 per cent think that it has been going up. There may be fewer giants than in the past, most MPs agree, but the quality of the average Member is improving.

But, perhaps, this influx of able, new and vigorous MPs will only add to Lieut-Colonel R. G. Grosvenor's diagnosis of Parliament's ills: 'Too many Members, with democratic freedom of speech, to be efficient.'

APPENDIX C

THE FACILITIES OF THE LIBRARY
OF CONGRESS

by WILLIAM HAMPTON

Introduction

The Library of Congress has far wider functions than its name
would imply, not all of which are relevant to any possible expansion of the Library of the House of Commons. It was
founded in 1800 'for the purchase of such books as may be
necessary for the use of Congress at the said city of Washington, and for fitting up a suitable apartment for containing
them',[1] but it has developed both into the national library of
the United States and into a major research centre for scholars
and the general public.[2]

It is still, of course, the Congressional Library, providing an
unrivalled reference service to the legislature, and it also
serves as the general library for the Federal Government as a
whole (unlike the British lack-of-system of Departmental Libraries, varying greatly in size, quality and accessibility).
During the nineteenth century it became the depository for
foreign government documents and for American copyright
deposits, and it has now the largest collection of books in the
country, going far beyond the direct needs of Federal agencies and Congress. The Library also acts as a national biblio-
graphical centre, developing systems of classification and sell-
ing millions of catalogue cards to other libraries, both for
economy and uniformity. Thus the Library is, as it were, the
Library of the House of Commons, that of the Lords (which
is also the archive of Parliament), the departments of Printed

---

[1] Sixth Congress, Session I, Chapter 37, Section 5.
[2] For the History of the Library of Congress see the *Report* of
the Library of Congress, 1946, the chapter by David C. Mearns.

Books and of Manuscripts of the British Museum, and all the Departmental libraries of Whitehall rolled into one.

Admission to the library is free, and no introduction or credentials are required. All persons over school age may use the reading rooms. The policy of the library is to encourage the widest use of its collections *consistent with* their preservation and with its obligations to Congress and the Executive.

It is important to bear in mind this vast range of activity when considering the Library of Congress, but for the purpose of the present study we may concentrate our attention on the one department that deals specifically with inquiries from the legislature: the Legislative Reference Service.

Legislative Reference Service

This department, which originated in 1915, was given increased status, financial support, and staff, following the Legislative Reorganization Act of 1946. Section 203(*a*) of this Act provided that within the Library of Congress a Legislative Reference Service should be established with the duty:

'(1) upon request, to advise and assist any committee of either House or any joint committee in the analysis, appraisal, and evaluation of legislative proposals pending before it, or of recommendations submitted to Congress, by the President or any executive agency, and otherwise to assist in furnishing a basis for the proper determination of measures before the committee;

'(2) upon request, or upon its own initiative in anticipation of requests, to gather, classify, analyse, and make available, in translations, indices, digests, compilations and bulletins, and otherwise, data for a bearing upon legislation, and to render such data serviceable to Congress, and committees and Members thereof, without partisan bias in selection or presentation;

'(3) to prepare summaries and digests of public hearings before committees of the Congress, and of bills and resolutions of a public general nature introduced in either House.'

Although authorized to conduct research on its own initiative the Legislative Reference Service has been fully occupied in fulfilling the directives of Congress and in meeting the requests initiated by members or committees.

Under a continuing congressional directive, the Bill Digest Section of the American Law Division is responsible for the publication of a digest of Bills introduced, and for the indexing and digesting of the Acts passed by Congress and signed by the President. Similarly, indices and summaries of State Laws are prepared. During 1962 this Division began to prepare a revised edition of *The Constitution of the United States —Analysis and Interpretation*. The last edition of this work was published in 1952 and the new edition will incorporate all the US Supreme Court's decisions on constitutional law since that date.

The Legislative Reference Service also supervises the Congressional Reading Room, which contains standard reference books and a working library in the field of the social sciences. This reading room is reserved for the use of Members of Congress and Congressional employees.

Although all sections of the Legislative Reference Service, and indeed the Library of Congress as a whole, deal with inquiries by Members, the Service contains six subject matter divisions who conduct the bulk of the research. These are: American law, economics, education and public welfare, foreign affairs and national defence, history and government, and agriculture and natural resources.

In 1961 a new unit was established in the Library Services Division to deal with inquiries which Members receive from constituents and forward to the Legislative Reference Service for answer. The Service had long sought to conserve its research facilities for requests made by Members or Committees on their own behalf. Previously this had been done by forwarding only the more readily available material in answer to constituency inquiries. The new unit acquires and stocks prepared materials, which may be sent in answer to such inquiries after consultation with subject specialists to ensure the suitability of the materials selected. This unit answered some two-thirds, or 31,750, of the constituent inquiries in 1962. The remainder, not being suitable for such handling, were referred to the subject matter divisions.[3] In Britain an MP will commonly send such inquiries *directly* to the Department of

[3] *Annual Report of the Librarian of Congress*, 1962, p. 21.

State concerned, who will provide a typed answer on House of Commons' notepaper ready for his signature—a wonderful testimony of trust in the Executive.

In 1962, 223 people were employed by the Legislative Reference Service. The Act of 1946[4] provided for the appointment of senior specialists within broad fields of research that included Public Law, education, full employment, labour, international affairs, housing, and various aspects of economics. Some of the eighteen senior specialists appointed in 1946 were University Professors of their subjects and all of them are research workers of a similar high calibre. By 1962 their number had reached thirty. Other staff members will be graduates in one of the social sciences. There is a tendency for these to be young, few are over forty, and many go on to make careers on the professional staff of Congressional Committees or in departments of the Executive. Some return to the universities.

By comparison we may note that there are thirteen Library Clerks in the Library of the House of Commons who will 'look things up for Members', of whom six 'researchers' concentrate on written replies.[5] It must be remembered, however, that in addition there are twenty-six graduates in the department of the Clerk of the House who service committees of the House, though these would not engage in research in the manner of the Legislative Reference Service.

Use made by Congress of the Legislative Reference Service

The same Act that reconstituted the Legislative Reference Service also provided for improved service to the Congressional Standing Committees. Each committee, other than the Appropriations Committees, is authorized to appoint not more

[4] Legislative Reorganization Act of 1946, Section 203(*b*).
[5] See the evidence of the Librarian of the House of Commons to the *Select Committee on Nationalized Industries,* Questions 196–98, HC Paper 276, Session 1958–59, and to the *Select Committee on Estimates,* HC Paper 168, Session 1960–61; see also pp. 68–70 above.

than four professional staff members (which it will recruit itself) in addition to the clerical staffs.[6] The Legislative Reference Service does not, therefore, need to provide staff for the committees. Senior Specialists may on occasion act as consultants to a Committee for a time, but in general the work of the Service is directed to specific requests for information.

These requests from Committees will commonly involve the preparation of detailed reports which may include some historical background, the presentation of arguments for and against some policy question, a bibliography, and a collection of related readings. Many of the more important reports prepared for Committees are subsequently published as Committee Prints or House or Senate Documents. Such comprehensive studies may also be made for individual members of committees or even individual Members of Congress, though if the research is likely to take several weeks the Congressman's notice would be drawn to this fact. Delay is their defence against excessive demands.

The range of the requests for information is very wide and very little is excluded. Members of the service could not write a purely political speech defending or attacking a political party, but they may 'on request' defend or attack *policies*. In fact Robert Elder has written that 'almost no request is "off limits"'. While the Service:

> 'Would not knowingly answer a question . . . for the benefit of a constituent participating in a quiz contest for a prize. It does occasionally do bibliographical work on masters' or doctors' theses, where an "enterprising" scholar has asked for such assistance through his congressman or senator. It avoids writing dissertations or major parts of them.'[7]

Such abuse, for personal or family requests, of the facilities available is not, however, a great problem. The bulk of the inquiries are of immediate relevance to the efficient working of the Congressman or Senator. This is true even of inquiries

[6] Legislative Reorganization Act of 1946, Section 202(*a*).

[7] Robert E. Elder, 'The Foreign Affairs Division of the Legislative Reference Service: Organization and Functions of a Professional Staff', *The Western Political Quarterly*, March 1957, p. 170.

from constituents, which make up nearly half the total handled. The member of Congress is assumed to have neither the time nor the knowledge to deal with all the questions his constituents ask him and, failing the Legislative Reference Service, he would need to hire a personal staff or neglect his mail.

Besides asking the Service for facts, for selected readings on a subject, for general reports, or for assistance in tracing quotations or references, the member of Congress may obtain background information on people or countries he intends to visit in the course of his duties. He may, too, receive help in the drafting of speeches. The work that goes into these drafts is obviously thorough. It has been suggested that three days would be taken to prepare a fifteen minute speech; and a week to prepare a thirty-five to forty-five minute address, although this might be reduced considerably during periods of peak demand.[8]

TABLE A

LEGISLATIVE REFERENCE SERVICE

Fiscal Year	No. of requests dealt with	No. employed at end of year
1946	22,765	n.a.
1950	42,144	161
1954	51,586	165
1958	67,843	195
1962	99,430	223

n.a. = not available.

Source: The *Annual Reports* of the Librarian of Congress.

Note: These figures do not reflect the full extent of the questions answered for Members by the whole Library of Congress. For example, in 1962 some 43,000 requests for service were met by departments other than the Legislative Reference Service. These, however, will tend to need little or no research for their answer.

[8] *Ibid.*, p. 173.

The number of specific Congressional inquiries dealt with by the Legislative Reference Service in 1962 was 99,430. This was an increase of 15,235 or 18 per cent over the number answered in 1961. The number of requests answered by the Service has increased steadily over the past thirty years. During the past ten years the number has increased annually by an average of 8 to 9 per cent. Table A gives an indication of the growth of the Service since its reorganization in 1946. In addition some 43,000 requests for service by members of Congress were met during 1962 by other departments of the Library of Congress.

TABLE B

HOUSE OF COMMONS LIBRARY

Written inquiries dealt with by Research Department

Year	General Research	Statistical	Total
1949	248	n.a.	248
1950	192	n.a.	192
1951	207	n.a.	207
1952	309	162*	471
1953	324	216	540
1954	378	216	594
1955	310	229	539
1956	387	300	687
1957	398	289	687
1958	388	317	705
1959	573	338	911
1960	615	329	944
1961	572	400	972
1962	519	370	889
1963	581	384	965

n.a. = not available. * 8 months. *Source:* HC Paper 246, 1960–61.

Of the inquiries dealt with by the Legislative Reference Service in 1962, 30,650 were answered by telephone and 57,800 by sending materials. This left almost 11,000 to be answered in report or other written form or by personal conference, and these must represent the bulk of the detailed research undertaken.[9] The steady growth in the number of inquiries reflects in part the increase in the volume and complexity of Congressional responsibilities, but in part it is a natural growth as members of Congress become practised in the use of the facilities available. It is generally true that a good library creates, as well as satisfies, demand.

Again for comparison we may note that in 1963 the number of questions answered by the Research Department of the House of Commons Library was 965. This figure does not include the many verbal questions answered in other departments of the Library (and includes answers to non-Members —about 100 a year over the last three years), but any minor faults of comparability are overshadowed by the *qualitative* difference in the figures of the two countries. It may be seen from Table B that the number of questions dealt with is steadily increasing. This shows that even a limited staff is serving a growing demand.

Conclusion

The difference noted above is not accidental, nor is it a consequence of the differing political systems of the United States and the United Kingdom. It is the result of definite policy decisions in recent times (in America associated with the period of political reform following Wilson's election in 1912). It is true that the development of the Legislative Reference Service has always been connected with the jealous regard of Congress for its independence of the Executive, but this is only a part of the impetus behind its growth. The other aspect is the realization that the elected representatives of the people deserve a status and the facilities which enable them to act

[9] All figures from the *Report of the Librarian of Congress* (1962), p. 20.

efficiently as guardians of their trust. And the Executive itself
has found it convenient to share many of these facilities with
Congress.

In Britain the attempt is made to maintain the status of the
Member of Parliament by emphasizing, in rhetoric, his individual ability. The Library Clerks are to provide the books,
references, and occasionally, statistics, but the Member does
his own work. The suggestion that 'briefing' for speeches
should be conducted in the Library is met with a dismissal
tinged with disgust.[10] When one considers that the largest
occupation group in the House of Commons is that of lawyers,
this is all the more puzzling and absurd.

In the United States, the British concept is regarded as unrealistic. If a representative is to follow, even in general, the
far-ranging activities of modern government, possibly specialize in some aspect of them, and, in addition, maintain contact
with some tens of thousands of constituents, then he will have
little time to act as his own research worker.

The recognition of this fact by the House of Commons need
not be seen as the importation of an Americanism that will
erode the special relationship existing between the legislature
and the executive in the British system of government. There
is plenty of room for the expansion of the modest facilities
provided by the Library of the House of Commons before we
come to *that*.

[10] See the Reports of the *Select Committee on Estimates* on the
House of Commons Library (1960–61, HC 168), and the Obser-
vations of Mr Speaker's Advisory Committee (1960–61, HC 246),
especially p. 8 of the former.

APPENDIX D

These summaries are given to show the usefulness of such work and the nonsense of asserting that such investigation and criticism interferes either with Ministerial responsibility or the normal operating of the Department—in this case, Board. Plainly both Ministers and Boards are affected by such exceptionally well informed criticism—which is as it should be (but is not so over almost all other fields of administration); but plainly they do not give way if they think it important not to do so—which is again as it should be (the Minister takes political responsibility for really important matters, or the Board refuses to be drawn into politics). This committee may be the 'thin end of the wedge' as some feared when it was set up; but then it is as well to examine the wedge with care. If Nationalized Industries were felt to be a special case, which would not challenge any Minister as closely and persistently as, say, a committee on Home Office affairs, then in fact this hope has not proved true: the Select Committee has frequently examined and challenged the decisions and the influence of the Minister—but none the worse for that.

REPORT ON SCOTTISH ELECTRICITY BOARDS, 1956–57
(HC 304 [vii])
(*Minister's Reply, 581 HC Hansard 103, 1957–58*)
    (all relate to N. of Scotland Hydro-Electric Board)

Principal recommendations:

(1) The Board should endeavour to obtain more fixed price contracts—the Board agreed.
(2) The Board had been in the practice of dividing its contracts for Water Wheels and Turbine Alternators between

three firms that had been encouraged to settle in Scotland. The Committee recommended that this work should now be subject to competitive tender. The Board agreed.

(3) The Committee was concerned that estimates for capital expenditure had proved hopelessly wrong in past years and suggested attention should be paid to this and to giving more figures relating to projects and estimates in the Annual Report. Board agreed.

(4) The Committee recommended that more publicity be given to the Consultative Council to ensure greater use is made of it when causes for complaint arise.

REPORT ON NATIONAL COAL BOARD, 1957–58 (HC 187 [vi]) (*Minister's Reply, 591 HC Hansard 825, 1957–58* [*see col. 842–45*])

Principal recommendations:

(1) Investment—The Ministry of Power should be able to make a greater financial check on the Board's investment schemes than they do at present. The Board should present full details each year of those schemes likely to be least profitable. Minister accepted this.

(2) *Investing in Coal*—This is the basis of investment in the industry. In their Annual Reports the Board should make a comparison of the results achieved with the estimates made in *Investing in Coal*. Minister agreed.

(3) Man power—The Board seem less concerned now with the total number at work than with the number of attendances of each man. The Board agreed to include in future reports information on the progress made in Work Study, job analyses and standard costing.

(4) Prices—The Committee agreed generally with the Board's policy on prices but made two general points:

(*a*) Coal Prices should cover the full cost of depreciation on a replacement basis. Minister agreed in principle but thought any large increase in price to meet this would be undesirable.

(*b*) The Committee did not like the informality of the 'Gentleman's Agreement' by which the Minister of Power exercised control over fuel prices—this dated back to wartime conditions; the Committee felt that such power should be exercised by directives and its use therefore disclosed to Parliament. The Minister disagreed: the relations between the Government and the Board must be based upon 'constant and confidential consultation'.

(5) The Committee felt that the limit given to divisional authorities for capital expenditure should be increased. The Board promised to consider this but had doubts about it.

(6) Other points on stocks, large and small coal and uneconomic pits were couched in such general terms that no comments were necessary to answer then specifically.

REPORT ON THE AIR CORPORATIONS, 1958–59 (HC 213 [vii])
(*Corporations' and Minister's Reply, HC 339, 1959–60* [*vii*])

A very long and detailed report. Principal recommendations:

(1) Consideration should be given to standardization of the requirements for civil and military aircraft. The Minister noted this point.

(2) Fares are controlled internationally, the Committee felt this should be pointed out when fares are increased and that British airlines should strive to reduce fares. Minister agreed.

(3) Services that are run as 'social services', e.g. to the Highlands and Islands, should be specifically subsidized by the government if it wishes them to continue. BEA agreed. The Minister thought there was no immediate problem as an overall profit was made.

(4) Such social service routes should be itemized in the accounts. Agreed by BEA and the Minister that some indication should be made of such losses but feel that it is better that this should continue to be done in the Annual Report.

(5) The Committee spoke of the financial dangers of a premature re-equipment race between airlines. The Minister thought the airlines had little option but to maintain their competitive position even if re-equipment led to capital losses.

(6) Aircraft Utilization—the Committee felt that this could be improved. BEA thought this doubtful.

(7) The Committee felt that not enough had been done to reduce operating costs which were higher than those of rival airlines. The Corporations replied that they were doing their best.

(8) The Committee thought it wrong that BOAC should be required by the government to invest in uneconomic subsidiaries, e.g. Kuwait Airways; such investment should be

subsidized as part of Government policy, not made a burden on a commercial undertaking. BOAC agreed. The Minister refused to reconsider the Kuwait Airways case, but said they would consider the matter if future cases occurred.

(9) Consideration should be given to pruning uneconomic subsidiary companies. Replies—the matter is under constant review.

(10) The Committee raised the question of the fixed percentage of traffic that is allocated to the Corporations and private concerns and suggested competition might be better. The Minister blocked this point.

(11) The Committee were referred to non-statutory controls exercised by the Minister and suggested that it would be better for him to act by Directive. The Minister stressed that the political and economic implications of the Corporations' decisions made Government control necessary, but he ducked the point about directives.

(12) The Committee felt that increased co-operation, but not a merger, would be to the Corporations' advantage. Both Corporations and the Minister agreed.

SPECIAL REPORT OF SELECT COMMITTEE ON
NATIONALIZED INDUSTRIES,
1958–59 (HC 276 [vii])

This Report considered the various proposals for giving expert assistance to the Select Committee.

The Committee accepted as general principles that any staff working for the Select Committee should be the servants of Parliament and not of the Executive, and also that any increase in staff should not lead to interference in the working of the Nationalized Industries.

The proposal for an officer of the stature of the Comptroller and Auditor General was not advocated as it would seem to be leading to a 'Grand Inquisition' of the Nationalized Industries. Other proposals were turned down on grounds of practicability, difficulty of recruitment for such a spasmodic job, or for other reasons.

Finally the Committee recommended that they have the services of an additional clerk and that the Senior of their two Clerks should have worked with the Special Committee for a number of years. This has since been implemented.

REPORT ON BRITISH RAILWAYS, 1959–60 (HC 254 [vii])
(*Reply by British Railways and Minister,*
HC 163, 1960–61 [*vii*])

(1) The Committee was critical of the British Transport Commission (BTC) and felt that the Railways should be organized as a separate entity. This has been done. British Railways would not comment at the time.

(2) Wagon turn-round—the Committee felt that not enough attention had been paid to this in the past; improvements needed to be made and made quickly. British Railways agreed, though sought to avoid criticism.

(3) The Committee stressed the importance of work-study. British Railways agreed.

(4) They thought that an increase in the number of highly trained technical staff was necessary and that a central register was necessary. British Railways agreed to first part, but did not think a central register was needed as the Regions kept them.

(5) General criticism of management: 'a serious shortcoming in management, the full effect of which it is impossible to gauge'. Specifically the Committee criticized the BTC for continuing with a costing system and accounts that made it impossible to ascertain the profitability of Regions and particular services. British Railways thought the criticism unjust. These matters were under consideration and considerable time had been spent on them.

(6) The Committee recommended that the utmost use should be made of the assets of land and property owned by the BTC. British Railways agreed and commented that they too had made representations on this matter to the Minister, *but* it might be more profitable to British Railways to participate in the development than to dispose of the property outright.

(7) Recommend that where Government action causes a Nationalized Industry to incur a specific loss or specific expenditure which it would not otherwise incur, then the Government should take steps to compensate the industry.

(8) Transport Tribunal—the Committee considered that there was no need for the Tribunal in areas where competition was effective. Perhaps it was still needed for suburban services. Tribunal should give reasoned decisions. Changes have since been made in the Tribunal. British Railways agreed.

(9) It should be for the Government—not the BTC—to decide when the social needs of the community or the needs of the national economy or defence, prescribed the continued running of services at a loss. Such services should be given an open subsidy, in advance. The accounts should make this quite clear. This would enhance the parliamentary responsibility of the Minister, and the Commission. British Railways in reply agreed in principle but pointed out the difficulties of deciding *which* services were to be subsidized and which were making a loss.

(10) The Committee reiterated a point made in their report on Coal that the Minister of Transport and the Treasury should receive a breakdown figure of the amount of capital investment planned. Not only the average return but the return of the less profitable investments also should be specified, so that the Government could judge 'where the public interest lies'. The BTC in their reply sought to defend themselves on specific points but in general accepted the views of the Committee—at least there was no open disagreement or controversy between the two bodies.[1]

REPORT ON GAS INDUSTRY (HC 280 [vii]) (*Reply by Industry and Minister, HC 218, 1961–62*)

This is a long and technical report. The principal recommendations are:

(1) Research—the Committee felt that expenditure had been too low in relation to turnover. The Industry denied that they had been lax in this matter and gave examples of their work.

(2) Organization—the Committee felt that a thirteenth board should be constituted to undertake large-scale production and other gas supply schemes. Both the Minister and the Industry agreed with the principle but did not accept the details. A joint investigation by the Ministry and Gas Council into the structure of the industry was set in hand.

(3) This Committee, like previous ones, stressed that the Government should lay down minimum returns needed before specific investment was undertaken. The Minister considered that the Gas Council must be allowed discretion

---

[1] Transport Act, 1962, White Paper, Cmnd 1246, and see note in *Public Administration*, Winter 1962, p. 436.

within its overall obligation to fulfil statutory requirements (*see* White Paper Cmnd 1337).

(4) In connection with this last point the Committee interpreted Para. 29 of the White Paper—'The Financial and Economic Obligations of the Nationalized Industries'—to mean that the Minister *had* interfered with the fixing of prices by Nationalized Industries and that this 'informal' practice, which has no statutory authority, would continue. The Committee recommended, therefore:

(*a*) That a written statement of any Ministerial intervention on tariffs should be laid before Parliament;

(*b*) An Amending Gas Bill should be introduced to give the Minister the necessary authority.

The Minister said the Committee had misinterpreted the Government's intentions. The function of the Minister was only to draw the attention of the Council to the Government's view of the National interest. The Council had the duty to fix tariffs at the level it considered suitable.

(5) There was considerable discussion of the merits of Methane and production by the Lurgi process. The Committee criticized the Council who did not accept the criticism and defended themselves with reasoned argument and facts.

APPENDIX E

THE WORK OF THE HOUSE OF LORDS

i. *Table of Bills Considered in the Lords originating in the Commons with the Number of Amendments and their Fate (and a list of Bills which needed no Amendment), Sessions 1948–49 and 1961–62.*

ii. *List of Bills Initiated in the House of Lords, Sessions 1948–49 and 1961–62.*

iii. *List of Divisions in the Lords, Sessions 1948–49 and 1961–62.*

iv. *List of General Discussions and Debates, Sessions 1948–49 and 1961–62.*

These Tables and Lists are set out in dull detail to make overwhelmingly clear how indispensable is the work of a Second Chamber, how little it gets in the way, and how readily it could do more to assist the Commons and to inform the public.

i. *Table of Bills Considered in the Lords originating in the Commons with the Number of Amendments and their Fate (and a list of Bills which needed no Amendment), Sessions 1948–49 and 1961–62*

Amendments accepted are, of course, mostly Government sponsored. Rejections, that is when there is a division, are rare (and so are separately studied in Table 3). But the significance of Amendments Withdrawn is to be seen less in their fate than in that they enable a subject to be fully discussed and publicized. Bills found to need no amendment are subject to just as much initial scrutiny—and need it—as the others: the bulk of them are Consolidation Bills involving issues of draughtsmanship and clarity, not policy. This Table excludes Private Bills.

SESSION 1948–49

Name of Bill	Amendments		
	Accepted	Rejected	Withdrawn
Cinematograph Film Production (Special Loan)	1	—	1
Consular Conventions	—	—	1
Coal Industry	25	—	9
Agriculture (Miscellaneous Provisions)	2	—	5
Agriculture Marketing	3	1	2
Commonwealth Telegraphs	—	—	2
Adoption of Children	38	—	2
Juries	8	—	3
Landlord and Tenant (Rent Control)	34	1	18
Lands Tribunal	8	—	2
Iron and Steel	88	10	65
Ireland	1	—	3
Licensing	50	—	7
Legal Aid and Advice	—	—	2
Housing	44	—	5
Legal Aid and Solicitors (Scotland)	3	—	11
Law Reform (Miscellaneous Provisions)	25	—	1
Housing (Scotland)	4	—	2
Local Government Boundary Commission (Dissolution)	—	—	1
Married Women (Maintenance)	5	—	2
Prize	1	—	—
National Service Amendment	—	—	1
Pensions Appeals Tribunals	—	—	1

Public Works (Festival of Britain)	4	—	—
National Parks and Access to the Countryside	149	—	84
National Health Service (Amendment)	5	—	—
Recall of Army and Air Force Pensioners	1	—	4
Wages Councils	3	—	—
Wireless Telegraphy	23	—	8
Special Roads	33	—	19
Water (Scotland)	22	—	8
Tenancy of Shops (Scotland)	1	—	2
Representation of the People	1	—	—
Superannuation	4	—	1
War Damage (Sites)	7	—	3
Parliament Square (Improvements)	3	—	—
Airway Corporations	—	—	2
Auxiliary and Reserve Forces	9	—	3
Distribution of German Enemy Property	1	—	5
Festival of Britain (Supplementary Provisions)	7	—	1
Electoral Registers	5	—	—

Bills found to need no amendment: Colonial Stock; Civil Defence; Administration of Justice (Scotland); American Aid (Financial Provisions); British North America; Consolidated Fund (No. 1); Army and Air Force (Annual); Debts Clearing Office; Expiring Laws Continuance; Education (Scotland); Export Guarantees; Docking and Nicking of Horses; Finance; Expiring Laws Continuance (No. 2); British Film Institute; Cockfighting; Colonial Loans; Colonial Development and Welfare; Judges Pensions (India and Burma); House of Commons (Indemnification of Certain Members); Isle of Man Customs; India (Consequential Provisions); Minister of

Food (Financial Powers); Merchant Shipping (Safety Convention); National Theatre; Profits Tax; National Insurance; Overseas Resources Development; Savings Banks; Solicitors and Public Notaries, etc.; Social Services (Northern Ireland Agreement); War Damage (Public Utility Undertakings, etc.); Slaughter of Animals (Scotland); Telegraph; Public Works Loans; Consolidated Fund (Appropriation); Coal Industry (No. 2); Armed Forces (Housing Loans) Bills.

SESSION 1961–62

Name of Bill	Amendments		
	Accepted	Rejected	Withdrawn
Army Reserve	—	2	8
Civil Aviation (Eurocontrol)	—	—	1
Commonwealth Immigrants	16	5	7
Health Visiting and Social Work (Training)	—	1	7
Housing (Scotland)	—	3	3
Local Authorities (Historic Buildings)	—	—	1
Local Government (Records)	1	—	—
Lotteries and Gaming	6	—	—
Sea Fish Industry	1	1	1
South Africa	3	1	3
Transport	185	36	76

Bills found to need no amendment: Agricultural and Forestry Associations; Air Guns and Shot Guns, etc.; Carriage by Air (Supplementary Provisions); Coal Consumers' Councils (Northern Irish Interests); Coal Industry; Colonial Loans; Commonwealth Settlement; Consolidated Fund; Consolidated Fund (No. 2); Consolidated Fund (Appropriation); Drainage Rates; Education; Expiring Laws Continuance; Export Guarantees; Family Allowances and National Insurance; Finance; House of Commons Members' Fund; International

Monetary Fund; Jamaica Independence; Landlord and Tenant; Law Reform (Damages and Solatium) (Scotland); Law Reform (Husband and Wife); Local Government (Financial Provisions, etc.) (Scotland); Marriage (Wales and Monmouthshire); National Assistance Act, 1948 (Amendment); Penalties for Drunkenness; Police Federations; Recorded Delivery Service; Shops (Airports); Southern Rhodesia (Constitution); Tanganyika Independence; Trinidad and Tobago Independence; Uganda Independence.

ii. *List of Bills Initiated in the Lords, Sessions 1948–49 and 1961–62*

The period between the Second Reading (2 R) and the Royal Assent (RA) is given for this shows the typical length of a Bill, for this is relevant to any consideration of the proper length of any period of delay. The time spent in Committee is time saved for the Commons in a direct sense in this class of legislation: rarely do the Commons find need to re-do this work of the Lords.

SESSION 1948–49

British North America (No. 2) Bill

2 R (Second Reading), 22 November, 1949. RA (Royal Assent), 16 December, 1949.

Support by all parties as a recognition of the complete self-government of each member of the Commonwealth. Two formal speeches of support on the Second Reading, but no real debate.

The Committee Stage was dispensed with and the Third Reading made the same afternoon.

Coast Protection Bill

2 R, 25 November, 1948. RA, 24 November, 1949.

General support on the Second Reading; a strong desire to discuss the allocation of costs during Committee.

Committee stage: two afternoons. Many amendments both drafting and material. Much expert knowledge, e.g. Lord Stansgate has served on Catchment Boards and spoke for their interests.

83 Amendments were received from the Commons and accepted en bloc. Lord Llewellyn (a Conservative leader) said: 'In this case the other place have acted as a very good revising Chamber to our original work.'

Amendments in the Lords: A (accepted), 121; R (rejected), 0; W (withdrawn), 56.

Colonial Naval Defence

2 R, 18 January, 1949. RA, 9 March, 1949.

To make further provision for Naval co-operation between the Colonies and the training of personnel.

Amendments: A, 1; R, —; W, —.

Consolidation of Enactments (Procedure) Bill

2 R, 13 April, 1949. RA, following session.

To facilitate the preparation of Bills aimed at consolidating the enactments referring to any subject; providing, inter alia, an extra branch of the Parliamentary Counsel's Office. A highly technical Bill for which agreement was reached by mutual Party consultation before introduction.

General support and no debate in Committee.

On the formal Third Reading two of the Law Lords stated their support and discussed how its conditions would preclude new law from being made under its powers.

Criminal Justice (Scotland) Bill

2 R, 30 November, 1948. RA, 16 December, 1949.

To amend the law relating to the probation of offenders and powers of courts; to abolish certain punishments and obsolete sanctions; criminal courts, prisons and kindred matters.

Formal all-party support but much discussion of detail; a good technical debate on the Second Reading by experts in the law of Scotland.

A typical Committee Stage: 1, Opposition amendment accepted; 31 withdrawn (usually only raised to make the Government explain a point); 17 Government drafting amendments; 1 Government amendment of substance withdrawn after discussion.

On the Report Stage 3 Opposition amendments agreed to; 2 withdrawn; 38 Government amendments, drafting, consequential or other amendments, and of minor substance, many to meet points raised in Committee.

Amendments: A, 85; R, —; W, 38.

Justice of the Peace Bill

2 R, 12 July, 1949. RA, 16 December, 1949.

A major Bill to amend the law relating to the distribution, finance, and procedure of magistrates' courts (and stipendiary magistrates) and to make provision for the payment of expenses for probation and care committees. A full debate on the Second Reading; most of the Law Lords attended; a highly informed discussion with much criticism of detail. The Committee Stage lasted four days with a full day on the Report.

Amendments: A, 299; R, 5; W, 54.

Married Women (Restraint upon Anticipation) Bill

2 R, 5 July, 1949. RA, 16 December, 1949.

To render inoperative restrictions upon the disposal or leaving of a woman's own property. (Introduced to cover the general case of such as the Mountbatten Estates Bill, privately promoted and withdrawn in favour of this Bill.) One full afternoon in Committee.

Amendments: A, 1; R, —; W, 1.

Milk (Special Designations) Bill

2 R, 14 December, 1948. RA, 31 May, 1949.

To improve and extend the standard designation of certain types of milk in the interests of public health. All party general support, but an expert and very close discussion of the details.

Amendments: A, 15; R, 2; W, 14.

New Forest Bill

2 R, 9 December, 1948. RA, 24 November, 1949.

Based on the findings of an independent Committee. To bring the ancient law and custom of administration of the New Forest more into line with modern conditions. A full and expert debate on the Second Reading (Lord Robinson was Chairman of the Forestry Commission; Lords Radnor and Beaulieu, the two largest owners of 'common rights' in the Forest; and Lords Teynham and Hagan were also residents).

Referred to a Select Committee—previously before the Second Reading, it had been published that interested parties could bring evidence before the Select Committee. The Minutes of Evidence were laid before the House. Reported, with amendments, to the Committee of the whole House.

In the Committee Stage the amendments of the Select Committee were agreed to en bloc. One full afternoon. Much give and take on substantial amendments.

Amendments: A, 34; R, —; W, 4.

Nurses Bill

2 R, 3 May, 1949. RA, 24 November, 1949.

General all-party agreement. Full and detailed discussion on Second Reading and Committee Stage.

Amendments: A, 55; R, —; W, 9.

Nurses (Scotland) Bill

2 R, 7 July, 1949. RA, 16 December, 1949.

To bring Scotland into line with the impending Nurses Act, 1949. The Bill was much improved during the passage through the House.

Amendments: A, 22; R, —; W, 1.

Patents and Designs Bill

2 R, 29 March, 1949. RA, 16 December, 1949.

Strongly criticized by judicial experts on Patent Law on the Second Reading, but not actually opposed.

Two full days in Committee. Much give and take over important provisions. Numerous drafting, consequential and minor amendments. Many amendments on the Report Stage also. In all they much improved the Bill.

Amendments: A, 55; R, —; W, 9.

Prevention of Damage by Pests Bill

2 R, 18 November, 1948. RA, 30 July, 1949.

Broad Opposition agreement to the Bill but much criticism of the wide powers it gave to the Minister. Much bad and ambiguous drafting cleared up on a full one-day Committee Stage.

Amendments: A, 47; R, —; W, 9.

Railway and Canal Commission (Abolition) Bill
2 R, 9 November, 1948. RA, 9 March, 1949.
No opposition and little discussion on the Committee Stage.
Amendments: A, 1; R, —; W, 2.

USA Veterans Pension Administration Bill
2 R, 2 June, 1949. RA, 14 July, 1949.
To enable the Minister of Pensions to administer, for the
benefit of certain US ex-service men and their dependants
in the United Kingdom, pensions and other sums which are
payable by the Administration of Veterans' Affairs in the
USA. All-party support. No discussion. The Committee stage
was avoided by suspending Standing Order XXXIX and the
Third Reading was held the same afternoon as the Second
Reading. No amendments.

Marriage (Enabling) Bill (Private Member's Bill)
To enable a person to marry certain kin of the spouse
whom that person has divorced; for the husband (or wife)
to be able to marry the sister (or brother) of the divorced
party. This was very strongly supported but opposed by Can-
terbury and York. Withdrawn owing to Governmental refusal to facilitate its passage, i.e. to find time for a Committee
Stage and Third Reading. Also the Conservative leader advised Lord Mancroft, a Conservative, to withdraw it as part
of an understanding to facilitate the passage of a Private Bill
by a Conservative MP. The support for it may have influenced
the Government, together with Mrs Eirene White's Bill in the
Commons on the divorce laws, to appoint a Royal Commission on the whole topic of the laws of marriage and divorce.
(This is a typical example of what happens to a Private Member's Bill.)

Also there were 11 Consolidation Bills, consolidating the
law on such diverse topics as Agricultural Wages, Civil Aviation, Electrical Law, and Patents Law; and 18 Private Bills,
mostly sponsored by Local Government Authorities and including two applications to alter the terms of a Charitable
Trust registered with Parliament.

SESSION 1961–62

Acts of Parliament Numbering and Citation Bill

2 R (Second Reading), 25 January, 1962. RA (Royal Assent), 19 July, 1962.

Support by all parties. Two formal speeches of support on Second Reading, but no real debate.

Formal Committee Stage.

Criminal Justice Administration Bill

2 R, 13 November, 1961. RA, 29 March, 1962.

To give effect to such of the recommendations of the Interdepartmental Committee on the Business of the Criminal Courts as required legislation.

Supported by both parties and the Lord Chief Justice.

Debates took place on Second Reading, Report and Third Reading, and amendments were made both in Committee and at the Report Stage.

Amendments: A (accepted), 21; R (rejected), 1; W (withdrawn), 5.

Licensing (Scotland)

2 R, 21 November, 1961. RA, 1 August, 1962.

A major Bill dealing with Sunday drinking and the permitted hours. The Bill followed the First Report of the Committee on the Scottish Licensing Law.

The Opposition welcomed the Bill but thought it too timid. A full debate on Second Reading went into detail on the interpretation of the Bill.

Two afternoons were spent in Committee, and further amendments were proposed on Report. There was a debate on Third Reading when further amendments were proposed.

Amendments: A, 50; R, 4; W, 13.

Northern Ireland

2 R, 1 February, 1962. RA, 3 July, 1962.

To make amendments to the Constitution of Northern Ireland made desirable by changing circumstances.

Supported by all parties. A short but informed debate on Second Reading with a contribution by Lord Denning on a legal point.

Amendments proposed in Committee, on Report, and at Third Reading.

Amendments: A, 5; R, 1; W, 1.

Pipe-lines Bill

2 R, 13 March, 1962. RA, 1 August, 1962.

To enable the Government to control cross country pipe-lines in the public interest and in the interest of safety; to enable people who wish to construct pipe-lines to obtain land compulsorily without having to promote Private Bills; and to establish that pipe-lines in England and Wales are rateable.

A long and complicated Bill that received detailed consideration. The Opposition did not divide on Second Reading, but were critical of the scope and drafting of the Bill. They suggested that pipe-lines should be considered a public utility and were therefore suitable candidates for public ownership.

Three afternoons were spent in Committee. On Report it was objected that the Government had not given sufficient time to consider the detailed proposals for improvement put forward in Committee and the Government's proposal to accept the Report was defeated. Two afternoons in the following week were then spent on the Report Stage and substantial amendments made.

A further debate took place on Third Reading and further amendments were proposed and made.

Amendments: A, 78; R, 8; W, 64.

Road Traffic Bill

2 R, 14 November, 1961. RA, 1 August, 1962.

To make further provisions for road safety. There were several contentious points in the Bill, e.g. those dealing with automatic disqualification after three specified offences within three years, and the testing of drunken drivers.

Two afternoons were spent in Committee.

Amendments: A, 7; R, 6; W, 13.

West Indies Bill

R, 7 March, 1962. RA, 18 April, 1962.

An enabling Bill to allow action to be taken consequent upon the breakdown of the Federation of the West Indies, and to allow the Government to grant new constitutions to the constituent territories.

During the debate on this 'melancholy Bill' the Opposition attacked the failure of the Government's policy but did not oppose Second Reading.

Amendments: A, 6; R, —; W, 3.

Animals (Cruel Poisons) Bill (Private Member's Bill—Lord Cranbrook)

2 R, 30 January, 1962. RA, 3 July, 1962.

To make illegal the use of certain poisons that cause lingering death to the pests they are designed to destroy.

Little opposition to the principle of the Bill, but some discussion.

In Committee drastic amendments were made on the instigation of the Government. These amounted to a re-drafting but the original principle was preserved.

Amendments in the Lords: A, 8; R, —; W, —.

Boxing Bill (Private Member's Bill—Lady Summerskill)

Defeated on Second Reading 10 May, 1962. Voting, 22 to 29.

Several hours were devoted to a full discussion of this Bill to make professional boxing illegal.

British Museum Bill (Private Member's Bill—Lord Hurcomb)

2 R, 15 March, 1962. RA, 18 April, 1962.

To enable the Trustees of the British Museum to lend certain works of art for exhibition in Vienna.

Supported by the Government and all parts of the House. Formal Committee Stage.

Racial Discrimination Bill (Private Member's Bill—Lord Walston)

Defeated on Second Reading, 14 May, 1962. Voting, 21 to 41.

To make discrimination by reason of colour, race or religion, a criminal offence.

After a long debate their Lordships 'while acknowledging the sincere motives that have prompted the noble Lord to introduce the Bill, denied it a Second Reading'.

Consolidation Bills

Building Societies; Education (Scotland); Telegraph; Town and Country Planning; Vehicles (Excise).

iii. *List of Divisions in the Lords, Sessions 1948–49 and 1961–62*

A division carried against the Government forces the House of Commons to reconsider something. Usually if the Government then rejects the Lords' amendments, the Lords withdraw; only in the Parliament Bill and the Steel Bill was opposition pressed to the limit. So properly to gauge the amount of obstruction over helpful scrutiny, the circumstances of each division must be considered. The list includes some votes on general resolutions, not on amendments to legislation; though even here divisions are the exception rather than the rule.

SESSION 1948–49

Coal Industry Bill Committee

Among the provisions of the Coal Industry Bill, amending the Nationalization Act of 1947, was a grant of power to the NCB to engage in overseas activities in competition with private firms. The Opposition moved that it should only be granted such powers by gaining, in each instance as it arises, the approval by resolution of both Houses. The resolution was carried against the Government by 49 to 18. The Commons disagreed with the amendment. The Lords changed their resolution to make the exercise of such powers by the NCB depend on a Ministerial Order which would be made in the form of a Statutory Instrument to be laid before Parliament in the usual way. This was agreed to by the Commons.

Economic Policy

In November 1949 the Lords debated Economic Policy on a Government resolution stating approval for 'the lines of action to deal with the present economic difficulties as outlined in the Prime Minister's statement of 24 October'. The Conservatives amended to censure the Government's alleged failure by 116 votes to 29 after a two-day debate.

Exchange Value of the Pound

Parliament interrupted the Summer Recess to debate devaluation. The Lords debated a Government resolution of approval for two days before amending it to one of criticism by 93 votes to 24.

Ground Nuts and Oil Seeds Scheme

The Opposition moved for an independent Commission of Inquiry into the Ground Nuts Scheme. It was carried by 57 votes to 27. Here the cumulative effect of criticism of the scheme was influencing public opinion.

Women Peers

A motion by Lord Reading (Conservative) to express the hope that future legislation would enable Peeresses in their own right to take their seats in Parliament. A free vote was taken that cut across Party Lines. 45 for, 27 against.

Housing (Scotland) Bill

A Conservative amendment was carried by 44 votes to 14 to ensure that grants in aid for rural housing should be so applied as to tie the houses to use by people in the agricultural industry—an offshoot of the tied cottage controversy. The Commons rejected the amendment and the Lords withdrew it rather than delay the whole Bill.

Justices of the Peace Bill (House of Lords)

A non-Party measure. Two amendments were defeated, and one in the report stage, the voting cutting right across Party lines.

Landlord and Tenant (Rent Control) Bill

Two Opposition amendments, one to provide that the abnormally low rents caused by people having to leave their houses for war service, should not be assessed as the standard rent for such people's property; and the other to allow Tribunals to increase rents in respect of increase in the price of services. Both were carried against the Government by, respectively, 58 to 19 and 40 to 15. Rejected by the Commons, they were withdrawn by the Lords.

Lands Tribunal Bill

An amendment was moved against the Government on the Report Stage to give people the power of appealing to a tribunal against any development charge by the Central Land Board under the Town and Country Planning Act, 1947. Carried by 68 votes to 22, but withdrawn following Commons rejection.

Licensing Bill

Some of the Bill's provisions directed that the sale of intoxicating liquor in the State management districts of the New Towns in licensed premises and clubs, should be restricted to people acting on behalf of the Minister of State. Conservative amendment was carried by 40 to 18 to exempt clubs from the provisions, but withdrawn following Commons rejection. There was a fear of discrimination against political clubs.

Married Women (Restraint upon Anticipation) Bill (House of Lords)

A Government Bill of a non-party controversial matter provided largely a lawyers' debate. Lord Simon moved an amendment against the Government, desiring the same effect, viz. allowing women to leave personal property as freely as men—but claiming that his method was more practical. It was defeated by 28 votes to 23, some Conservative and Liberals voting with the Labour Lords.

National Parks and Access to the Countryside Bill

On this measure, in the Committee Stage, over 300 amendments were before the Lords; drafting, consequential and of substance. It was three days in the Committee Stage, two on the Report Stage while previously two on the Second Reading. Two amendments were pressed against the Government: one to provide a power to set up a uniform system of bye-laws over all the National Parks—carried by 42 to 15; and the other, to enforce local Planning Authorities, before providing extra accommodation facilities for meals, camping sites, etc., to satisfy themselves that no other person is able and willing to provide them. Carried by 44 to 13. These were accepted by the Commons together with 140 other non-contested amendments in the Lords.

Nurses Bill (House of Lords)

In general this was a non-party Bill. But the Conservatives pressed a division to ensure that Teaching Hospitals receive their grants direct from the Minister and not from the Regional Boards, defeating the Government by 48 to 19. This amendment was left in the final Act by the Commons.

Parliament Bill. See pp. 122–31 above.

Parliament Square (Improvements) Bill

A comprehensive and, at first sight, non-contentious, Government scheme to improve Parliament Square, was so amended by the Conservatives as to make the scheme unworkable because it refused to allow a road near the Statue of Canning—carried by 57 votes to 28. The amendment was rejected by the Commons, the Lords accepted the rejection.

War Pensions and Disability Allowances

A Conservative motion: 'That in the opinion of this House, the time has arrived to hold an inquiry as to whether the existing rates of war pensions and disability allowances are adequate to meet requirements under the conditions at present prevailing.' The Government would not accept the motion as being unnecessary and an implied criticism. Carried by 47 votes to 30.

Wireless Telegraphy Bill

A Conservative amendment was moved to a section of the Bill aimed at preventing electrical apparatus interference with wireless. It was carried 42 to 23. A similar amendment relating to appeals against the Postmaster-General's powers to eliminate interference, carried 44 to 17. Both amendments were rejected by the Commons and then withdrawn by the Lords.

Iron and Steel Bill

After many days in the Committee and Report Stages, twelve amendments of substance had been carried against the Government. The Commons rejected them all. The Opposition, by agreement, withdrew all the amendments except one that delayed the vesting date to June 1950 instead of May so that a General Election would intervene and give the public a chance of stating its mind.

SESSION 1961–62

Army Reserve Bill

A Bill to retain for a further six months and, if necessary, recall certain National Servicemen in view of the critical international situation. In addition the Bill provided for the creation of a Territorial Army Emergency reserve.

The Opposition sought to add a clause providing that any person so retained would be entitled to receive a Bounty equivalent to one hundred days' pay to compensate for inconvenience caused to him. This was defeated by 57 votes to 32 votes.

Boxing Bill (House of Lords)

This Private Member's Bill was defeated on Second Reading by 22 votes to 29 votes.

Commonwealth Immigrants Bill

The Opposition pressed two amendments to this Bill, both of which would have given a right of appeal to immigrants refused entry by an immigration officer. The amendments were defeated by 30 votes to 55 votes, and 27 votes to 51 votes respectively.

Defence, Amendment to Motion for Resolution

This was a general debate on Defence initiated by the Government. An Opposition amendment expressed no confidence in the Government's policy and it was defeated by 24 votes to 71 votes.

Government Assistance to Universities

This debate was on a motion critical of the Government's policy towards the Universities. At end of the day's debate the Motion was defeated by 32 votes to 49 votes. The Opposition were joined in the minority by a few Peers from other parts of the House. It was remarkable in that no one spoke in support of the Government.

Health Visiting and Social Work (Training) Bill

Lady Summerskill moved an amendment to enable grants to be paid to trainees from central as well as from local funds. Although she was supported by Lady Elliot from the other side of the House, the amendment was defeated by 39 votes to 86 votes.

Licensing (Scotland) Bill (House of Lords)

Two amendments were pressed against the Government. One would have extended Sunday opening to Public Houses as well as Hotels (defeated 24–63), and the other would have extended Sunday opening hours in Hotels from 9 p.m. to 9.30 p.m. (defeated 35–44).

London Government

Lord Morrison of Lambeth initiated this general debate on the Government's proposals for London Government reform. At the end of a full day's debate the motion was defeated by 21 votes to 59 votes.

Manchester Corporation Bill

Lord Birkett moved that 'it be an instruction to the Select Committee to which the Bill may be committed to leave out Part III (Waterworks) of the Bill'.

This was agreed by 70 votes to 36 votes in a division in which the leaders of the Labour Peers voted with the Government in the minority.

The Opposition to this Private Bill, which concerned an alleged threat to natural beauty spots including Ullswater, was later withdrawn and the order committing it to a Select Committee discharged.

National Health Service

Lady Summerskill initiated this debate on the 'grave shortage of qualified dieticians, occupational therapists, physiotherapists and radiographers in the National Health Service'. On the motion being pressed to the vote it was carried *against* the Government by 24 votes to 21 votes.

Pensions of former Colonial Service Officers

Earl Listowel moved this resolution urging the Government to increase the basic rate of pensions paid to former Colonial

Service officers and their dependants. After debate the resolution was carried *against* the Government by 21 votes to 19 votes.

Pipe-lines Bill (House of Lords)

This Bill sought to regulate the provision of underground pipe-lines and to provide, under certain conditions, for compulsory purchase of land in connection with their construction.

Four divisions took place. An amendment to enable the British Transport Commission to construct and operate pipelines was defeated by 17 votes to 59 votes. The Report was not accepted the first time the Government moved it on the grounds that insufficient time had elapsed since the Committee Stage to enable amendments to be prepared. The voting was 19 to 63, many Conservative peers voted against the Government. On Report the Opposition again pressed the amendment mentioned above and it was defeated by 15 votes to 51 votes. The Opposition also pressed that the responsible Minister should be the Minister of Transport instead of the Minister of Power and this was defeated by 31 votes to 53 votes.

Queen's Speech

An amendment by the Opposition regretting the failure of Her Majesty's Government to take any effective steps to remedy the grave state of the economy of the nation was defeated by 88 votes to 28 votes.

Racial Discrimination Bill (House of Lords)

This Private Member's Bill was defeated on Second Reading by 21 votes to 41 votes.

Road Traffic Bill (House of Lords)

Three amendments were pressed to the vote when this Bill was in Committee and all were defeated. One dealt with the methods used to test drunkenness while driving (voting 41–66); another sought to remove speeding from the list of offences which incurred automatic disqualification after three convictions (voting 11–50); and the last one sought to introduce a local inquiry into the procedure by which a Minister might vary or revoke locally imposed speed limits (voting 23–81).

There was some cross-voting on these amendments.

Salaries of Nurses and Midwives

Lady Summerskill moved to call attention to the inadequate salaries paid to nurses and midwives and to the existing shortage of recruits to these professions. The Government moved an amendment defending their policy and this was carried by 73 votes to 35 votes.

Sea Fish Industry Bill

An amendment was moved to bring Shell Fish within the scope of this Bill and it was defeated by 46 votes to 61 votes. Another amendment to exclude from receipt of a grant any vessel built outside the Commonwealth was carried in Committee by 45–44 votes against the Government, but this decision was reversed on Report by 116–48 votes.

South Africa Bill

An amendment to extend the period within which South Africans could choose British citizenship from 1965 to 1966 was defeated by 38 votes to 72 votes.

Transport Bill

This major Bill was pursued tenaciously through the Lords by the Opposition. Seventeen divisions were pressed against the Government in Committee and on Report. All were defeated.

The debates were mainly on strict party lines but they were enlivened by a small group of canal enthusiasts led by Lord St Davids.

iv. *List of General Discussions and Debates, Sessions 1948–49 and 1961–62*

Half as many again discussions in 1961–62 as in 1948–49, even though the House has recently been more politically in tune with the Government, shows the growing need for such —on the whole—cross-bench discussions of relatively specialized matters. Useful though they can be, how much more so would they be if a Second Chamber had direct access to expert opinion and research facilities, or was debating the reports of sensibly constituted and staffed Select Committees on many of these topics. There would be a strong case for a reformed Second Chamber to integrate this aspect of its work with many of the inquiries and topics in Appendix F.

SESSION 1948–49

Afforestation

African Colonies

Utilization of Rural Land

State of, and importance of British Air Power

Humane Slaughter of Animals

Armed Forces Court Martial Procedure

Artificial Insemination and Legitimacy

Atlantic Pact

Treatment of British Subjects Abroad

Administration of Civil Aviation

Eire and Commonwealth Citizenship

Horticulture Industry

Distribution of Industry

Japanese War Crimes

Livestock Industry

Situation in Malaya

Organization of Nationalized Industries

Shortage of Nurses

Police Pensions

Road and Street Planning

Voluntary Action for Social Progress

Totalitarian Diplomacy

Increase of Crime

British and Western Union Defence

Defence Policy

Diplomatic Privilege of Press Agencies

Ground Nuts and Oil Seeds Scheme

Teachers for Technical Colleges

Home Grown Meat Supplies

Foreign Affairs

Position of Small Traders

Hand Woven Tweed Industry

United Nations Commission on Tanganyika

Work of UNESCO

Trusteeship Territories and the United Nations

Water Resources

West African Administration and Economic Situation

SESSION 1961–62

Agriculture
Agriculture Act, 1947
Air Estimates
Army Estimates
British Claimants under Anglo-Egyptian Agreement (twice)
Price of Building Land
Central African Federation
Civil Aerodromes and Air Navigational Services
Civil Aviation
Civil Defence
Commercial Broadcasting
Commonwealth Consultation
Disarmament
Shortage of Doctors
Economic Situation
Care of the Elderly
European Economic Community
Licensing of Firearms
Housing
ICI and Courtaulds
Industry and Exports
International Situation
Kenya
Mental Health
Murder
National Health Service (Shortage of Dieticians, Occupational Therapists, Physiotherapists and Radiographers)

National Productivity Year
Nature Conservancy
Navy Estimates
North Atlantic Treaty Organization
Pensions for Ex-Regular Members of Polish Forces
Pensions of Former Colonial Service Officers (twice)
Planning Appeal Inquiries
Population Growth in Asia
Smoking
Space Research
Aid to Underdeveloped Countries in Commonwealth
Wales and Monmouthshire
National Water Policy
Youth Service
Broadcasting
Defence
Hospital Plan (Scotland)
London Government
Tall Buildings in London
National Health Service
Salaries of Nurses and Midwives
Probation Service
Rival Ideologies
Government Assistance to Universities
Administrative Inquiries

APPENDIX F

A LIST OF COMMITTEES OF INQUIRY INTO SOCIAL AND ECONOMIC MATTERS APPOINTED FROM 1958–1962

The following table is taken from HC *Debates* 675 (cols 237–42), 2 April, 1963, which was put into the official record by the Prime Minister in answer to a question from Sir Barnett Janner, MP (Labour). Some of these subjects might seem purely technical; but many, if not most, whether technical or not, involve issues of public policy on which one might normally expect MPs to be consulted, not excluded.

Appointed	Subject	Chairman	Total number of Members	Members of Parliament	Time to report (in months)
Royal Commissions					
Jan. 1960	Police	Sir Henry Willink	15	2	17
Mar. 1961	Press (1961–62)	Lord Shawcross	7	None	18
Committees of Inquiry					
Jan. 1958	Tenancy of Shops (Scotland)	Mr Ian H. Shearer, QC	5	None	5
Feb. 1958	Funds in Court	The Hon. Mr Justice Pearson, CBE	11	None	15
Mar. 1958	Superannuation of University teachers	Sir Edward Hale, KBE, CB	12	None	21

Appointed	Subject	Chairman	Total number of Members	Members of Parliament	Time to report (in months)
Committees of Inquiry—continued					
Mar. 1958	Co-operation between Electricity and Gas Boards	Sir Cecil Weir, KCMG, KBE, MC, DL	9	None	12
May 1958	Composition of Milk	Mr J. W. Cook (now Sir James Cook)	15	None	26
May 1958	Examination of Steam Boilers in Industry	Sir George Honeyman, CBE, QC, JP	5	None	24
June 1958	Drug Addiction	Sir Russell Brain, Bt.	8	None	30
June 1958	Business of the Criminal Courts	The Hon. Mr Justice Streatfeild, MC	9	2	30
June 1958	Grants to Students	Sir Colin Anderson	16	None	24
July 1958	Matrimonial Proceedings in Magistrates' Courts	The Hon. Mr Justice Davies	11	None	5
July 1958	Medical Staffing Structure in the Hospital Service	Professor Sir Robert Platt, Bt.	11	2	30
Sept. 1958	Human Artificial Insemination	The Earl of Feversham, DSO	9	None	22
Nov. 1958	Youth Service in England and Wales	The Countess of Albemarle, DBE	13	None	12
April 1959	Solid Smokeless Fuels	Mr N. M. Peech	4	None	12
April 1959	Coal Derivatives	Mr A. H. Wilson, FRS	8	None	16
May 1959	Sheep Recording and Progeny Testing	Mr Ivor R. Morris, JP	14	None	21

Date	Subject	Chairman			
May 1959	Probation Service	Sir Ronald Morison, QC	14	None	31 (36 mths supplementary report on approved hostel system) 13
June 1959	Experimental importation of Charollais cattle	The Lord Terrington, KBE	4	None	
July 1959	Consumer Protection	Mr J. T. Molony, QC	12	None	33
July 1959	Operation of the Truck Acts 1831 to 1940	Mr David Karmel, QC	9	None	20
July 1959	Control of Public Expenditure	Lord Plowden, KCB, KBE	4	None	21
Aug. 1959	Scottish Licensing Law	The Rt Hon. Lord Guest, QC	12	None	16 (1st report.) Not yet reported finally
Sept. 1959	Replacement of the 'Queen' liners	The Rt Hon. Viscount Chandos, DSO, MC	3	None	8
Sept. 1959	Rural Bus Services	Professor D. T. Jack, CBE, JP	12	None	18
Nov. 1959	Milk Distributors' Margins	Sir Guy Thorold, KCMG	6	None	24
Nov. 1959	Levy on Betting on Horse Races	Sir Leslie Peppiatt, MC	7	None	5
Jan. 1960	Issue of *subpoenas* to secure attendance of witnesses and the production of documents before disciplinary tribunals	The Rt Hon. Viscount Simonds	3	None	4

Appointed	Subject	Chairman	Total number of Members	Members of Parliament	Time to report (in months)
Committees of Inquiry—continued					
Jan. 1960	Oriental, African, Slavonic and East European Studies	Sir William Hayter, KCMG	5	None	16
Jan. 1960	Company Law	The Rt Hon. Lord Justice Jenkins	14	None	29
Feb. 1960	Need for further research into the effects of toxic sprays in agriculture	Professor H. G. Sanders	10	None	20
July 1960	Magistrates' Courts in London	His Honour Judge Aarvold, OBE, TD	7	None	16
July 1960	Future of Sound and Television Broadcasting	Sir Harry Pilkington	11	None	21
July 1960	Policy and Arrangements for Dealing with Fowl Pest	Professor Sir Arnold Plant	7	2	18
Oct. 1960	Legal Education for Students from Africa	The Rt Hon. Lord Denning	21	None	3
Oct. 1960	Difficulties in the Port of London concerning Ocean Shipowners' Tally Clerks	Mr H. Lloyd-Williams, CBE, DSO, MC	3	None	1
Oct. 1960	Sugar Confectionery and Food Preserving Wages Council (Great Britain)	Sir George Honeyman, CBE, QC, JP	7	None	9
Jan. 1961	Limitation of Actions in cases of Personal Injury	The Hon. Mr Justice Davies	11	None	19

Date	Subject	Chairman			
Feb. 1961	Higher Education	The Lord Robbins, CB	12	None	Not yet reported
Mar. 1961	Scottish Electricity	Mr Colin Mackenzie, CMG	7	None	18
Mar. 1961	Docks and harbours of Great Britain	Viscount Rochdale, OBE, TD	5	None	16
April 1961	Selection and Training of Supervisors	Mr D. C. Barnes (Under-Secretary Ministry of Labour)	16	None	12
April 1961	Shipping Services to Northern Ireland	Mr D. V. House	3	None	18
May 1961	Law relating to Children and Young Persons (including that relating to Juvenile Courts in Scotland)	The Hon. Lord Kilbrandon	13	None	Not yet reported
June 1961	Grouping of London post-graduate institutes and hospitals and their joint use of facilities	Sir George White Pickering	6	None	15
July 1961	Sunday Observance Law	The Lord Crathorne	8	4	Not yet reported
Oct. 1961	Transport needs in the next twenty years	Sir Robert Hall, KCMG, CB	12	None	16
Nov. 1961	Award and withdrawal of teachers' certificates in Scotland	The Rt Hon. Lord Wheatley	22	None	Not yet reported
Dec. 1961	Baking Wages Council (Scotland)	Professor H. S. Kirkaldy, CBE	7	None	12
Dec. 1961	Traffic Signs on roads other than motorways	Sir Walter Worboys	12	None	Not yet reported
Dec. 1961	Decimal Currency	The Earl of Halsbury	6	None	Not yet reported

Appointed	Subject	Chairman	Total number of Members	Members of Parliament	Time to report (in months)
Committees of Inquiry—continued					
Mar. 1962	The administrative and clerical staffing arrangements of the hospital service	Sir Stephen Lycett Green, Bt. JP	7	None	Not yet reported
Mar. 1962	Scottish Salmon and trout fisheries	Lord Hunter	7	None	Not yet reported
April 1962	Marketing and Distribution of Fatstock and carcase meat	Sir Reginald Verdon-Smith	7	None	Not yet reported
Oct. 1962	To study contractual methods in the building and the civil engineering industries	Sir Harold Banwell	12	None	Not yet reported
Oct. 1962	Recruitment for the Veterinary Profession	The Duke of Northumberland, KG	7	None	Not yet reported
Nov. 1962	Demand for Agricultural Graduates	Mr C. I. C. Bosanquet	9	None	Not yet reported

APPENDIX G

THE CASE FOR NOT TELEVISING
PARLIAMENT

by ALLAN SEGAL

There has recently been mounting pressure for a Select Committee of the House of Commons to look into the possibilities of televising the proceedings of Parliament. Mr Robin Day has written: 'it was more than a hundred years before Parliament granted reporters a bench in their own right. How long will it be before television takes its inevitable and rightful place in the Press Gallery?'[1]

So far the Government has been disinclined to act on the matter, while trying hard not to appear unsympathetic to television. Sir Alec Douglas-Home replied to a request for an inquiry, made by Sir Norman Hulbert, MP (Conservative), that 'at present I am not convinced that the House as a whole would wish a Select Committee to be appointed'.[2] (In reply to an earlier request for an experimental closed circuit televising of the House, he said that 'I do not think it would be right to conduct experiments unless I was sure that the House as a whole supported in principle the idea of the proceedings being televised.'[3]) Nevertheless, Mr Selwyn Lloyd as Leader of the House spent some time 'sounding out' the opinions of MPs which, according to *The Times*'s political correspondent, may have begun to change: 'at the beginning of his inquiries he felt that he sensed a growing readiness among MPs to let the television camera into the chamber. Now he has changed his mind; he finds opposition beginning to strengthen'.[4]

Of the several reasonably precise schemes that have been

[1] Robin Day, *The Case for Televising Parliament,* with a Foreword by the Right Hon. R. A. Butler, CH, MP (Hansard Society, 1963), p. 23.

[2] 684 *Hansard Debates,* 19 November, 1963, col. 1.

[3] 685 *Hansard Debates,* 5 December, 1963, col. 1360–1.

[4] *The Times,* 13 December, 1963.

suggested, Mr Day rejects the idea of a continuous transmission of proceedings in favour: 'A late evening "Television *Hansard*", which would be an edited recording of the day's proceedings, varying in length according to what had happened . . . It would not monopolize a special channel . . . and would enable Question Time and important afternoon speeches to be seen.' But before we accept even on these relatively realistic terms, the 'inevitable and rightful' entrance of the television camera into the chamber at Westminster, it might be well to ask if such a venture is wise or even desirable, either in principle or practice.

The first difficulty lies in the adaptation of parliamentary debates for the viewing public. Newspaper reporters and other professional commentators are able, however imperfectly, to summarize the main arguments of a parliamentary speech in language which is intelligible to the viewing public. If we are to televise the speeches of MPs direct, then we must accept the fact that MPs are not speaking primarily to the public, but to their parliamentary colleagues—and in a style, usually informal, not seldom verbose, and which often includes technical references that are readily understood in the House of Commons, but not among the general public. News stories, with suitable adaptation, can be gleaned from a long speech, but it is to be doubted whether all long speeches (and there are many of them) can be edited into an intelligible, say, three minutes' worth for each MP. The position may well arise where statements are made which are of profound, political or economic importance, but which are useless for public consumption until they are suitably interpreted by a TV journalist.

The second difficulty is the question of editing. All agree that Parliamentary sittings would have to be tele-recorded and edited if infinite hours of boredom resulting from procedural wrangles are to be avoided. Who is to ensure that the events will be edited in a spirit of impartiality? The issue of deliberate bias does not really arise. Those entrusted with such a task would soon be fired if it was seen that blatant favouritism was being exercised on behalf of Government or Opposition. Day rightly points out that even if all views cannot be satisfied at one time, then this will be corrected over a period of time. But there is a danger of bias due to the Parliamentary system itself. Oppositions in the House of Commons have a natural advantage in being newsworthy over the Government of the day because it is their job to attack—not defend. This has already been seen to be evident in the present system of television interviews. If the Minister announces to the House that there is to be an increase in public expenditure, Oppositions cry 'extravagance'. If on the other hand he announces cuts in public expenditure, then the shout of 'cheeseparing' goes up. On a TV screen the Opposition would appear to have a natural advantage over Government spokesmen, no matter how cleverly Government replies were interposed. The public, knowing little of the 'game' of politics, might be forgiven for believing that, for the most part, the Opposition has the upper hand. Day has admitted that this tendency has already occurred in the present method of TV interviewing: 'The inevitable but not intended result has been that the effect of some programmes may have appeared biased against the Government. The longer the Government has been in power the more noticeable and more natural has this tendency become.'

If this is true at present, how much more true would this have been had the Profumo Debate been seen in ten million homes? And if bias of any sort is to be totally excluded from a 'TV *Hansard*' (supervised, of course, by a Parliamentary Committee), might not the result be chronic dullness and a boredom that is totally unrepresentative of the real House of Commons at work?

There is also a contradiction of interests between Parliamentary debates and news items as such. This can be seen most clearly in the sphere of Defence. The revelation that millions of pounds of the taxpayer's money has been wasted on a 'Blue Streak' or a 'Blue Water' missile may make for good viewing as well as a good news story in the press. But it may be that equally important Defence matters, such as NATO exercises, or lack of conventional weapons or troops in Germany, are omitted from a 'TV *Hansard*' because they are not newsworthy enough. In a speech where important information is being laid before the House, there is a danger that the visual aspect of gestures, mannerisms, and facial expressions will both dominate and obscure the information being provided and will divert (in every possible sense) public interest. And we must consider how many MPs and Ministers are just plain bad orators, who leave even their parliamentary colleagues little inspired, even though their contribution may be important. Also it is recognized that the television camera would have to be precluded from showing any Member except the one actually on his feet. Otherwise some MPs feel, as *The Times's* political correspondent put it, that they would have to be 'sitting to attention' all the time they were in the Chamber (and never permitted even to yawn, much less to doze off). Poor television would almost certainly be the result —a Pyrrhic victory. Whatever may be said, television must still entertain (and in this sense it is to be taken as being interesting) even in parliamentary reporting, or the faithful will switch off (or over). What is important is not always entertaining, and might possibly be omitted in order to maintain the TAM ratings. Television executives do not like to be told that their programmes are at the bottom of the popularity charts, and if they are, then the sensational items may to some measure gain preponderance over the important but dull. (Perhaps if Parliament ever came near to accepting Mr Day's proposals in principle, he might find it far more difficult to get the various television authorities to accept such a burden than to get Parliament to provide the means.)

Television is to be commended for the skilful way in which it presents the views of many MPs and Ministers as news. But this is all done under studio conditions, studied well beforehand, and almost always with carefully timed and prepared questions. Studio interviewing of MPs is a skilled occupation acquired only by the giants of TV journalism and under test tube conditions. It is to be very much doubted whether the views which MPs express to their colleagues in the House (where the TV camera would only be an onlooker) can be suitably edited into a newsworthy form.

The argument that some speeches in the House are so long that it would be difficult to summarize them, Day rejects by saying: 'This would not always be too difficult, but in any case it is likely that television would have the wholly desirable effect of making parliamentary speeches a good deal more succinct than they are now.' More crispness on the part of many MPs is indeed most desirable. But behind this there is the possiblity of some very gentle pressure to arrange parliamentary proceedings to suit the television cameras. Whilst the technical and procedural problems of putting equipment into the Chamber need not be insurmountable by themselves, the cumulative prospect of the combination of strong lights, 'succinct' speeches and powdered parliamentary faces is perhaps a little horrifying even for strong nerves. And it is to be remembered that the suggestions of the Select Committee on

Procedure, 1959, to reserve an hour in major debates for 'five-minute' speeches proved highly unpopular among Back-benchers themselves—one Member called it a 'Parliamentary Children's Hour'.

The notion that television would encourage stunts and exhibitionism is, indeed, dismissed by most of those who want Westminster to be televised. 'Television,' says Day, 'has the remarkable effect of making public figures behave—and argue —more reasonably.' This is to be doubted. There is little room at the present time for an MP to be an exhibitionist in a TV interview—virtually all he can do is to lose his temper with the interviewer (and hope that he is not called into the Whips Office in the morning). But in the day to day business of the House of Commons, many hitherto closed doors are opened. The classic case is at Question Time. It is true that by tele-vising Question Time constituency grievances could be aired in full view of the public, though it is also true that most of them would be unintelligible without explanation. Where there are genuine grievances this is all to the good, but this is not always the case. Take the many questions, for instance, which are raised in the vexed area of the Nationalized Industries (where authority is divided between the Minister and the Board) that could have been more quickly dealt with had the MP written to the Chairman of the Board instead of raising the matter in the House. As a result many constituency claims against public utilities are brought to the floor of the House, when they need not have been. A television camera at Question Time could precipitate a larger number of con-stituency questions, many of which should never have been raised at all but dealt with at the appropriate level. Indeed the whole nature of Question Time may be changed into a forum for the discussion of predominantly local issues instead of queries concerned with national policy. MPs are subject to the normal temptations, and there may well be a few who would 'hog the camera' once they had realized the possibilities that it offers. No one would argue that the House would be reduced to a comic farce, but the temptation of a few to boost their public image by perhaps a little foolery now and again is not too hard to imagine. Mr Quintin Hogg's famous inter-view on the Profumo affair was talked about precisely because it caused a sensation. Notice is taken of George Brown on television because he has a tendency to become a little larger than life on occasions. The passive interview and the meek question in the House arouse no public comment. How much greater will be the urge for an MP to rise above the everyday 'hum-drum' questioners and burst into prominence with a well-timed tantrum?

If this can be applied to Question Time, it can equally be applied to minority opinion, the lone dissenter. Day says: 'With the cameras in the House he would catch the public eye on television more often than he is able to at present.' This regard for the underdog is a noble sentiment indeed. But the facilities that this affords to sensationalists, especially those disowned by the Whips, needs more careful attention than the summons to a 'free for all'.

What is even more surprising is Day's belief that: 'Television would stimulate the House of Commons to modernize its procedure and improve the standard of debate.' He argues that if the antiquated procedures of Parliament were exposed on the screen, public opinion would be aroused for 'Parliamentary reform'. This is to put the cart before the horse with a vengeance. The present conservatism of the House is unlikely to grant any form of increased facilities to television. If there were to be any such scheme at all, the House would first have had to reform itself more generally, and then not for the sake of television, but for the sake of generally informing itself to inform the public better. A reformed House of Commons might indeed make better television; but television will not create Parliamentary reform.

Finally one must consider the time of day that such a 'TV Hansard' would be shown. Day has suggested late evening —10.30 p.m. This would enable 'important afternoon speeches to be seen in the evening by a much bigger audience'. What, one may ask, will be done with important evening speeches which are too late to be included in the day's video-tape recording? If kept to the following day there may be too many immediately topical items that must be included. The possibility of a little pressure on the parliamentary time-table to have more newsworthy items debated earlier in the day cannot be excluded. In the debate on the Profumo scandal, the adjournment was not taken until 9.50 p.m.—too late for an adequate summary of the arguments to be included in any 'TV Hansard' that day. We may well have reason to fear at least some pressure on the Government to reorganize the order of business so that important matters can be 'taped' in time for the evening viewers.

There is certainly a very strong case to be made for better coverage of political events by television, but the obvious remedy is largely in the hands of the television authorities themselves: more time should be allocated to parliamentary affairs and to political programmes and reporting in general. Granada Television, for instance, has already made some advances in this field, such as its excellent coverage of the Rochdale by-election of 1958. Perhaps this dearth of political reporting will be partly rectified by the BBC's Channel 2. But certainly Parliament should clarify the meaning of the provisions of the Television Acts 1954 and 1963 which require 'due impartiality' on the part of commercial companies (and which has always been followed by the BBC as a matter of convention).

This has led, rightly or wrongly, to the practice that all or none of the candidates in each particular constituency must appear on a programme, so that one Party's refusal to co-operate precludes a programme being built round the others. And Parliament should be more helpful, both to itself and the public, by providing facilities for a studio in the Palace of Westminster or in the new Bridge Street site, so that MPs who have made important speeches could repeat the gist of them in a quick television interview without having to travel half-way across London to do so, which would also be a great convenience to MPs themselves for their normal appearances in television interviews and discussions. It is indeed ludicrous, as Day says, that to cover the debate on the Profumo scandal of 17 June, 1963, the BBC had to huddle MPs 'underneath dripping umbrellas' in Parliament Square by Lincoln's statue, and the ITV to gather them up in a 'makeshift studio in a nearby pub' (although his case would be stronger if their desire for instant coverage arose on even slightly more normal occasions, or if both their forethought and their sense of the importance of Parliament had already led them to rent suitably dry and sober premises nearby). But there is a fundamental difference between the original claim of *Hansard* to report debates, and the claim of a right and a public need to televise them. The public already has available to it reports of debates in the press, and can judge the views of MPs on normal, specifically arranged television programmes. The facilities available to television need to be extended; but this does not constitute a case for televising the proceedings of Parliament. The claims of the camera to a place in the Press Gallery of the House of Commons must be such as to outweigh the disadvantages that many think will accrue from such a venture. Day has put the case for the camera in the Gallery cogently and forcefully, but he has passed over the disadvantages far too lightly. The 'rightful' place of the camera must be proved, even if the 'inevitable' cannot.

Indeed, looking at the problem strictly from a television viewpoint, hardly anything could be imagined less likely to make 'good television' than a parliamentary debate. This raises the suspicion that what is at stake here is not the enhanced prestige of Parliament, but of television.

INDEX